D0557507

The Best Jobs in
The Music Industry

The Best Jobs in The Music Industry

Straight Talk from Successful Music Pros

People in the music industry
tell you firsthand
what they do for a living.

Michael Redman

Hal Leonard Books

An Imprint of Hal Leonard Corporation

Copyright © 2013 by Michael Redman

All rights reserved. No part of this book may be reproduced in any form, without written permission, except by a newspaper or magazine reviewer who wishes to quote brief passages in connection with a review.

Published in 2013 by Hal Leonard Books
An Imprint of Hal Leonard Corporation
7777 West Bluemound Road
Milwaukee, WI 53213

Trade Book Division Editorial Offices
33 Plymouth St., Montclair, NJ 07042

Printed in the United States of America

Book design by Michael Kellner

Library of Congress Cataloging-in-Publication Data is available upon request.

ISBN 9781476817019

www.halleonardbooks.com

This book is dedicated to my two daughters, Grace and Julia, who entertain me on a daily basis and share their love so freely, and my surfing, guitar-playing son, Tyler, who is making his own way in our world.

If it's a career in the music business you want, and you don't want to be a performer, you have limitless options. Engineering, like I have done, or producing, mixing, artist representation . . . there are plenty of ways to make a good living in the music business, just find your passion.

Ours is an industry of passions and emotional connection. A lot of people don't realize what it is they really want out of a career, what will satisfy them personally, until they've tried something new; so don't be afraid to try. —Todd Rundgren

contents

preface

IT'S DARK, VERY DARK. The excitement and anticipation in the room is electrifying and the audience is on the edge of their seats; you have been waiting years for this moment. The lights come up and the applause is deafening as a lone figure walks to the stage, and says, "Please welcome the Berklee School of Music's graduating class of 2013."

When the ceremony is over, with your room packed and you catching a flight home to Peoria, some scary thoughts of hoped for employment opportunities and a career that generates income for you and your future family weigh heavily on your mind.

- *What will I do if I can't make enough money playing trumpet to afford to live on my own?*
- *What if I still need to live with my parents?*
- *What if I need to get a job bagging groceries to survive until I'm famous?*
- *Crap! What if my hair falls out and I don't look good on camera playing my guitar and shaking my hairless head?*

If you have questions like these bouncing around that cerebrum of yours, then I certainly hope you will read this book cover to cover. The music business is stronger, with more opportunity than ever, and with a little planning you can be quite successful while staying close to the music you love. You won't need to work in a grocery store, sell water purification systems door to door, or even stand in a manufacturing line punching out little metal parts for some refrigerator door.

In my life I've been a drummer, guitarist, banjo player, saxophonist, singer, songwriter, publisher, studio owner, composer, recording artist, jingle writer, audio engineer, producer, serial entrepreneur, technologist, consultant, filmmaker, and the list goes on. I've been told it's my ADD, but I prefer to think of it as an overabundance of creativity flowing through these bones of mine. I want you to live your dream as I have and experience the ever-changing path of musical magic.

The dream: What's yours? Do you dream of being onstage in front of thousands of adoring fans screaming your name? Or do you live and breathe for music's sake? The pursuit of music is a lifelong passion for many of us and not a one-shot deal.

I have but one goal with this book, and it's to open up the world of music and the music business to you—not just the microcosm of performance, which makes up a mere 10 percent of the business.

A music career today looks very different than it did ten years ago. Our parents typically worked at one job for most of their lives, and companies promised to take care of them after thirty years of service; there was loyalty on the part of the company and employee alike, but like everything else, times change.

Companies no longer have the desire or luxury to keep employees one day more than they are needed. They instead opt for outsourced, freelance, and part-time workers to avoid paying benefits and supporting their workers during slowdowns. It's Wall Street that demands a return on investment and company growth of 15 percent year after year that drives this particular change. To accomplish this goal, companies are faced with an unsavory solution: cut costs. The easiest way to cut costs is to reduce the workforce, which is just what they've done. Employees have lost favor with the company and the company has lost the loyalty of employees.

Today's employees also look very different from where I sit. They're not interested in working if the job has no meaning; they have more of an entrepreneurial spirit, are willing to take more chances, are faster on the uptake, and have a curious confidence in themselves and the future.

Like everyone else, musicians today might be working at five different jobs and loving it . . . like one of our contributors, Paul Ill, to make ends meet. Your career will undoubtedly lead you down a very exciting path if you allow your spirit to take control and appreciate the music industry as a whole.

Musicians exhibit the unique ability to encapsulate expressions of the human experience like no other artists, and I must say that I'm still filled with wonder when I listen to the Beatles and peer into the soul of a young Paul McCartney and John Lennon through their lyrical windows that were far beyond their years. For the many years I've worked at writing music and I have yet to bridge the lyric and melody combination they seemed to possess naturally.

This book is not about my life, challenges, and successes, or for that matter me at all. It is, as they say, all about you and your music. It's about keeping you in the game and positioning you to make a good living; it's about shortcuts to positions and careers that will keep you close to the music.

I wrote this book as a guide for all of you who love making music but who might not become the next Led Zeppelin, Justin Timberlake, or Marc Broussard for that matter. You won't find any business speak (EBITDA—*earnings before income taxes and depreciation* or RIO *return on investment*) or flamboyant literary twists, so you won't need a dictionary to comprehend what's written here.

There are many levels of success that are attainable in the music industry, and stardom is but one of them. The simple fact is that with 13 million bands worldwide, only about 2,000 make a great living. That leaves the rest of us to make hard decisions down the road when and if stardom eludes us.

For our purposes, I am going to concentrate on what I call "career enlightenment." I understand that musicians as a group don't like to read books when they could be playing their instruments, so I'll try to stay on task and get right to the point whenever possible.

In this first volume, we will cover many of the more prominent and well-known jobs in the music industry. I'll share a few of my comments followed by interviews I've conducted with people who have been very successful in their particular jobs, and interview myself in jobs where I have personal experience. I believe this is the best way to deliver straightforward information, rather than *my* doing research and then presenting that research with *my* slant. I will also use stories that involve famous artists you may know, but won't use their names. This book is *not* about name dropping and I don't want to get any nasty letters from their lawyers.

I've been fortunate enough to be financially successful making music and blessed to have had enough experiences for more than ten people. Some of the experiences I will share I'm not too proud of, but are needed to illustrate common pitfalls of being popular and often things you may want to avoid.

When I sat down to write this book, I made the conscious decision to focus on jobs that are still viable in today's economy and digital world rather than pontificate on every possible outshoot of the music industry. I also decided early on that I wouldn't promote some elusive target that you could never achieve.

I encourage you to read every section of this book to gain a fundamental understanding of all the different jobs offered, and then jump around at your leisure and read at will. There is no specific beginning and end to this story, just ideas shared by people just like you who have been successful—very successful—in the music business.

acknowledgments

I WOULD LIKE TO OFFER my sincere thanks to all of the contributors to this book. I know you have busy schedules as successful music industry people and finding time to share your experience and knowledge is much appreciated.

I'd like to thank Greg Sims, my partner of the past six years and a very positive influence on my life. Also, many thanks to Melissa Pantel-Ku, John Branch, and Bobby Andrews. Without their tireless assistance this book would never have seen the light of day.

The Best Jobs in
The Music Industry

Introduction

I'D LIKE TO SAY AS A PRELUDE to the many opinions expressed in this book that to be successful in the music business, you need the same essential skills of any person in any industry. First and foremost, you must love what you do and do it for the right reasons. If your sole intention is to make lots of money, you will be sorely disappointed.

The term "starving musician" refers to a condition that artists of every type suffer. There is the popular opinion that musicians don't work—they play music—and therefore shouldn't be respected or compensated for their efforts, at least until they have gained a level of popularity. Then and only then are they worthy of making a living at their art. You might laugh at what I just said but remember another truism for painters: *"Your work is only valuable after you're dead."* Hmmm . . . if you ask me, that's not much to look forward to.

A Quick Story

Many years ago I lived in Florida and had a band called Headlines. We played in bars and often at the University of Florida in Gainesville (a well-known school where drinking heavily and acting stupid is encouraged) for fraternity parties A client asked me why we charged so much because we just "played" music and it wasn't like a real job.

I proceeded to tell him that to play their party our day went something like this:

- Pack the trailer for one hour
- Drive two hours to Gainesville
- Set up and do a sound check for two hours
- Play for four hours
- Break down and pack for one hour
- Drive home at 2:30 a.m. for two hours
- Unpack the trailer for another hour

I told him, "So to 'play' your crappy little party, we put in over thirteen hours. You're getting a great deal, and no, we're not playing. We're very serious about what we do"

Okay, back to the traits of a successful person in this business: love what you do, have a measure of expertise at what you do, and cultivate a personality that engages others, has true compassion for others, a positive (glass half full) attitude, and an ability to stick to your path even when others don't support you. This last element is a tough one for many of us, as sticking with the music business is not always the path of least resistance.

Before we move on, let's briefly look at each one of these traits.

Love What You Do

I believe you should love what you do in this life because our time here is limited. Don't settle for less or you'll regret it. If you love what you do, it's not work; everything else will fall into place and you will have a lot of great memories.

Expertise

This is a big subject covered very well in the book *Outliers* by Malcolm Gladwell. With expertise comes success and longevity. If you play guitar, practice until you are the best you can possibly be. If you're a composer of commercials, write hundreds of them and hone your craft until it's second nature. If you're a sound designer, create your own unique sound library. If you're a music producer, go ahead and be a perfectionist; don't settle for less than your artists can deliver. You get the drift.

Positive Attitude

Without a positive attitude, everything you do is likely to end in failure and disappointment. Always be the problem solver and go into the job or project with success in mind. Turn bad situations into good ones; support your friends and colleagues. I can't tell you how many young people I have hired because they had incredible attitudes and others wanted to be around them just to soak up the positive vibes.

Open Personality

People like to be around interesting people, so share your expertise and your life, and you will be liked by others. Simple but true, most of the opportunities that come your way will be from people you know or have casually met along your journey. Go out of your way to help others, and you'll also be helping yourself.

Compassion for Others

Believe it or not, *it's not all about you.* Nothing matters more than compassion for others. You can't fake it, and at the end of the day you are judged by who you are. Your character is displayed through your treatment and empathy for others.

Perseverance

You've heard this many times, but you can't hear it enough: *never, never, never give up.* The perfect job may come from the next phone call, text, FB post, or e-mail, and you need to be there to receive it. I was once told that "If you work hard enough, you *will* get lucky." I live by those words.

How to Read This Book

Each description of a job starts with a short summary designed to help you decide right off the bat if this might be something you want to explore further. This is followed by the real stories, paths to success, and challenges you may face, all in the words of those I consider to be industry experts, people you can believe and should listen to. Read and learn from these people who have lived in the music industry and navigated it well and been successful. It is their words and thoughts you should reflect upon, not my interpretations—*even though some of my thoughts might be helpful.*

Each job section includes "Rapid Fire," a simple overview like the one below constructed from my experience and confidential information supplied by my contributors.

Rapid Fire

> **Skill Set**—Specifically what you must have to succeed
> **Hours**—Self-explanatory
> **Upside**—What's good about this job
> **Downside**—What could be a challenge
> **Financial**—$($15K or less)–$$$$ ($100K and up)
> **Location**—Best places to live for this job
> **Future**—What does it look like for this job?

Self-Evaluation

Before we jump into what I hope will be an enlightening path to a long, successful career in music, we have a few important considerations to address. So let's complete a reality check. We need this reality check because there are many jobs in the music industry and some of them, though not glamorous, will pay your bills while allowing you to follow your musical dreams.

To begin the process of deciding what musical career path makes the most sense for you, let's start with some big questions. Based upon your answers, I hope you will begin a thought process that will help you narrow down your options to find the job where you will be the most comfortable, effective, and have the highest chance of success.

1. Are You a Good Musician?

Try to answer this question honestly because it's the basis for everything we are talking about here. One thing we are *not* talking about is self-deception. If you don't understand what this means, just watch the auditions for *American Idol* or *America's Got Talent*. It's all very entertaining (if you have a slightly sick sense of humor), but doesn't make for a career in music.

So are you a good musician, a great one, or just aspiring to be great? You probably already know that you don't need to be the greatest guitar player or singer to be successful in the music business, just remember what the Wizard said: "What have they got that you don't?"

2. Money

How much money do you need to live *now*? If you know how to use a spreadsheet, this might be a good time to break out your laptop and create a simple, realistic, big picture budget. When it comes to my own finances, I am the worst. But you really need to understand your current financial situation. Don't forget to include rent, food, guitar strings, and all other necessities, including your party materials. Let's be honest.

How much money will you need or want in *twenty years*? This is a tough question, and one you might ask a friend who has completed at least a couple years of finance, accounting, or economics to help you figure out. We've all heard our grandparents talk about going to a double-feature movie for 50 cents and having enough money left over for popcorn, but time marches on and so does inflation. If you don't understand what *inflation* means, look it up on Wikipedia. If you are making $500 a week now, you will surely need to make $2,000 or more a week in twenty years just to remain in the same place you are today. Explaining the nuances of money and finances is beyond the scope of this book, but it's something for you to consider as part of the process.

How much money will you need to *retire*? A better question might be, "What do you want to do later in life?" This includes travel, helping others, teaching music, writing a book (as I am), or sailing your private yacht around the world. This will require you to again ask your financial friend for assistance to project your life's income over a very long period of time. Plan on being very happy, healthy, and financially successful. It all costs money, so a little time spent now will be well worth it later, even though your plans and circumstances will surely change over time.

3. Education

Are you a trained musician who reads music as easily as reading *Musician* magazine? Trained musicians, especially those who have taken some music business classes, have the most career options within the music industry.

Are you an untrained musician who finds reading music to be like reading **Greek?** This is where most musicians I know live: *the great in-between.* It's a hard place to be and where I struggled for many years. As you read on, you will see its impact, depending on what you might like to do.

4. Play by Ear?

Guitar players know this joke: *"How do you get a guitarist to turn down?"* "Put a chart in front of him." In the long term, ear players and singers need to work harder than anybody else to stay in the performing side of the business—unless your name is Keith Richards, Joe Walsh, or maybe Danny Elfman.

5. Are You Currently a Working Musician?

I ask this because there is a difference between loving music and playing it. If you *must* play music, read carefully to find a career option that will allow you time to do so.

6. Is Music Your Hobby?

This is the music lover's stepping-off point. I've known many successful audio engineers and producers who don't play professionally, but without them we musicians wouldn't have an opportunity to blossom commercially.

7. Success

What does success look like for you? This question should also be considered along with question #2. Do you see yourself with 100,000 adoring fans crowding the stage just to get a glimpse of you? Or with a long career creating the music you love and connecting with others who love music? Or both?

Maybe it's money, enough money to do whatever you want whenever you want: to help yourself, your family, and others? I'm not here to push you in any specific direction, but you should visualize your goals so you'll know exactly what your target is, and just as importantly, when you have reached it. Many people accomplish their goals and don't even realize it, only to be unhappy and feel that they've failed. I like reaching a goal, celebrating it, and then having another one ready to go. It sounds easy, but believe me when I tell you it's not.

So let's get started and talk about your goals for a minute. More questions, I'm afraid, but what I hope to accomplish with this book is to help you *think* about a career in music from many different view points, and not just as a vehicle to making money.

Do You . . . ?

Do you just love playing music and your particular instrument? What I mean here is, are you happy just playing and don't really need to make a living, although it would be nice?

Do you like to play for your friends and entertain them? My brother was never a professional musician but knows the guitar chords and lyrics to over 200 songs. By contrast, I was a professional musician in every sense of the word and can play about, oh, *one* song at a party.

Do you:

- Have something to say emotionally, socially, spiritually, or politically in your writing/composing?
- Want to make lots of money?
- Want to travel the world?
- Want to be on the big stage?
- Want fame?

This is the question I will attempt to help you answer *if* you read this book: ***Can you make a good living in the music industry long term?*** The answer is a resounding *"Yes, you can!"* You may need to put together multiple music-related jobs to create the revenue stream you desire, but ultimately with the help of the relationships you make along the way, you can develop a rewarding full-time career in the music business.

A Life in Music

In my opinion, there are right and wrong reasons to pick music as a career. I believe there is only one *right* reason to think about music as your lifelong partner and companion: *love*. You must love music, love the way it makes you feel, and love the connection music makes with the world around you.

Conversely, there are many reasons not to look to music as your career path, and they include fame, fans, and riches. This doesn't mean that you won't ultimately become rich and famous, but if you choose music for these reasons alone, you'll probably look back and wonder why the heck you ever decided to be in the music industry in the first place. Be honest with yourself and think it through. Try meditation—I can't do it, but maybe you can!

My story is typical and somewhat humorous. When I was seven years old, I was sent home from school for banging on the desk and my parents were summoned to talk to the principal. "Your son is disruptive to the entire class," he said. "He's always banging on the desk and you need to get him under control or find another school!" So my mom took me to a shrink, who told her, "Michael has lots of nervous energy and my suggestion would be to get him some drum lessons or something where he can redirect all that extra energy."

A week or so later, I met my first drum teacher, a marine with a roughly shaven head and a grimace that never left his face, who says, "We are going to start with rudiments. Here's your book, and I want you to learn these first ten pages by next Tuesday. Good-bye." Despite the fact that he scared the crap out of me, I was very excited to have something to bang on, so I worked like a dog all day, every day, to make sure he would be happy with my progress.

At my next lesson, he sat very quietly and said, "Okay, play for me." I did the best I could, not really knowing what I was doing because he hadn't taught me what quarter and eighth notes were. Then without warning, BAM! He smacked my knuckles with a drumstick and I screamed. "That's not right!" BAM! again. "I told you not to hold the sticks that way." I was crying, and then he scolded me for crying; in the span of about one minute, I hated this man, the drums, and music.

When mom picked me up, she asked why I was crying and I told her what had happened. She turned the car around and headed right back to Congressional Plaza and the music store. "What the hell do you think you are doing hitting my son? I'm going to call the police." She was really mad. At any rate, after two drum lessons I was done.

The next day, we went to another music store and she bought me a set of bongos; they were to become my best friend. We went everywhere together and I bet I played those bongos ten hours a day, much like you probably did with your instrument when you first fell in love with it.

On my eighth birthday, mom said, "Let's go to the music store and see if we can get a little upgrade to those worn-out bongos before they totally fall apart." Off we went and returned home that afternoon with a brand-new Ludwig black pearl snare drum and a sixteen-inch Zildjian cymbal. It was so awesome, and they received as much play as my bongos, but something was clearly missing. I needed the entire set, but we didn't have the money to purchase them, so I cut grass, washed cars, whatever I could do to earn money. Over the next few months, I saved about $90.

December rolled around, and on Christmas morning there was a matching black pearl bass drum, hi-hat, and tom-tom under the tree. Eight years old with my own set of drums in the basement and permission to play them whenever I wanted: it couldn't get any better. I learned to love music that year. I didn't dream of being John Bonham in Led Zeppelin or even of being in a band at that point; I was in it for the beauty and serenity of the rhythm.

So my question to you is: Why do *you* love to play music?

Contributors

Probably the greatest joy I found in writing this book—aside from the potential to help you find your path in the music business—was the people I had the pleasure of interviewing. They are like you in that they love music and have passion for what they do. They are hopefully like you in that they never gave up on their dreams of being successful in the music business.

From David Newman, who is a very articulate, busy, and a somewhat serious composer, to Randy Mease, a hardworking audio engineer running a successful one-man shop in Orlando, it was refreshing to hear the passion in their voices as they welcomed the opportunity to share their thoughts and advice with you.

The opinions you will read here are from the horses' mouths, so to speak. They are insights from those who have pursued the dream, lived it, and most importantly been successful, both personally and financially.

As you read on, be sure to look up their names on Google or imdb.com as this may give you a framework and help you understand more about them and their jobs.

1

Audio Engineer

Rapid Fire

Skill Set—You will need a good ear, a strong (but not too strong) opinion, the ability to work long stretches with little sleep, a supportive spouse, enough creativity to understand how a song or audio track will sonically stand the test of time. Education is very helpful but not required.

Hours—Hmmm, they run from bankers' hours to the night shift and everywhere in between. If you are dead set on recording music, be ready to flip your schedule upside down and work from 9 p.m. to 4 a.m. on occasion. You need to bend your schedule to fit your artists. I once talked with Stevie Wonder's engineer and he lived in an apartment at Stevie's house because he was on call whenever Stevie felt like recording. He told me it was not unusual to get a phone call from him at 3 a.m. "I have an idea and I want to lay it down. I'll be in the studio in fifteen minutes."

Upside—The opportunity to create a sound canvas that may become a masterpiece for a song, film, TV show, or even a radio spot. There are many different areas of audio engineering in which you can make a nice living. While some roles like the traditional big studio staff engineer are disappearing, others, such as a post-engineer or tech-based audio engineer, are growing.

Downside—The pressure to continuously deliver fast, high-quality audio product can be stressful. When something goes wrong in the studio, it's your job to get it corrected quickly. The long hours when you're working on crap and politics can also be a problem. There is also the issue of the job market. You will need to be creative and entrepreneurial in nature because there is a lot of competition.

Financial—$$ to $$$$ I know engineers that pull in $250,000+ a year and those who top out at $60,000. It is generally a good job and even more so if you can fund your own studio and find a great little niche or company to work with on a regular basis.

Location—Technology advancements allow you to live anywhere, depending on the specific type of audio work you would like to do. However, most major film, TV, and advertising is located in the Big Three—New York, LA, and Chicago. You can live in other metropolitan markets, but you should realize you will not be working on these types of projects very often.

Future—The future is good for the entrepreneurial recording engineer and not so much for the traditional label-type music engineer, with the exception of those individuals who are already in the system and part of the major label fabric. There will always be a need to have something recorded professionally.

A DISTANT RINGING. "What is that nasty sound?" I think, as the sound grows ever louder, closer, and more annoying. Finally, as I wipe the sleep from my eyes, I see this pulsating blurry '5'-something flashing—flashing and getting brighter. Crap, it's 5 a.m.! I just want to smack that clock and drift back into my dream about the girls, the lake, and the big green egg, but no, I have to be at Starke Lake Studios for my first day on the job as chief engineer.

I had decided beforehand that if the downbeat (recording start time) was 9 a.m., I should be there by 7 a.m., leaving me enough time to set up the recording studio "A" room at ease and time to fix anything that might creep up and kick me in the butt. I showered and drove through the morning darkness, unlocked the doors to the studio, turned off the studio alarm, and broke out the microphone cases. I set up the room in a semi-circle because I thought the musicians would want to see each other. Mistake number one!

I should stop and tell you that my first-ever session in this studio was to record a twenty-eight-piece ensemble that included brass, woods, percussion, strings, and rhythm section. No big deal, *except* for the fact that to date I had only recorded four- to six-piece rock bands, no orchestral instruments, and had no experience with critical vocal recording.

I felt pretty good about the rhythm section and the number of players, but had no idea how to place the microphone or record a French horn, how much to pad a trumpet, or even what microphone to use on a flute.

I set up the chairs, music stands, headphone boxes, and all the other little electronic stuff you need in the studio and then proceeded to calibrate the two-inch twenty-four-track MCI tape machine. So far, it was pretty routine and I was way ahead of the clock. At 8:30 a.m. the musicians started arriving, as well as the composer and my producer/client. The composer looked at the studio and asked, "Michael, where is the conductor's stand? And why are the musicians all in a semicircle and not facing me?" Crap, I didn't know there would be a conductor; I just thought the musicians would read the music and I'd record it. "No worries," I thought. I was sure that I could get everything taken care of in time. I was very glad I had taken that shower!

The musicians sat down and started asking me *their* questions. "Is this a new way of miking the French horn?" to which I replied, "I'm just doing a little experimenting," because I had no idea what he was talking about.

I went into the control room and started working on the recording levels, sounds, headphone mixes, and the like on the MCI 636 console, which I had seen for the very first time the previous day. Everything was coming together; my blood pressure dropped and my breathing slowed as the clock struck 9 a.m.

The composer said, "Okay, Michael, let's take one," and I went into shock! I couldn't believe what I was hearing. We were at least four to six hours away from rolling tape in my mind. I was used to spending an hour or two just on the drums, not to mention all these new instruments I had never recorded. I scrambled like never before, assuming that if I could just get the music on tape clean and undistorted with some reasonable level of fidelity, I could later create some mixing magic. I don't think I ever had a more harrowing eight hours in my career as a sound engineer.

The short of it is that with very few glitches the session went just fine, and I learned more in one day than some audio engineers do in six months. Trial by fire, there's nothing like it. The funny thing is, I spent the next year dissecting every part of that session and perfecting my miking techniques, but had I been an intern for a great engineer, I would have learned those skills in just a few short weeks.

So . . . one thing you will need to be successful is confidence. The confidence to take chances, learn fast from your mistakes, and grow quickly, but not too much confidence because there *is* a fine line between confidence and stupidity. On this particular session I had that crossed the line into the stupid zone! I knew I could do the session but didn't do my homework, and didn't know what I was getting myself, or my client, into. It was a very important lesson. The upside of that session was that the composer and I formed a wonderful long-lasting relationship and worked together for many, many years.

I have never been one to say, "No, I don't know how to do that." Like so many of us, I always say, "Sure, I can do that," and then try to learn very, very fast. . . . Like the time I auditioned for *Annie Get Your Gun*, and they asked me if I played five-string banjo. "I sure do, but I left it at the house. Would you like me to go get it?" I went straight to the music store, bought a cheap banjo, tuned it like a guitar and passed the audition. Over the next couple of months, I became an adequate banjo player, which also came in handy when I decided to write country music!

I guess what I am saying here is that you shouldn't be afraid to stretch out and try new things. You may surprise yourself! It's made my career and life more interesting. By the way, did I mention that you will fail sometimes, but that the earth keeps spinning and life goes on? I was once told by my father-in-law, Chuck Ames, "Michael, I have invested in a company every year since I graduated college; some have done well while others have failed. You just hope that the ones that do well do much better than the ones that fail." No risk, no reward.

A recording engineer—a good one—is a rare find these days. To become a much sought-after engineer requires a unique skill set indeed. You must be a diplomat and technician, have incredible ears, thick skin, and be one step ahead of everybody else in the room. You must understand what "I want it to sound more red" means, know at least a few great musician jokes, be able to keep your eyes and ears open for extended periods of time, *and* leap tall buildings in a single bound.

As you will see in the interviews that follow, a career as an audio/recording engineer may take many forms. There are several interviews in this section because engineering covers so much ground and the job/skill set is diverse, as are the opportunities. There are multiple options in the audio engineering arena to be considered, ranging from audio post to music recording.

I spent much of my life juggling my music career as an artist while making a living as an engineer; being skilled in both areas has contributed greatly to my own personal success.

When I picked up the headset to Skype with Michael Semanick, I didn't know that much about what a re-recording engineer did other than create the final mix for a film and prepare it for theatrical release. After a few minutes, I was just fascinated and fantasized about starting all over and following his career path. Every movie that plays the theater circuit needs to be mixed for the theater environment and it takes a specialized team headed by someone who can focus for very long periods of time, has the patience of Job, and is a diplomat of gargantuan proportions. Michael is that guy.

Michael Semanick

RE-RECORDING ENGINEER (FILM)

Michael Semanick is a two-time Academy Award winner (The Lord of the Rings: Return of the King *and* King Kong) *and has been nominated six times for Achievement in Sound Mixing.*

Michael, What does a re-recording engineer do?

A re-recording engineer/mixer is a person who takes sounds prepared by the sound team (editors) and blends those sounds to produce the final mix that is released with the film. The sound team includes sound-effects editors, dialogue editors, music editors, and Foley editors. Sound-effects editors go out and record sounds that are needed for the film. This includes atmospherics, like birds, crickets, restaurant walla, bar walla, etc., and hard sound effects like guns shots, cars, doors, and horses, to name just a few. They edit these sounds into the picture.

Dialogue editors take the dialogue that was recorded during the filming and edit them into the picture; this may involve editing dialogue from various takes. They also supervise and edit the ADR. (ADR is dialogue the actors recorded in a studio after the film has been shot.) ADR (automatic dialogue replacement) is recorded because the production dialogue might not be usable, a performer was replaced, or lines changed.

Music editors edit all the music for the film. This can consist of the score or source music—like music in a club or restaurant. Foley editors edit the sounds created specifically for the film by the Foley artist. These sounds can consist of footsteps on different surfaces (dirt, gravel, concrete, wood floors, etc.), the movement of the actors, various things like cups being picked up and put down, door handles, chair creaks, and so on. The sound editors then bring these sounds to the dubbing or mix stage. As you can see, the sound elements for a film might be several hundred tracks wide.

Then comes the re-recording mixer's job. The re-recording mixer takes this pallet of sounds and blends them together to create the final soundtrack. The director of the film guides us into what he wants the film to sound like.

You need to be very organized to perform at this high level of production, don't you?

Yes, since there are hundreds of tracks of sounds, both the mixers and sound editors need to be very organized. There maybe five to six sounds just for one gunshot, or many sound elements just for a door close.

As the mixer, I'm comping down certain groupings of sounds and tracks so it's more manageable in what is called pre-dubbing. Taking many tracks that make up a sound like a gun battle, which would consist of gunshots from both sides (good guy, bad guy), the ricochet of each shot, the debris of each hit, the gun movements, shell casing drops, and combining those elements so it is more manageable in the final mix, so taking a gun battle that might start out as a hundred tracks and getting it down to like twenty tracks. Which requires combining elements together. It can be a lot of fun, very stressful, and very demanding. It is also very creative and collaborative, which I really enjoy.

So when you are mixing, do you work in a movie theater environment?

Yes, it is the same setup as you see in a movie theater but with fewer seats, and a very big console in the middle. Behind us there are lounge seats for directors and producers. We are also surrounded by computer workstations for the various sound departments.

That must be quite a sight! Do you work with another mixer as a team?

Most of the time I mix with a partner because there's just too much to handle with hundreds of tracks coming in. We split the duties: one will take dialogue and music, while the other takes all the sound effects. It varies, depending on who is mixing and what might be best for the film. I do feel that the whole sound team has to work together to produce a great soundtrack. The editors and mixers go hand in hand, but they are both two very different art forms. Occasionally we'll do a three-mixer crew with one guy for dialogue, one for sound effects, and one engineer for music.

It sounds like it varies from project to project. How long does one of your projects take to complete? Is there a typical, or average, length of time needed to mix a movie?

It depends on the movie, really. How long is it? How much action? How much is sound used to tell the story? How much ADR is being used over production? Was the production track recorded good or is it poor, requiring more work to try and clean the track up? So many variables, and of course budget. On average a film takes about ten to twelve weeks. Smaller films, indies can to be mixed in three to four weeks for budgetary reasons. They're also a little more sparse and rough around the edges. They play fine but I always want to go back and tweak them; unfortunately the budget limits what I can do. Because it's such a creative process and there are so many different stakeholders, it's all subjective and times can vary dramatically.

Are you a musician, Michael?

I started out playing in bands in elementary school and high school. Trumpet, French horn, and E-flat alto horn. I also played guitar. When I got to high school, I applied to the Berklee College of Music and got accepted. So the answer is yes, I am a musician, but I play for fun now.

What role, if any, did education play in your particular career choice?

I just wanted to be involved in music. When I got to Berklee, I fell in love with the recording studios and I decided what I wanted to do while I was there. "I want to capture musicians on tape. I want to capture their performances and work with them on songs." It was fascinating to me. At Berklee I majored in music production and engineering.

Even school can't prepare you for everything, can it? Speaking of which, what are the greatest challenges of your job?

The hardest thing is to discern the director's sonic vision for his/her film, and then to support that vision. I work with the same directors over and over again so it's very important to understand what they like and expect. We become friends and business associates. I do occasionally work with new directors and teams, but once you find a good groove, you tend to hang in that groove. I am lucky to have directors who are very loyal. That's an awesome feeling; when you find people who are that loyal! [*laughs*]

Has this job led to other opportunities for you?

Absolutely! Fantasy Studios, where I worked early on in my career, and its diversity in recording led me to working in film. That led me to work with Francis Coppola at his Napa facility, which led me to Skywalker Sound, which led me to Peter Jackson and working on *Lord of the Rings* in New Zealand.

Michael, it sounds to me like you are busier than ever! What were some of the coolest projects you've ever worked on?

One of my first projects was *Twin Peaks* with David Lynch. He took a huge chance on me, and gave me a stepping-stone. I also worked with Paul Thomas Anderson early on. He took a chance on me as well, and we have worked together ever since. The same with David Fincher and others.

What's a typical day like for you in the theater?

My day usually starts around 9 a.m. and stops about 7 p.m. I'll get in 8:30, and if it's the first day of a final mix, there's always a lot going on with everyone running around trying to make sure visuals and audio are playing back correctly, getting the same sample rates, etc.

For me it's a question of, do I have the right track? Do I have access to everything I need to make this happen—the reverb and dialogue chains and the sort? What we will normally do the first day is just open all the channels with the director and play it through in its entirety. It's usually a train wreck [*laughs*] but we get broad strokes from the director this way.

"I want this ethereal here, quiet here, we need to rethink the music cue here, and now that we have all the sound effects in, things aren't working for me." The director is also being pulled a million directions, so we work out the basic blends and present a first pass to him a day or two later. We'll start by playing the reel (15–20 min. long) and then you fix more and move to the next reel.

"I need a different sound. Those sound effects aren't great there." Or it could happen this way: "It's great!" And it's on to the next reel. It's a constant, all day long, easing sounds in and out until about 7 p.m. But as with anything, there are always deadlines and people procrastinate along the way, so you can end up working twelve hours a day towards the end of a project to get it to what the director wants. It's costly, but in the holistic scheme of a theatrical film it's one of the least expensive line items! [*laughs*]

What does the future of the re-recording engineer as a job look like?

Honestly, I think it is a healthy career, but I don't know because I'm busy and just want to work. I'll keep going until they tell me I can't mix anymore, or the phone stops ringing. I want to mix for my buddies and find a different direction; maybe that's speaking to and passing the baton on to the next generation. I'm not sure if I'm at the point yet, but I know it's coming because as I get older, the directors I grew up with are getting older too. Some of them will continue to make movies into their seventies/eighties, but I don't know if I'll hang in there that long! [*laughs*]

RE-RECORDING IS BUT ONE of the many types of recording and mixing jobs to be had in the music business. If you want to be directly involved in music creation, you might want to consider working with bands and artists.

Even though most artists today have a home studio running Logic or Pro Tools, many smart artists will enlist the help of a professional to record or mix them. Think of it like the homeowner and the carpenter. Let's say I own a hammer and nails are easy to come by, but I wouldn't try to add an addition to my house if I ever expected to sell it to someone! Owning the tools does not make you a carpenter.

More and more artists are realizing this and hiring engineers when they can afford them in all sorts of capacities, including the guy that just records the tracks, the person that mixes them, or the mastering of the final product. There are also the special folks that do it all for a package price and produce, record, mix, and master your final tracks.

Jimmy Douglass is one of these people, with many years of experience under his belt both as a successful engineer and producer.

Jimmy Douglass

RECORDING ENGINEER (MUSIC)

Jimmy Douglass, also known as "The Senator," is a four-time Grammy-winning recording engineer and record producer whose career has spanned more than four decades. His clients include Aretha Franklin, Hall & Oates, Led Zeppelin, Foreigner, AC/DC, the Rolling Stones, Justin Timberlake, Snoop Dogg, Kanye West, and Ludacris.

Would you explain the role of a recording engineer when you started in the business and how that role has changed?

When I started with Atlantic Records, the engineer was someone who could control the whole room. Production quality was included in that as well. Most engineers could play an instrument and contribute in some fashion musically, much more than just getting sounds.

Today, the role of the traditional audio engineer is almost nonexistent because the technology has changed, fine-tuned, and self-contained the process. Take drums, for instance; the drum manufacturers have it down to a science and kits sound great before you even start playing. Back in the day, drums sounded like a crappy mess, and you had to spend days to get a good sound.

Today, you also have the benefit so much expertise, years of people messing around learning how to mike a drum set, and they share all that information. You can watch YouTube and learn how to get any sound.

Why did you decide to pursue engineering?

As it turned out, engineering found me. I was looking for a job. I knew Jerry Wexler's wife and daughter, and there was an opening at Atlantic Studios to do tape copying. I thought I could start in high school and continue part-time when I went to college. It was an easy job because you'd put a tape on, walk away, and do your homework. In the back of the record company they'd be doing recording sessions, so little homework got done. That's how I got into it. I was a musician but I didn't even know what a studio was. I totally fell in love with the recording process.

What's the best part of your job today?

Everything—I'll never stop doing this. I have two traditional, proper studios, one at home and one on my laptop. It's what I do and it's what I'm always thinking about. I'm always trying to find something new to create.

What's a highlight of having your dream job?

I'm happy when people acknowledge what I've done. Kids look up to me. I love that part, but when they tell me I'm a genius, I always respond, "I was just trying to keep my job." When you're sitting behind the board and Aretha Franklin starts belting out a vocal, my job was to figure out a way to keep her from distorting. An engineer is a problem solver.

The one item that I do miss in this new world of engineering is to problem solve, quickness, to adjust, read, and just to keep the ball moving. The urgency factor is missing, and I think it's missing in music as well. A lot of times great ideas and music happen spontaneously because of the urgency factor.

You've clearly worked with incredible talent throughout your career. What's a day in the studio life of Jimmy Douglass like?

I work out in the mornings to stay in shape and get blood flowing, then I go to the studio and start mixing, go through e-mails and music sent for me to listen to. I might look up some new bands on the Internet, or listen to the radio to hear the latest sounds. What's sonically correct changes every seven years or so. Like the 808 drum sounds, in the '80s, then all of a sudden they went away and in the late '90's they were back again.

I have two studios, and two different producers that work with me who are incredible beat makers—young kids that produce. I also have one or two artists signed that keep me busy.

Where does most of your work come from?

It comes from all over the place because the model is changing so fast. The problem is that there are only twenty artists that the labels are spending the big bucks on and there's at least a hundred engineers running around LA fighting for the same twenty records.

At the next level, you have a whole new world of artists who are doing things without "professionals," and others looking for engineers that will work at a lower rate because they can't yet afford them.

These artists are the talent of tomorrow and I'm always scouting these indie artists. When you go for the big ticket, they have four, five different people test-mix a track and there's no joy. You may get paid, and you may not if they don't pick your mixes.

Let's talk about money for a moment. How does one get paid as an recording engineer?

The easiest/best way is to get paid by the day, rather than the hour or by the mix. If you're working with a band that's too particular and you charge said band by the mix, you will lose every time. You have to pick your poison carefully.

How long does a typical recording project last?

Back in the day, we all got together for a month and laid it down as one cohesive package, but it's changed an awful lot. I rarely do a project from start to finish anymore. Lots of artists record in stages. For example, Kanye does a track, and then sends it to Ludacris to add to, and then they send it to someone else, like me, to mix it. That's an extreme example, but that's what can happen these days. So the short answer is that it might take a few days or a few months.

That sounds like quite a challenge, because it effectively means you have multiple people to answer to on a job that might be in two different places! Aside from those kinds of logistics, what are the biggest challenges for recording engineers these days?

I believe that music engineering as a sole profession is shrinking because everybody can pretty much record himself or herself. In most cases, they don't understand what a bad job they're doing, nor does the listener. So if that's cool with everybody, who am I to say what's good and bad. I have a nice Neve console, and most bands don't even want to hear that old soggy sound.

What advice would you give to someone starting out with aspirations to engineer music in today's industry?

Know your instrument and know your craft before you go out there to tell the world what you're doing. You have to be better than anyone else. It has to show in your work, not in your mouth.

What does the future of the music business look like to you?

The landscape is all-encompassing, and what most of us can't quite figure out is how the money stream is going to continue to support so many people.

For example, I've noticed that in radio play—they're only playing ten records, so not many people are getting paid, and on the Internet nobody is being charged. There is no organized way of accounting web plays. The clubs have also gotten out of hand. There are clubs everywhere,

DJs everywhere playing music and the artists aren't getting paid there either. DJ-s are becoming more important than the producers, engineers, or in some cases the artists themselves.

I believe you're going to see the advent of live music again, but it's going to come through the backdoor and maybe with DJs as the new front person. They're going to add live singers and instruments to their DJ thing. Drummers may be out of luck because they won't be needed. The rhythm thing is covered, and the live people will be on top like icing on the cake—new clubs will expand to live performance.

It will be different, but exciting for sure.

WHEN I MEET WITH PEOPLE WHO are looking for my advice about some music-related endeavor, I always recommend education and experience, because that's where it all starts, at least for those of us who have been successful. In other words, do your best to become an expert. You can't do anything that's meaningful in this life without knowing what it is you're trying to accomplish, and the self-made, self-taught road is a long one.

There are a million books on the subject of music and how to make it as an artist. These publications cover everything from building your Facebook fan base to the best way to print one-off T-shirts for your band. There are also a handful of terrific books that take an in-depth approach to the real-life education of musicians and artists and great places to start your journey. One of these books is *Behind the Glass* written by the extraordinary Howard Massey. Howard uses the shared advice and experience of producers to deliver a powerful message. I asked Howard to share his thoughts as a recording engineer and author.

Howard Massey

RECORDING ENGINEER (MUSIC), AUTHOR

Howard Massey is a recording engineer, producer, musician, and music journalist. He was formerly an editor at Musician *and* Performing Songwriter *magazines and is the author of* Behind the Glass.

In your book, Behind the Glass, you interviewed some of the greatest engineers of our time. What are your personal feelings about making a living as a recording engineer today?

It could be tough going [*laughs*], if you're going to *just* be an engineer. You have to have a more diverse skill set to put several revenue streams together because the rules have changed so dramatically. Many musicians today have their own Pro Tools rig at home and think they know how to engineer, but most can't. Part of the myth that prevails is, "If you buy this new tool, you too will be a great engineer."

We haven't reached a point where it's apparent that the only people who can make great records are skilled engineers, but I believe at some point we will.

Would you talk about some of the other types of audio engineers? Audio post-production, film and TV scoring perhaps? There are still a lot of different engineering opportunities out there.

Scoring and post-production are industries that are still expanding. It's a competitive field and it's primarily centered in one city (LA), but it's an area where there's work and a demand for talented engineers. It's also intense work because you need to be able to work very fast, which is another skill entirely.

Calm under pressure, technical chops, for sure! What other traits might make someone successful in today's industry?

Developing great people skills! [*laughs*] If you're an ass, no one will want to be in a room with you. If people are comfortable in your presence, they'll let you get away with messing things up . . . once in a while, anyway. People skills, psychology, and knowing when to keep your mouth shut are top of my list.

[Engineer] Jim Scott once told me a story about how tough he is on assistant engineers in his studio. If they can't make great coffee or know to keep the pencils sharpened, his theory is that they'll never be detail-oriented enough to make good records. That attention to detail, and knowing when to melt into a room, are the things that no school can teach you. Your role is to be completely invisible sometimes. I'd rather spend a month on a project with a nice guy who's not that good than a jerk who's great.

What are some of your best experiences?

One was with [engineer] Humberto Gatica, who was working in the studio at the time with Carole King and we had scheduled an interview for the end of their session. Carole was still there when I arrived, and she said to me, "Do you mind if I stick around to hear the interview?" I said sure, but before we started Humberto decided he wanted to play me a surround mix he'd just completed for Celine Dion.

So I'm sitting at the mixing board with Carole King and Humberto Gatica listening to this amazing mix, and about halfway through I hear Carole King literally sobbing next to me— that's how much the mix moved her emotionally. The hairs on the back of my neck stood up. When the lights came up, she turned to Humberto and said, "Why don't you make *me* sound that good?" [*laughs*]

Also, as part of the preparation for Geoff Emerick's autobiography (which I co-authored), I got to see London with him and visit places from his childhood. Here I was walking down the corridors of Abbey Road Studios with the guy who recorded the Beatles' *Sgt. Pepper* album as he pointed to spots saying, "John Lennon was standing here when we had this conversation, and this is where we moved the drums when we did that track"—amazing stuff!

Several years ago when I opened RedHouse Inc., we hired interns to help fill the holes in our team and generally help us out. There were a few exceptional interns who stood out to my partner Tom Faulkner and me. One was a young guy who brought a smile to everyone's face on a daily basis. He would stick his head in my office three or four times a day: "Hey, Mr. Redman, can I help you out with anything?" Randy should have started a school called How to Succeed as an Intern, because without even knowing what to do, he *did it* naturally.

Randy was the best intern to ever grace our doors and was to become one of the best audio engineers ever to walk through them as well. He soaked up engineering like a sponge, instinctively knew how to make our clients feel special, and just may be the fastest Pro Tools editor on the planet, and that's saying a lot because I thought I was! Randy blew us away on a daily basis, caring for everyone around him as he humbly created some of the best work to come out of our company.

Randy wasn't with us more than a month when we were invited to "become more convenient" by the Disney brass and open an office on Disney property at Celebration. We opened a beautiful studio fully outfitted with two video edit suites, audio, and graphics to service our Disney clients only to find that we were now "too close." You see, our clients wanted to leave the office for the day so they could hide from the watchful eye of the Mouse, but since we were only a block away it was too convenient to call them back to the office. Our studio failed miserably, but Randy took it all in stride, working every day through the turmoil and loneliness of an empty studio for the three months it took us to shutter the office.

When I closed RedHouse in 2007, Randy was faced with the same decision I had made several years earlier and chose to go into business f[...]
Randy has prospered in Orlando.

Randy Me[...]

Recording Engineer (Audio[...]

Randy Mease specializes in music and sound d[...]
and a variety of advertis[...]

Randy, was there a point in your life when you c[...]
going to do for a living"?

I got out of high school and was still playing m[...]

music, but didn't know what to do with it for a career. Then of course you have bills to pay. I heard about a recording school in Florida and that's where it took off.

You learned engineering skills in school?

Yes, I went to Full Sail University in Winter Park, Florida, where I was taught audio engineering. After attending Full Sail and learning about recording, and seeing the different areas that audio engineering could take you, I decided to follow the path of post-production audio. Here I am.

It sounds like it was a good experience for you. How did you make the transition to engineering?

I felt the best way to start my career in engineering was to intern. Once I got the internship, I saw just what working as a post-production engineer really meant. It's a different type of audio engineering altogether. There are a million music studios that all pretty much do the same kind of work day in and day out, while post-production studios are much more elaborate. In post-production, you use all the different mediums of audio, not just music, so I was attracted to that aspect.

What are some of the skills somebody needs to be successful in the audio post world?

I can't say enough about people skills. You need to make your clients feel great about what you do and they need to trust that you are an expert and can achieve the desired end product. That's always been very important for me.

Do you work a lot with your clients in the room or do you primarily work in an unsupervised setting (by yourself)?

It's a mixed bag. Many times my clients will just say, "Give this a stab," and I'll have a chance to explore and experiment, which is a big part of what we do in audio post. I'd say that having the freedom to work unsupervised is one of the best things about my job, but also having the opportunity to work with great producers is as rewarding.

...ike you need great client skills and have a knack for diplomacy; being ...round the politics of a session is an extremely valuable asset. ...ut that?

...idea to yell and throw things. [*laughs*] Working in audio post is kind of like ...ust have fun and put things together because it's the last part of the ...nts are ready to see it all come together. My part is usually adding ...t sound sweet. That's why we call it "sweetening."

It also sounds like a lot of what you do is solve problems. What are your thoughts?

Sometimes it's like a jigsaw puzzle for sure. You're getting ideas from editors, musicians, composers, directors. Audio elements can come from anywhere and everywhere and it's the audio editor's job to create a consistent sound canvas and smooth out all the edges. More and more I see my work as a craft like that of a painter, carpenter, or artist. It's meticulous and time-consuming work.

What type of client do you normally work with?

It varies. . . . Being an audio-post house in Orlando, which is not a large media production market, my client base consists mostly of advertising professionals. I've pretty much seen and done every type of audio work you can imagine here, from on-hold messages to national commercials to Disney films.

Is there a reason you chose to strike out on your own as opposed to working at a larger company or post house?

Post houses are great because you get to work with a team where you have graphic designers, video editors, and everybody can work together. The economy has shut down most of the large post houses and there are a lot of one-man shops. I guess the main reason I'm on my own is having the freedom to direct my own business and the fact that good gigs at large facilities are not as attractive anymore.

Are you able to make a good living as an audio post engineer?

Yes, I'm fortunate that I have. When you open your own shop, obviously there is an investment in equipment and shop expenses like phone lines, ISDN, and maintenance . . . there are just a million things you have to look out for. If you can take care of that end and find a good accountant to keep you on track, you'll do all right. Obviously our industry is driven by geography, but with technology and a strong marketing plan, you can pretty much live and work anywhere you want to these days.

Clearly, keeping your client roster healthy is probably the best way to stay in this business. Do you find yourself looking for variety of project types, or simply for more clients for one type of work (i.e., sound design for corporate advertising, as you mentioned earlier)?

It's always nice to have a variety of different clients with different audio needs. There is no reason to just focus on one type of client or project; for instance, you might be able to work on some music projects here and there to fill in the holes in your main post-production schedule.

Do you have some advice for someone who is entering this business or wants to become an audio engineer?

Research! Try to get into a facility where you'll be exposed to all the different areas of post, like editing, graphics, shooting, etc. Obviously future employment is important too. . . . If a place hires interns out of their positions and into paying gigs, get in there, do a great job, and make yourself invaluable to them. Just keep showing up. . . . If you can do that and make great coffee, everybody will be happy!

HAVING A VERY FAMOUS FATHER HASN'T STOPPED DAMON from becoming one of the hardest-working people in the entertainment business. Even though he rarely toots his own horn, he is one of the most respected scoring engineers in Hollywood, combining passion and expertise to capture the orchestra the way it was meant to be heard. Just listen to the recording of the score on *Rabbit Hole* and you'll know exactly what I mean. Having come from an engineering background myself, I can really appreciate Damon's work, dedication, and attention to detail, not to mention that he's a very welcoming fellow.

Damon Tedesco

SCORING MIXER

Damon Tedesco is an award-winning, independent music-scoring mixer for film and television, whose credits include Six Feet Under, Call of Duty, Kill Bill: Volume 2, *multiple Super Bowl commercials, and* Xbox Halo 3.

Could you explain in some detail what the job of a scoring mixer entails?

Typically a composer gets hired by the production company to score a film and that composer hires a scoring mixer that they trust to record and mix their music for their film. Normally I work with the composer and get everything prepared ahead of time in Pro Tools; that's the way most everything is recorded nowadays.

To do this, you'd build a few elements in Pro Tools, including your click, synth pre-records, digital video, and MIDI tempo maps, which give you the bars and beats. Then the composer will check to make sure everything is in the right place, so when you get on the scoring stage there's not much guesswork. Things always change but at least you'll have a game plan.

Once you get to the scoring stage, you record all the music to match your picture and there'll be directors and producers in the room working alongside the composer to make sure it's exactly what they want. You'll make sure everything is good on the recording, take notes, and make sure you have your selected takes; however, you may or may not do your editing there. Most of the time, you'll leave the session with a hard drive full of musical material and take it to a mix facility to create the final mix in 5.1 surround and in stereo.

What special skill set have you developed that's specific to this process as opposed to someone who records bands?

I think I lean towards orchestral recording and get hired to do that sort of thing as a specialty. I've spent over fifteen years on scoring stages assisting other scoring mixers, being onstage with live orchestras every day, and I really understand what an orchestra is supposed to sound like. It really helped train my ear and understand the scoring process thoroughly.

So do you mix the music for the final version of the film?

Not typically. What I would do is prepare all the stems and give them 5.1 electronics, 5.1 percussion, 5.1 orchestra, and so on.

In an ideal world, everything would be set to unity and they would just set their faders to zero. That would be the mix that I prepared for them. It's a safety net, so if musical elements are battling the dialogue and need to get rid of a low drown or a high-pitched element, they can just duck one element instead of the whole score. The process is always a dance and the key is to understand that the dialogue is, and always will be, king of film. Do not fool yourself into thinking the music is going to win. [*laughs*]

Would you consider the role of scoring mixer to be a creative one?

There's a lot of creativity involved in the available musical choices, recording techniques, and the mix. I think that creativity really starts to develop when the relationship between a composer and engineer becomes a trusting one. You start to anticipate what that composer would like and really hone in on it.

Tell me about your normal workday. You get up in the morning and then what?

Once again we'll pretend it's a live scoring session. First of all, live scoring is what I live for. It is my favorite thing to do in the world. A friend of my calls it "gig heroin"; you do a job and it will keep you high for a couple of weeks, but ultimately you go searching for the next one.

So if it was a double session, which would be musicians from 10 a.m. to 5 p.m., you get to the scoring stage at seven or eight in the morning and bring your hard drive full of material. You might even get there the day before and bring all that stuff you've prepped. You'll look over the stage setup. On large-format sessions, I would have already faxed a drawing, including the stage setup specific to microphones, preamps, channel faders, Pro Tools, reverbs, video, and all the technical specs.

You make sure the Pro Tools is working, test headphones, etc. What you are really doing is making sure that everything's tested because once you start recording, the cost per minute is gigantic with an orchestra. You can't be fumbling around with the click track or having problems with video or out-of-sync dialogue because everybody is already very anxious. You work all day, back up to external hard drives, and start all over again the next day. Hopefully it's longer than a day session! [*laughs*]

How long is a typical film in recording days?

It used to be five to ten days of recording, but I think those days are over. Today you're seeing that most films are recorded in a few days due to budget. What will happen many times is the composer will prepare all their stuff on synths and treat it more like a sweetening session where they'll record brass, wood, and strings.

Dubbing has changed and they want much more control over the instrumental mix and you can't really do that if everyone's playing at the same time.

Would you tell me about some highlights for you personally as a scoring mixer?

The thing that I love about my job is that every session is different. Recently I enjoyed mixing some of the music for the *Wolfman* movie with Conrad Pope because it was such a challenge. There was fair amount of drama with composers being hired and fired and we had to fill in the gaps in the existing score, so it was a true challenge. Conrad Pope was the composer on the film and he really knocked it out of the park. I think he was great. I didn't record it but I mixed it in 5.1 in my own studio.

I just finished the *Rabbit Hole*, which stars Nicole Kidman and is out right now. The composer was Anton Sanko and that was also a fun score. We did small strings on a pretty intimate score and it's exposed. It's a very quiet film with dialogue and not a lot of effects, so it's really music heavy. I loved it!

How long does it take you to mix a score?

How long you got? [*laughs*] Most of the time there's a package where they'll hand a composer a bulk sum of money, $50,000 or $25,000, and say, "Here's your production budget and you need to figure out how you're going to deliver a forty-five-minute score to us." So the first call from the composer is like, "Hey, ya know, how long's it going to take for us to record and mix all this stuff?"

It might take four or five days to record and another five, six days to mix. I think on *Rabbit Hole* it was six days total. So it's a difficult call because all it takes is one little bit of a snag with the director not liking something and you're into rewrites, and before you know it, you're over budget. There is not the wiggle room with budgets any longer, so it is pretty stressful on the composer.

Since you brought up budget, does a composer call you specifically or is he kind of bidding you against other guys in your profession?

It really depends. It's a very team-oriented sport. Usually the composer likes working with you and is a fan of your work. That's the best scenario. The worst scenario is, "Hey, this guy wants to charge $100 an hour. What can you do for me?" Because then you know you're screwing somebody else, and I'm not a fan of that way of doing business.

So yes, you do get people pitted against each other as far as budget and price and really all you can do is put your best foot forward—is it your talents, your speed, is it your studio, is it the microphone collection you have? For me personally, speed and efficiency is usually why I get hired, because I can get the job done quickly and efficiently, which in turn saves them money.

Another advantage for me is my studio. About eight years ago, I built this wonderful 5.1 mix room, seeing the coming demise of the bigger studios. Budgets were shrinking so quickly that you couldn't go and record somewhere and then spend five days just mixing in a big room.

You've said that your specialty is recording orchestra. If somebody decides to do an orchestral score, they may just switch their scoring mixer, right?

That's true. There are plenty of people, and yes, I'm going to name names that I respect, love their work, and I love the teams they're surrounded by. A team is usually made up of the composer, scoring mixer, music editor, copyist, and orchestrator. I'm talking about a small team of five to seven people that can really crank out the scores.

I really enjoy the music of Randy Newman, Chris Lennertz, Michael Giacchino, and Walter Murphy. Walter writes the music for *Family Guy* and gets to record a live band every week! These are guys I'd love to work with at some point.

Damon, I was an engineer for about twenty years and I know exactly what you mean. It leads to my next question. Like most professions, a scoring mixer is pretty competitive. Is there something special you do to position yourself or service that's unique?

I think every session should be fun. Almost every composer comes to me with a lot of stress, anxiety, and that look of fear in their eyes. Sometimes we've got sixty-five minutes of music and it's due in a week and a half.

I would say my demeanor is calm, fun, and supportive. A lot of this comes from my work ethic. You can't treat the low-budget projects like garbage and then kiss butt on the big-budget projects. Music is music. We're going to get it done. We're going to have fun. You're in good hands. Don't worry, it's going to work out. And above all treat everyone around you with respect. I don't think that it's unique, but it's the way I work and the way I am.

Damon, as with most businesses, music is extremely relationship-oriented. Do you find yourself using social media networks for business purposes?

I think as far as Facebook is concerned, I use it to show friends, the watchers, the work I'm doing. It's also helpful when composers that you work with tag you in photos. It's a delicate balance between letting people know what you are working on and just being a pompous show-off.

How do you think the job of a scoring mixer might change in the future?

In the last ten years, the business has shrunk dramatically, and it's only going to continue to shrink unless things turn around here in Los Angeles. You can't put all your eggs in one basket, so I do live sound at different venues, live recordings, classical recordings, etc. You can't rely on just one thing; you have to understand dialogue editing, music editing, sound effects, and sound design too. I'm not saying you have to be Jack-of-all-trades, but you should have a strong understanding so when you get a call and they ask, "Do you do dialogue editing?" your answer will be a confident yes.

That said, there is a lot more media content being created, and it is my hope that there will always be a need for someone to record the music.

Is there some wisdom you'd pass on to someone headed down your path?

I was mentored by Armin Steiner, Bobby Fernandez, Danny Wallin, and Tim Boyle. These are scoring mixers that are still working and kicking ass, but they were able to take me under their wing and show me stuff. I feel like the mentor role is going away, unfortunately. Lots of people are working by themselves, staring at their screen, and not learning from anyone else.

As far as advice is concerned, go to school for engineering and music because I think it's smart. A lot of people underestimate the difference an education can make, whether it's a university or trade school.

ONE THING THAT JUST DOESN'T HAPPEN ENOUGH in our industry is reaching out and lending a helping hand to those in need, in need of a break, to be heard, or to be fed. I felt that need to get involved when I decided to write this book and hopefully help some artists live a life in music and not be forced to give up that love to pursue the dollar.

There are those of us who have a calling beyond ourselves, a calling to help other musicians be heard and share their music with the world. It is a tangible gift that transcends all cultural boundaries and racial divides. When I called on one of these people, Eric Gast stepped forward and simply said, "Sure, Mike, I'll help, what can I do?" I was immediately drawn to this guy because he stands for everything I endeavor to be!

Eric Gast

MIXING ENGINEER (MUSIC)

Eric is one of those people who has his fingers in all aspects of the music business. As an engineer, he has worked with Billy Ocean, Will Smith, Britney Spears, and Kid Rock, to name a few. He should be an inspiration to all of us musician types who use our gifts to help our world.

Eric, would you explain the role and purpose of a mixing engineer?

A mixing engineer is a large part of the production process because it's about producing the sounds.

A mixing engineer has a palette of frequencies and a stereo spectrum to work with, and a bad mix will simply ruin a song. There are only so many frequencies, so it's all about placement and where you put sounds. Some of the bigger records that have made a difference in your life, like Steely Dan or Earth, Wind & Fire or the Eagles, have a sound canvas that is like a fine painting and they take you to a whole different world. Without that sound, they would still be brilliant records, but wouldn't have the longevity and impact they still have today.

Maybe you could tell me a little bit about how you switch hats when you're producing and engineering at the same time on a project. How do you talk to yourself?

I think of it as almost like quarterbacks in the NFL that can throw and run just as well. I'm creating sounds from the beginning, and you know where you want them to sit in the mix later. I may be doing some untraditional EQing but I also know where it's going to land in the mix as the producer. So I can see both sides of the coin in that scenario.

It's the production of sound and it's all part of the same vehicle. I think it's helpful when you're doing both because most really good mixers are one step away from being the engineer *and* the producer anyway.

What type of equipment do you use?

I used to have a studio in my house, but now it's just a museum-quality collection of equipment. These days I'm using an HD Pro Tools rig but still love analog tape. I still do my drums and guitars to analog tape at 15 ips [inch per second] and then bounce it over to my Pro Tools rig. I love that tape compression. I also love Neve consoles. If I can find an old-school Neve and be able to track something on that, I'm a happy guy! I love tubes—warmth and fullness.

I recently interviewed a guy, who said, "I've got a $400,000 Neve console in one of my studios and none of the new artists will even let me turn it on." Isn't that amazing? I never realized it before, but they've grown up in a digital world that doesn't like that warm sound.

No, they don't, which brings me to something else . . . it's a very different world now and a little disconcerting. You hear music that you mixed and some kid downloaded it from somewhere and plays it to you on his iPod in mono; the sad part is they don't seem to care [*laughs*]. You have to wonder what we're becoming because we'll sit and obsess over a mix that nobody cares about!

As a recording engineer, do you get involved with an artist beyond the recording process and sometimes help them place their music, try to get deals, that kind of thing?

Yes, I've done that many times with newer artists, especially if it's somebody I really believe in. If they are on a small label, I might help with my connections. Also, if it's a project that I've worked on and [am] proud of it, then it encourages me to get it to where it needs to be.

I once worked with a Celtic band called Seven Nations that were just great. They were on a smaller label but wanted to get on a bigger label like Atlantic. They had this system and were making a lot of money playing festivals. They were just like a machine, turning out money and had a huge following, so I told them, "You really shouldn't mess with this formula because you already have it." They got the deal with the major label and ended up making much less than they ever had before.

Everyone wants to be on a big label, but it's very different nowadays. Labels are basically banks, and if they are not doing tons of marketing for you, then you simply don't need them, you really don't.

What would you say is the most challenging part of being a music mixer, the things that scare you in a session?

There was a point as an engineer when you could cover the VU meters with tape and not worry about how hard you were hitting them. You would just use your ears and let them do the work.

It's a different world now, where everything is in a Pro Tools rig, but back in the day we used tons of outboard gear and we had to know everything. There was a lot of technical stuff to stay on top of, and you always had to know what the newest gear was. Just when you got comfortable and you got good at cutting tape, people stopped cutting tape! [*laughs*]

As you get older, you realize that the most important part of producing or engineering is knowing when to stop. There is a point where you're not making the music any better. You don't understand that until you get older or you've done enough records that you can say, "This one is right. I can keep nitpicking all day but it is right."

How do engineers get paid?

Typically they get paid per mix, but some of the older guys like me can get points on a single that we're mixing, almost like production points. Sometimes the label budgets are less, so they'll reserve a single's mix for someone who's a little more seasoned and pay them more. It's a weird thing to me because what that means is that record companies aren't making albums anymore; they are just making singles.

You no longer will hear a cohesive audio novel like *The Wall* or Zeppelin. Labels are worried about one track, banging it out, and the rest of it is a write-off. It's very strange thinking. . . .

Since you work mostly for record companies, are you available when you get a general call—"Hey, would you mix this for me?"

Sometimes. I try to split my year between music mixing/producing and my NPO. I need to pay my bills and make my rent on the months that I'm working, so being out there doing the typical mixing thing doesn't work too well. The months that I'm doing straight charity work I'm not getting paid.

It's quite a balancing act, isn't it?

Yes, it really is. When I originally had this concept for FM World Charities, there was much more work coming in through the music industry. Working only six months a year made sense at the time because that was enough for me. Today I have to be really careful about the projects I take on. In the past I would do jazz records. I love jazz, but they just don't pay [*laughs*], so it's very hard to do now.

When you look into your crystal ball, what does the future of the music industry hold?

To be honest with you, Mike, it's a new frontier, and even with the issue of monetization, I am very optimistic that someone with the wherewithal can make music in his house. And if it's good, and he can reach an audience, he won't be a slave to the labels anymore.

Basically the only thing that makes sense is to let people listen to music for free, but when you download it, you have a commercial. Let Reebok, Volkswagen, Doritos, [private industry] pay for it with brand messages like television shows do because music hits the specific demographic they want. Who needs to reach millions of people? . . . Those guys. You shouldn't need to sell out anymore to get paid for the music you create.

ONE OF THE MOST FAMOUS INNOVATIONS of motion-picture sound was developed by a fellow also known for some terrific wine and a series of films that have just been re-released in 3-D, thirty years after they changed the way all of us looked at outer space and our universe, the *Star Wars* trilogy.

In 1978, George Lucas founded what would become, and still is, one of the premier sound-recording studios on earth. Skywalker Sound has been the creative force behind hundreds of films, home to many thousands of recording artists, as well as the mix spot of choice for an untold number of TV commercials and series.

Many of the people who have contributed to this book have at some point worked at Skywalker. It is no small feat to become a working executive at a facility as renowned as the Skywalker Ranch.

Leslie Ann Jones

RECORDING ENGINEER (MUSIC)
DIRECTOR OF MUSIC RECORDING, SKYWALKER SOUND

Leslie Ann Jones is a multiple Grammy Award–winning recording engineer, and is also a past chair of the National Academy of Recording Arts and Sciences board of trustees, the organization that awards Grammys. Jones has worked with, among others, Bobby McFerrin, Herbie Hancock, Miles Davis/Quincy Jones, Boz Skaggs, B. B. King, and Dee Dee Bridgewater. Her video game scores include Star Wars, Pirates of the Caribbean, and more.

Leslie, you started out as a musician. Would you tell me how you decided to pursue a career as a recording engineer?

I originally wanted to be a record producer and an artist manager but thought that I should learn something about recording. I really enjoyed engineering and later started producing and managing. One thing led to another and I found that I had an aptitude for sound mixing and recording, at which time I stopped playing guitar and pursued a career as a recording engineer.

How about the skill set that's required for somebody to do this type of work?

I think the skill set includes the ability to work well with people under sometimes very stressful conditions, long hours, changing plans, and these days you have to have a good working knowledge of computers. You don't necessarily have to read music, although that's certainly a big help and it is also helpful to have played an instrument and understand orchestration, song structure, things like that.

Okay, so how important do you think it is to have a formal education in the industry?

Nowadays everybody that you're competing with for a job is going to a recording school, so it's kind of hard not to. We also have fewer and fewer large, multi-room facilities where you can get a job interning and work your way up. Most studios are single-room studios and owned by the engineer doing the work, so it's very difficult to learn on the job anymore. This is not the same answer I would have given twenty-five years ago; it's the answer that I give now.

Things are changing! So would there be an advantage to a customer coming to one of the larger facilities and working with experienced engineers, as opposed to somebody that has all the time in the world sitting in front of a Pro Tools setup?

I think there is always a benefit to working with other people because you pick up a lot more and you work on a variety of recording projects. Therefore, you get experience with all kinds of music and many different situations. I always believe it's beneficial to work at a larger studio, or at least a studio that has good project turnover with a diverse outside clientele.

It's a shame that large facilities are fading away; while I'm hopeful we'll see a resurgence. Another thing I have found surprising, while writing this book, is the lack of women in the technical side of our business. Why do you think that is?

I think that it's changing all the time, but in many cases it is simply the lack of exposure of our business to women, and general lack of effort in helping them understand that it is a real career option. For me, I was playing guitar in rock and folk bands and eventually just started doing live sound. There just aren't enough opportunities for women to see other women doing work behind the board.

Also, there are sociology studies done that explore what happens to young women when they are in middle school. They kind of go through this transformation from being eager beavers raising their hand in grammar school to being in middle school and paying more attention to what their friends think of them.

This is one reason I spend a lot of time with girls and young women, teaching them recording, lecturing, and things like that because the more they can become empowered, the better off they'll be at whatever they choose to do.

Leslie, what's your favorite part of the whole recording process?

I guess my favorite role is whatever I can contribute because every project needs something different. Sometimes it's more of my engineering expertise and sometimes it's my production experience—whether I'm producing the record or not.

As an engineer, you always have to be careful because if there is a producer, you certainly don't want them to feel intimidated in any way or less valuable because you may know more about what they're doing then they do! [*laughs*]

I work with a lot of new producers: people that are picked as producer by the artist for whatever reason. It doesn't necessarily mean that they really understand pitch and composition and things like that, so my favorite part of the process is when I feel that I've contributed in some way and they have benefited from working with me or here at Skywalker.

How has changing technology affected the way you do your job in both positive and negative ways?

I think more about editing now and what the creative possibilities of editing are. Having the ability to fix and change things is great, but I still try to record the way I always have, which is to capture a great performance. Just because I can tune things doesn't mean that I want to, or that I will. I would rather work with a singer or the artist and try to get the performance naturally in tune because ultimately, to me, that's what makes a great listening experience.

What's the best way for someone to work toward being a recording engineer?

I always try to talk to people about finding somebody who is also starting out as a musician or as a songwriter. The best calling card we have is word of mouth and people that will pass our names along to other people. I have told the same thing to many people who want to be scoring mixers: "Find a young director who is working on their first project and/or find a young composer who is working on their first project scoring a film." It's all about relationships and you need to make as many as you can!

WE ALL HAVE OUR FAVORITE MUSIC and artists who inspire us. The soundtrack from the movie *Silverado* has always drawn me in and rarely do I get tired of listening to it, as composer Bruce Broughton brings a classic Western story to life. I've also told you that I'm a fan of great R & B music, but what I haven't shared yet is my admiration and respect for Todd Rundgren. For you young musicians, his name may not ring a bell, but for many of us, Todd's work as an artist, engineer, and producer laid the groundwork for much of the music you enjoy today.

I first remember hearing Todd when I was in college in Maryland. The song was "Black Maria" and I was sure this guy was a genius. Well, Todd is still going strong today and the years have proven my theory to be true. He has been, and continues to be, one of the most progressive, hardworking, fan-supporting, creative musicians alive, *and* he is homegrown in the USA!

I talked to Todd from his beautiful home in Hawaii, not about Todd the artist but Todd the audio engineer.

Todd Rundgren

RECORDING ENGINEER (MUSIC), PRODUCER, COMPOSER, ENTREPRENEUR, ARTIST

After thirty-plus years, Todd Rundgren still maintains a full touring schedule to sold-out houses of adoring fans. There is something mystical about this guy, and he transcends the typical talents of even the greatest musicians.

Todd, something my readers may not know about you is that you are a very accomplished recording engineer. Could you tell me a little bit about how and why you started engineering?

When I first started making records with the Nazz, we had little experience in the studio and a lot of presumptions about where the responsibility for sound lay. We discovered very quickly that while the producer gets lots of credit for the final product in terms of making a record, that doesn't necessarily apply to the sound quality.

Early on, there was an engineers union, so they were the only ones allowed to touch the console, and producers weren't the creative people that we assumed they were based on George Martin's resume. At the time, they were actually in the studio to organize everything and make sure the session didn't fall apart or run over budget.

I realized fairly quickly that if I wanted to have a certain sound, or take control of our sound in any way, I wasn't going to do it by asking the producer. I'd have to learn what the engineer was doing so I could speak his language.

By the time we started the second Nazz album, I had my hands all over the console, and by the time we actually mixed it I was the engineer. That kind of hands-on opportunity allowed me to quickly gain experience that most artists don't have. I learned the hard way.

In most cases, you go to some sort of audio engineering school and intern; so in effect I was lucky and leapfrogged all of that. As a result, that allowed me to market my engineering services later on when I was doing album post work.

Were there some highlights? Any times you worked on a project and were just floored by how incredible the project was?

My very first gig was as an engineer with Robbie Robertson as producer on a record we made in Toronto by an artist called Jesse Winchester.

So there I am, in a studio I'd never been in before, and I had to take over all the engineering responsibilities. Fortunately for me, everyone was fairly happy with the end result. It was a little different than what I had been doing with the Nazz, which since I was a performer the engineer took care of all of the microphone placement and stuff like that. This was the first time I actually was supposed to pretend like I knew something about miking. I had to just lean on what I had picked up from watching him, and just move things around while diddling with the EQ. I combined a little bit of knowledge with very acute listening to what was coming out of the speakers. I learned very quickly where the mike should be relative to the instrument to get the best sound. So it was really a lot of on-the-job training in the beginning.

Do you still engineer your own material?

Yes, I do. With other acts it's an issue of whether or not I think I'm going to have trouble with the performance in the studio. If that's the case, I'll get an engineer because I just don't want to have to push the buttons constantly. But for the most part, I'm always the engineer because I discovered at a certain point there are projects where unless I am engineering I'm liable to fall asleep. [*laughs*] Also, in the past I would do projects where I knew that I had to engineer because the sound was so critical that I couldn't allow anyone else to even move the faders.

Do you find it hard to separate yourself as the artist from the producer, from the engineer when you're in the studio?

Well, early on in my career I tended to get a little too involved in helping people with their songs. Sometimes it was to an extreme, and would make the record tend to sound a little bit too much like my records. That's not necessarily a good thing when we're trying to figure out what's unique about the artist. So it's better for me to be minimally involved when it comes to material. Having said that, material is the most important part of any production, so I usually listen to the material fairly seriously before we even go into the studio to record it. That way, I'm not making those kinds of judgments or contributions but actually getting to the production itself.

You've always been an early adopter of technology, going way back to the introduction of MIDI in the late '80s. To what do you credit this interest in tech?

Well, to a degree it's a certain amount of curiosity, but I've always had a pretty good sense about when it's time for me to adopt a particular technology and that's not necessarily the same time [as] everyone else.

I will sometimes burn through technology before others even discover it, but then it will become very popular and I'll already be on to something else. So to a degree it's early adoption, but in other cases it actually may be late adoption.

As an example, I didn't start using sequencers to make my records until it was fairly established. They were Roger Powell's specialty, so by association I knew about and was working with sequencers and MIDI equipment. There was a point where I was letting other people do the work because it didn't seem like the technology was mature to the point where I wanted to adopt. Also, I've never felt the necessity to duplicate what other people are doing musically in this business.

Everyone that I've talked with has a somewhat different take on what they think the future of the music business will be. What's yours?

Well, it's started to become a little clearer, at least to me. I think a new collection of models that can work for the musicians and for musical entrepreneurs is where it certainly needs to go. For instance, I think that Rhapsody is going to become a serious competitor to iTunes, and that iTunes will have to change its model to Rhapsody's. Then everything is going to be fine.

In other words, the 99 cents a song model is bogus and will eventually go away, but the $10 a month subscription model is terrific and will become more and more popular. That's my belief.

Part of that is because for a long time I didn't have a device that would deliver Rhapsody to me and it was not available on Macintosh for some reason. Now I have Rhapsody on my iPad and all I need is some bandwidth—I'm downloading albums all the time and what it allows me to do is to listen to music I would never pay for. No advertising model. I just pay the $10 a month and I'm happy to do it.

As I've told you, I was an engineer and worked on hundreds of commercials, so I can say with some degree of confidence that it's a tough job. The stress can be intense, and the rewards come fast because you are recording at a breakneck pace, sometimes recording three or four different commercials a day. To stay in this arena for years takes a special type of personality and maybe some blood pressure medicine. I tracked down and interviewed Gary Chester on the recommendation of a friend in the advertising business who told me he was simply the best engineer he had ever worked with.

Gary Chester

RECORDING ENGINEER (ADVERTISING AND FILM SCORES)

Gary, you started out in studio maintenance but didn't really care for it. Please explain?

I started out in maintenance, but within three weeks they called me and said, "Gary, you're not really fixing anything." I said, "I don't know anything about tubes! I come from a world of schematics, diodes, gates, and resistors! I'm not qualified for this job. Do you have anything else?" They asked, "How would you like to be a mastering engineer?" And I said, "Great! What's that?" [*laughs*]

I then became a mastering engineer and I worked on a lathe cutting vinyl records. I used to listen to the whole album, make notes on the loud parts and the soft parts, and then make deeper grooves or narrower grooves based upon the volume and bass. It would take forever to make these works of art, which is what I considered them.

My goal was to make the loudest records I could and my client base grew. If you can't make it loud, you're the same as every other mastering engineer!

One day the studio manager asked me, "Do you want to do a session with us?" I had never worked in a studio before, so I told them, "Sure." I went into the studio and cleaned up the place, organized it, got rid of all the boxes, and we did a record. Soon I was getting more work with UA artists like the Belmonts, Funkadelic, War, and I that's how I transitioned into engineering. It was a wonderful accident! [*laughs*]

That was the beginning of an incredible career. So what are you doing these days?

I'm mostly recording film scores, and loving it. When music and picture come together, they always make the other better. The passion and emotion that is created can give you goose bumps and that's what I really enjoy. I get to do a lot of work in Prague with the Czech Phil.

Recording film scores is a lot like playing jazz because a lot of the engineering creativity is done during the recording. It is better to get the oboe solo up during the recording so it doesn't just sound like a fader move later, so the conductor will say, "Bring up the oboe in bar twenty-five and twenty-six, bring the cello down two dynamic levels," and you great a great mix during the live session.

You are a legend in the world of recording for advertising. Is working on commercials a more specialized job for a recording engineer? If so, in what way?

Yes. First and foremost, *speed!* Speed is crucial for an engineer in the commercial business. If your session's starts at 10 a.m. and the drummer gets there at 10, he sits down and you hit the record button; you don't have time to get drum sounds.

It's also being able to understand the communication by the creatives of agencies, being able to understand and decipher what they all really mean.

One time we finished a sixty-second spot, played it back, and the creative guy stands up and says, "Right there! Right there! Play that back—right there! I love that!" And I'm thinking, "I didn't hear anything wrong with it . . . what?" And he says again, "Right there, I love that!" And I said, "Okay, that's where the track modulates!" He replied, "Let's start it that way!" I laughed to myself, how do you start with a modulation? Advertising is a strange world indeed.

Another time we were tracking a sax solo, and the agency person says, "It sounds too frantic, too *Saturday Night Live*," so I said, "Maybe we should bring it down an octave, which we did, and then she said, "It sounds too bluesy, how about half an octave?" [*laughs*] There are many stories like that in advertising, not to mention people saying things like, "Can you make it sound more . . . magenta!"

Do you have any "I've been there" advice that might help someone learn about the business side of your job?

I do! Schools like NYU now have great engineering, production, and music business programs. They give their students a well-rounded introduction to the business, whereas my introduction was strictly from the street.

So you'd recommend, for someone who is thinking about engineering as a career, that they should attend Berklee, NYU, Full Sail, or another school and minor in business?

Either that, or don't forego a lawyer. When National Video in NYC took out a loan for $9 million, it used all of its distributaries as collateral. Even though I owned 45 percent of the audio studio and had paid $1.5 million plus interest for the construction, when the bank foreclosed on National I lost everything.

As a kid from the Bronx, I didn't understand what had happened. I couldn't even get my gold records or the pictures. I was pretty upset but thought to myself, "I started from nothing. I'm just going to kick back and get it going again." Pay for a lawyer before signing a contract! Don't get so excited you sign and regret it later.

How does technology play into your workflow now?

Any time I am working in a big studio, I have a Pro Tools operator working with me. I could operate it myself, but I really can't do a good job reading the music, mixing, getting sounds, *and* running Pro Tools. My son works on Pro Tools ten to twelve hours a day and is blazing fast; it's all about keystrokes and shortcuts.

What is the typical schedule for a scoring project in Prague?

It's unbelievably fast! [*laughs*] If it's a commercial, it will be one session with sixty players. We get on a plane Friday night in New York and arrive in Prague Saturday morning. Saturday afternoon I set up the studio and the Pro Tools rig. Sunday we do the session, and Monday we come home. That's it!

On a film like the *Camelot* miniseries on Starz that I just did with Jeff and Mychael Danna (from LA), it was five trips to Prague. Each trip was four sessions (three orchestral, one choir) over five months and it was all done with Source-Connect. They were in LA and I was in Prague and it worked out just great. It was such a wonderful experience working with them.

Booking Agent

Rapid Fire

Skill Set—Socially skilled, sincere, like long hours, have a thick skin, a strong belief in your gut and your artists, have the ability to negotiate a deal or walk away from one if it's not in the best interest of your band. It doesn't hurt to have a degree in counseling too because bands tend to bring their problems to their managers and booking agents.

Hours—Typically bankers' hours, except for going to clubs to support your artists and check out new talent.

Upside—Everything, as long as you keep your energy level up. Booking agents can enjoy a long run if they are consistent, organized, and deliver good, solid acts to venues as well as good, solid venues to their acts.

Downside—Sometimes, even when you are working hard at this job, you will get slammed by bands for gouging. It's usually because bands don't make much money to begin with and then they see the few remaining dollars getting sucked away . . . you are the closest target. Starting out could take you a while. You'll need to be aggressive, project a high level of confidence, *and* find bands that believe in you as much as you believe in yourself.

Financial—$$ to $$$$ People working full-time as a booking agent make between $50,000 and $150,000 (not including the superstars who pull in over seven figures). Like many of the jobs in this book, the smarter and more creative you are, the better you will do financially.

Location—There are bands everywhere. You should be looking at large metropolitan areas, especially tourist destinations and places that hold conventions.

Future—Bands today need to play live and tour more than ever before, so the role of the booking agent is, and will be, an important cog in the wheel of any successful music machine. If you want to, you can make this a lifelong career (one of the few that still exists).

MOST BANDS TODAY NEED TO PERFORM TO MAKE A LIVING, or at a minimum to connect with their audience. There are several ways to find places for a band to play and to book gigs, including personal meetings with club owners or managers, through friends and family, and even through one of the many online services. However, if you are in the music business working at a professional level, you probably have a booking agent.

Agents are those guys that many bands look down upon but at the same time rely on. You see, most bands are struggling, and they view the 15 percent booking fee most agents charge as outrageous. The fact of the matter is that without the agents, there would be no gigs for the bands, and just about every business transaction has a commission or fee of some type connected to it . . . hmmm. Seems like a lack of business savvy on the bands' part.

Booking agents are the conduit that connects a band with places to play. Performance venues vary greatly, including coliseums, clubs, conferences, meetings, private functions, and a host of other possibilities. Booking agents are typically contracted to fill performance schedules in these venues, and on the flip side represent bands and artists that would like to perform in these venues. It's a social profession that sometimes requires long hours, but it's a very viable career option with great long-term potential.

It was Saturday afternoon and the auditorium was packed—packed with talent scouts, sort of. These talent scouts were about sixteen years old and appointed by a school committee to check out bands and decide which one would play at their high school prom. They were a tough crowd, and for most of them it was the first time in their lives they had money to spend—and they wanted a lot for their money!

So the lights dimmed and a band started playing something that sounded familiar, but I couldn't make out exactly what song it was. All of the sudden a lone figure sprinted from the back of the room holding a doll and a knife, shouting, "Shattered!" This crazy guy, Chris Merrell, taught me that day just how good you could be as an entertainer. The band was the Malones and they landed almost every great gig that day.

My band at the time was Nova and we were very nervous playing after them, because we just couldn't compete with such talent. I think we contracted three proms, while the Malones landed twenty-two or something equally outrageous. Now, it didn't hurt that they were exclusively represented by Blade, a great little booking agency with two very aggressive agents that had put this showcase together. Our band was only part-time with the agency, and we suffered for it.

As a band matures and learns more about the music business, they usually gravitate toward one agent who best represents their goals. In the case of the corporate arena, which can sometimes be a gold mine for a band, the agent of choice in Orlando, Florida—which hosts the largest convention market—is Lloyd Hanson. Lloyd is a my mentor and longtime friend; he is also one of the hardest-working agents in the business.

Lloyd Hanson

PEYTON ENTERTAINMENT

Lloyd Hanson is an entertainment agent and a member of the Paradise Band, which has played at events with Ray Charles, Bruce Hornsby and the Range, the Commodores, and many other touring acts.

Lloyd, would you tell me what a booking agent in today's corporate entertainment world does?

It really starts with acquiring a talent database comprised of all styles of entertainment at all price points. The next ingredient is a client base that needs entertainment for special events, scheduled events, or ongoing events. Add to that some experience in the music industry to provide the perfect entertainment for each opportunity. Agents are the middlemen of the supply chain in the entertainment business. Proposals, contracts, follow-ups, etc.

How did you elect booking music as a full-time job?

As a bandleader, the business role of keeping the band working is really not much different than that of a talent agent. After pulling away from playing nightly in bars and moving into one-night gigs like conventions, country clubs, special events, etc., our band became quite popular. I found myself handing off a lot of gigs to other bands because we were already booked. It made sense to not only help other bands find gigs, but make extra money with commissions on these dates.

What has been the most satisfying part of your job as a booking agent?

I have always been fairly comfortable and resourceful at finding work for my band. Other musicians (quite often—some of the best musicians) don't have this skill, and providing work opportunities for them is quite rewarding for me personally. The other is hearing from a client that the entertainment I provided *made* their event!

While it might be a rewarding profession, I'm sure it's a taxing one as well. Tell me about the biggest challenge you've had to face as a booking agent.

Discipline! Providing consistent quality to regular clients as well as one-time buyers requires attentive listening, great note-taking, attention to detail, timely responses, and accurate follow through crossing the T's and dotting I's.

What are your hours like? I've heard you have flexible but long hours; is that accurate?

Well, it starts with something like a nine-to-five job, but you also need to attend some of the events and get out and hear new talent as well as meet with both established and potentially new clients. The longer your hours early in your career, the quicker you'll build a client base and a talent pool.

If you had to pick the single most important trait someone would need to be successful as a booking agent, what might that be and why?

I would think it's good communication skills. Sharing and imparting information with entertainers, buyers, managers, and event planners always needs to be honest and accurate.

What does the future of a professional booking agent look like?

Great question! I think the information highway is affecting every business, and ours is no exception. Entertainment of every kind can be found on the Internet if one decides to look for it. There will always be a place for talent agents because we not only book the talent, we take very good care of our clients as well. The future will be there for those who have a presence on the web and use all of the resources made available to us, as well as to entertainers and buyers.

On that financial side of things, how are today's agents compensated? Can you make a good living as a booking agent in today's uncertain economic climate?

Usually, in my experience it's been commission, based upon percentage of cost of entertainment booked; and yes, you can make a good living. If you work at it consistently and build a large clientele, you can do quite well.

If it's all right with you, I'd like to put you on the spot here and ask how much a moderately successful agent might expect to make annually.

A part-timer with little experience and not too much effort could make $20K to $25K per year. An agency owner who markets high-end entertainment, takes the risks, and has other agents working under him can make ten times that and more. I have always felt I could make more money if I focused only on being an agent, but I made the conscious decision to continue to play music—and it was a good one. I love the camaraderie *and* the music.

J. J. Cassiere

THE AGENCY GROUP

J.J., can you tell me about your role as a booking agent?

I primarily coordinate the artist's touring schedule, which helps create the overall master schedule for the artist. Some artists at the time when we sign them do not have management.

At that point, the agent will help set up management meetings for the artist, and most of the time the agent will give the artist some advice when they are ready to make a management decision.

Is your plan for a month, for a year?

Every agency is different, but I work at least three to six months in advance. If the band is touring major markets in January/February, maybe they should tour secondary markets in April/May. So it just depends on the time of the year, where the artist is in their record cycle.

So if I'm a band and I find a festival I'd like to play, part of your responsibility is to find out who's in charge of booking for the festival?

Yes, I'll find out who the buyer is for the festival, and then submit the band to the buyer for consideration.

What's a regular day like for you?

Generally I get to the office around 8:30 a.m. and stay till about 7–8 o'clock. I will leave earlier if I have a show to attend. Once I wake up, I'm like a machine. I normally grab my Blackberry while I'm lying in bed and check e-mails and voice mail. Once I get into the office, I create a to-do list for each client on my roster—what needs to be done immediately, and worked on for the coming months.

Do you spend any time at the bands' gigs?

I went to Tokyo for the first time this year with one of my clients, The Word Alive, just two weeks before the earthquake. Traveling is a huge part of being an agent. I love it!

You obviously love music. What separates a great agent from one that's not so great?

Comparing myself to Dan Shapiro, who is a terrific agent, I would have to say the main difference is experience. He has found bands and taken them from $100 a night to $10,000, then on to become $30,000-a-night acts. Developing an artist is a big priority, and what some agents forget about is the actual music. They get caught up in the commissions when they should be believing in the music and the long-term plan for the band.

So when you're developing a band, is that assisting, helping the band, and mentoring the band, telling them what's going to get them the bigger-dollar gigs?

Yes, it really is. The manager may come up to me after a show and ask, "Hey, how were we tonight?" And I try to be honest with them. Sometimes I have to tell them, "You've got to clean yourselves up." Advice can range from losing weight to trimming a beard. Mental, emotional, physical, everything.

Do booking agents make a good living?

Yes, especially now with the shortage of good agents. I live comfortably and I'm pretty sure all the other agents I know do as well.

Are you on a salary, and then receive additional commission based on a percentage of the band's income?

Yes, I am salary based. Most agents will then have a back-end deal in place for when they gross/net X amount of dollars.

So it's performance based; the harder you work the more you're likely to make?

Most of the time! [*laughs*]

If I had the right skills and wanted to start in the agency business, is there some advice you'd give me?

I believe the best way to start out is to learn about your local music scene. Try to meet a promoter, and intern with him, get on a street team, that kind of thing. Also find a band and find them gigs. Believe in your ears when you listen to a band, or spend some money to go to a festival and network. But always remember, you really have to like music and people because this is a social profession.

So what would you say is the hardest part of your job, J.J.?

Well, I have nineteen bands with about five to six members in each band. The hardest part for me is disconnecting myself. It's very hard on a Sunday to put the phone down and go to the beach and have a life away from my job. I have started to get better at it, though!

And the best part?

Not to sound cliché but this is my dream job, to be working at this company and to wake up every morning knowing I'm working in the music industry. I love watching a band grow from $100 a night to $5,000 and that they made it happen for themselves because they worked their asses off. But deep down inside we both know that I helped them create a living out of something they love—music.

Justin Bridgewater

THE AGENCY GROUP

Justin, would you explain exactly what you do as a booking agent?

In the most basic terms, a booking agent's job is to plan where a tour goes (city, state, venues) and to negotiate the artist's performance fee. There are a lot more details that go into making those decisions, but that's the basic duty of a booking agent.

How does a booking agent work with the artist's management? What's the relationship?

A manager is one of the most integral parts of a band's success, as they guide the artist's career in all aspects. As an agent I work closely with the manager to ensure that each band is making the best decisions in terms of the other acts they are touring with, along with the venues they play. I like to think of all of the different people I work with (manager, label, publicist, etc.) as the band's team. If you don't have everyone working toward the same goal, it will be difficult to lead a band to be successful.

Do you make a good living?

Yes, if you find the right bands who tour frequently and make good money on the road, there is definitely money to be made, but it's up to each agent to hustle and stay active in finding artists to work with and to keep getting them work.

Do you keep long hours?

It's really a twenty-four-hour job, as I'm responsible for my artists when they are out on the road. So if they run into any problems with the venue or promoter, I could get a call at any time of the night during the week or weekend.

What would you say are the most important qualifications of a great booking agent?

I think a great booking agent has to have a few strong qualities. Communication is one of the most important ones, as agents are constantly on the phone and sending e-mails with promoters, managers, so you need to be able to communicate effectively in order to get what you need out of the other parties you work with. This business is all about hustling and there are many different bumps in the road, so staying grounded and being patient is important. There are two aspects of being an agent that are important, one is being able to cut the best deal for your artist possible, and the other aspect is a creative element as to how to position your band and help guide their career.

What's the toughest part of your job?

The most difficult part of my job is trying to stay ahead of the curve on trends in the industry and to be a forward-thinking person. There have been a lot of changes in technology over the past few years that are dramatically affecting the way the industry operates. So staying on top of those changes and using them to further develop an artist's career is important.

How does someone prepare for a job like yours—school?

School can teach the basic elements in terms of cutting a deal and understanding the different type of deals, but experience as an intern or assistant is really the only way to truly understand what it means to be an agent and the duties that are associated with being an booking agent.

What does the future of the music business look like from where you sit today?

There are a lot of changes taking place in the industry, especially on the label/distribution side of things. Understanding how to expose your artists to the public is becoming a bit more challenging, since mediums like MTV and record stores aren't as strong as they used to be. However, I feel very optimistic that booking agents will be around for a long time, as people love to see live music, and as long as that remains the case, there will always be a place for a booking agent to exist.

3

COMPOSER

Rapid Fire

Skill Set—A formal education is helpful for most types of composing. You may be able to write for a TV series without a formal degree, but if you're really serious about a job composing, you might want to learn to read music. I would also recommend at least some basic arranging and orchestration classes or you may severely limit your potential. The ability to write lyrics is also helpful; software skills are a must, as are an understanding of your style limitations and social skills. And yes, you should be a highly creative, prolific composer.

Hours—This job can require long hours because of project deadlines and is not the best for raising a family in the early stages of your career. You are often the last person in the food chain working on a project and everybody is waiting on you. If you are lucky enough to have a great home studio, it can make the process easier. For TV you can expect to have a spotting session for most every episode, potentially deliver some rough sketches in a day or so, and then, depending on the type of music you are composing, a tracking session. You will also need time for revisions, changes, mixing, and so on. As you can see, this is not a 9-to-5 job, ever.

Upside—You are usually the master of your own universe—sort of. You usually get to work your own hours, even if they are long, and composing is personally rewarding as a musician, almost as much fun as having an applauding audience. The compensation can be very good as well. You get to watch TV a lot (without the commercials). Can be a long career, depending on your connections and your ability to stay current.

Downside—Composing is not a team sport from the perspective of the actual art of composing. You'll spend a lot of time with just yourself and your music (this could be an upside). It can be a chore, however, being highly creative on demand and on an ongoing basis. You may lose touch with reality. If you are successful, there's little time to sit back and smell the roses (or even enjoy listening to your music). Also, as this is a great job, the competition is crazy and the business can be hard to break into.

Financial—$$ to $$$$. This is totally dependent on your personal success. There are so many levels and positions in the composing arena that it's hard to nail down a number, but let's say in the top echelon composers get paid around $1.5 million a film with a very long tail. Original advertising music can range from $5 to $30,000 per track, and corporate work varies. I might be writing another short book with a specific focus on this subject.

Location—Chicago, LA, NYC, Minneapolis, Austin, Nashville, and Montreal, Canada. There are many places to live and compose music, but it also depends on the type of music and industry segment. You probably don't want to live in Austin and try to write film scores (at least until you can afford two homes). Always remember the social side of the business. Networking is extremely important, and it is through this channel you will find most of your work.

Future—Looking good for a long, long time. There's more visual media being created than ever, but sit down and develop a solid plan if you want to make it work.

ONE OF THE MOST CREATIVE, CHALLENGING, AND REWARDING JOBS in the music industry is composing music. For reasons that should be obvious, it's the next best thing to being a performing artist. You get to play your instrument, create music, and get paid for it—most of the time. For the same reasons, it is also very competitive, but the good news is that if you are truly talented, skilled, and a persistent networker, there is composing work everywhere.

I started writing not long after I learned my first few chords on guitar. I have always written music; it just seemed like a natural extension of myself and it wasn't until I found writing for production music libraries that I started making money composing.

Several years ago I met John Parry, the owner of Parry Music, while working as a recording engineer in Florida. We were recording music for one of his upcoming releases and I found it just fascinating. John would always tell me in his wonderful English accent, "Michael, this music must have extra reverb because it will always be played softly behind a voice," or, "Add extra bass to the final mix so that the track will sound full in the background." One day I asked John if I could try writing some music for his library and he agreed to give me a shot. He liked the first tracks and kept offering guidance. "Michael, library music must always have an ending." Well, that was almost twenty years ago, and I still go to the mailbox and collect royalties for that music. Thanks, John!

In the years that followed, I made quite a good living composing music for everything and everybody, from Disney and Universal to NASA and major ad agencies. For me, composing music is probably the single most fulfilling mental activity I've ever experienced, and I've been known to write fourteen hours straight, just grabbing an occasional glass of water or coffee and loving every minute of it!

Today, with the enormous amount of media being created (YouTube uploads over forty-eight hours of video every minute of every day, and it's growing at a rate of 50 percent per year), there are opportunities to compose music for an ever-growing array of projects. It's not just film and TV as you might think. The long list includes gaming, industrial, marketing, documentary films, production music, advertising, in-flight entertainment, webcasts, theme parks, radio, podcasts, indie projects, and on and on. I bet if you sat for thirty minutes, you could make a list of over fifty possible markets that use original music on a regular basis. For the purposes of this book, we are focusing on a few of the higher profile markets so you can get an idea of what's out there and what the jobs are like.

It's question time again. Do you really listen to the score of a film when you watch a movie? I was told that there are really only two types of film scores: the ones that will be released as soundtrack recordings and the ones you never hear. You never hear them because they are there only to expand upon the emotional experience of a visual scene. On the other side of the coin, you have a classic John Williams score that is rich with memorable thematic lines running throughout, dancing from instrument to instrument, modulating, inverting, and making their own space in the film.

For the most part, film composers fall into one category or the other, but on rare occasions you find one that is equally as comfortable supporting the image as they are creating a memorable theme. Today I had the pleasure of speaking with one of these composers, the dedicated and prolific David Newman.

David Newman

FILM

David Newman has scored more than a hundred films, ranging from War of the Roses, Matilda, Bowfinger, *and* Heathers, *to* The Spirit, Serenity, *and* Alvin and the Chipmunks: The Squeakquel. *He was nominated for an Academy Award for his score to the animated feature* Anastasia.

David, would you explain your path to composing for film?

I had very European classical-music training as a young kid and my main instruments were violin and piano. I attended USC as a piano major but ended up as a violin performance major. When I got my degree it was in violin performance, and subsequently continued my education, receiving a masters in conducting at USC.

Once I graduated, I started doing film and television work as a session violinist. I played on many of Jerry Goldsmith's and John Williams's films, a host of television series and records. At the time I had no intention of doing any composing because my interests were entirely in conducting and performing.

At some point, though, I changed my mind and decided that I'd like to compose.

I'd been closely watching how the process worked and had some experience, but I learned more sitting in the orchestras watching and listening than I did from my family. [David comes from a long line of film composers, including [Randy, Alfred, Emil, Lionel, Thomas, and Joey Newman]. You used to be able to go in the control-room booths when they would do playbacks, so I just sort of stayed in the background and watched and listened.

I decided scoring was something I could do, so over the course of the next three years I composed and recorded a demo that was extremely difficult at that time because there were no synths. I couldn't afford to hire an orchestra, so I got all of my musician friends together and we recorded an orchestral demo cue.

Eventually, I got an industrial film job, and then some small B movies. It was a slow process and it took me five or six years to get anything really going. I kept working, doing sessions for about three of those years, and then just stopped and lived the best that I could for a couple of years until I broke in. I figured that the financial rewards could be quite good, so it wasn't all that risky.

It sounds as if a lot of time and effort was required just to get the ball rolling. Is that accurate?

Yes. But eventually you collect enough samples of your music, and then it either happens or it doesn't; I was determined to *make* it happen. I think that *not giving up* is the most important part of the career process. Whether it happens or not, it's never going to happen if you don't push for it and give up.

David, you've scored over one hundred films. How has the process of film scoring changed since you started in the business?

The technology has changed in a way that allows composers who were not formally trained to score films. That's opened a kind of pop-music production style of film scoring, and the people who do commercial music and can't read music can now do film scoring. It's also changed how you show a director your music. Now a film composer must do what's called a "mock-up" of the cues, which is a sample-based performance of the cue. I also have seen that young directors are used to using whatever music they can find and cutting it into their films before hiring a composer. This used to be very difficult, but with the advent of Final Cut and GarageBand it's available in a fairly simple format. I believe that technology has greatly influenced the content of film music. It's at once more egalitarian and less content driven. As more non-music artists are influencing what music goes into the film, the process changes. This of course is due to the advances in technology that make this way of working possible.

How does technology affect your personal process?

It's really the same thing. It's just orchestra music, or a hybrid of orchestra music and electronic music. Electronic music isn't really a good word for it, I suppose. . . . Some of my films use a big orchestra while others are sample-based with some live instruments added.

I think it's how film music has really changed and not the process of scoring a film. You still need to sit down and write a cue, and get it approved. You have to get every single note approved. You didn't need to do that when I started. There's a little more micromanagement nowadays than in the past. The bottom line is that they either like or don't like the music; it's that simple. If they don't like it, you have to figure out a way to fix it and change it up so that they will.

Do you have directors who want to come into your studio and want changes on the spot?

Oh yeah [*laughs*]. . . . They don't sit there while you make the changes; you'll just take notes and resend the music to them. You need to do everything you can to properly prepare before you go to the scoring stage. You do the best that you can to mock it up with samples.

You've told me a little bit about your education, David, but how important was it, and what role does it play, with what you're currently doing?

How would I ever know how to compose if I never took a composing class? [*laughs*] For me, it was training and it didn't come naturally. I had great training, and the ear to be able to figure it out so I knew when I heard something that was right and that I liked. I had also done a lot of conducting, and I played in orchestras from the time I was eight years old; I know the orchestra really well.

Would you give me an overview of a normal day when you are in composing mode?

You just get up and start going! I compose in a linear form and don't know how else you would do it.

It all starts with a list of tasks that you have created with the director while viewing a rough cut of the film. Each cue is a task. So I pick a cue to get started. I start at the beginning of the cue and work my way straight through to the end. Because there's so much mathematics involved, synchronizing to a picture, which is not going to change, I don't jump around a lot. So at least 99 percent of the time you're just going from the beginning to the end.

You also have these horrible deadlines, so you have to work a lot of hours, be calm and thick skinned about the process, but as we know, no one is thick skinned. You get yourself pumped up and ready for an emotional ride. I think the emotional ride is the hardest part about scoring for movies. You have to be willing to open yourself up to write something that is good, but that also means that you've opened yourself up! So when someone doesn't like it or they say something derisive, it's painful. So multiply that process by the thirty to forty cues and you have to know that you're going to get upset, but that you also have to keep going.

The hardest thing with composing (and everyone will tell you this) is just getting started. Some people have it wired: they get up at six or seven in the morning, have breakfast, and start working. However, most people procrastinate. I'm a huge procrastinator, so I have to really sit down and get started and lose myself in it. Once I have committed to the process, I start writing the music, and then, lo and behold, find myself finished with the cue.

What would you consider the most stimulating part of composing for film?

Well, for one, you get instant feedback about your music. You write music and a couple of weeks later you're recording it, and I don't know of any other musical endeavor where you write a piece for an orchestra and two weeks later you're getting it played by very high-level professionals; the speed with which this happens is intoxicating.

It's great! Movies are great! They're wonderful artistic statements, and most of the people who work on movies are very professional artists. When you look at a movie over and over again, even the ones that are not very good, you find what's good in them and you bond to that; on top of it all, you get to add your two cents musically. Your music can change the way a scene plays for the better. It's a very exciting job.

How do film composers get paid, and would you touch on the residual income?

There are so many different ways of getting paid, but if there is just one thing I would like your readers to take home from this interview, it is this: you should never ever, ever, *ever,* EVER sign a contract without running it by a lawyer or you *will* be kicking yourself later.

Let's say you're starting out, and you'll do *anything* to do a movie. As an example, you're writing the music for *The Blair Witch Project,* just some movie that no one thought was anything, and then it makes hundreds of millions of dollars and you did it for free, got your publishing or something small, but that's all. You would be feeling quite sick as you watched that film top the charts, knowing that you didn't get to participate in the success and cash in.

It doesn't need to be upfront money when you're starting out either. There are all types of other ways that you are paid. You're paid via a public performance when you sign up for BMI or ASCAP, and if the film is a big hit, you're going to get a lot of money from the performance royalties.

If you can get a CD made, anything that you own, you're going to automatically get 50 percent of the publishing revenue. There are also ways to do something for nothing and still get paid. The bottom line is that the more films that you do, the bigger your royalty checks are going to be.

It seems to be logarithmic, so it's good to do as many films as you can do in terms of making money, not necessarily artistry and career-wise, but simply on the making money front. The more movies you do, obviously, the more money you're going to make in the long run.

David, I'm a huge fan of your work and I believe composing music for comedy is probably one of the hardest compositional styles. Do you have a specific thought process when it comes to composing for comedy?

There is a story about *Throw Mama from the Train,* which was the first big studio movie that I worked on. This film was a dark comedy and, in some ways, they're easier than the straight-up comedies. The straight-up comedies can be really hard because there's nothing to hang your hat on.

I wrote a main title and it was very Bernard Herman-esque, very dark. The director, Danny DeVito, took days to process the music. He came back to me and said, " David, I just don't like it," so we talked a little bit about what I might do, but ultimately I had to start over and re-write the entire cue. (By the way, I was devastated by his comments.) I went back and wrote the new cue, and it turned out so much better that it completely solidified my relationship with DeVito, which is what you want to do! I went on to write music for many of his wonderful movies.

I remember that time as the worst I'd ever felt scoring a film, and also the best I've ever felt. The thing that's so cool about movies is that you never know what's going to happen. Right around the corner you could be offered a huge studio film, or you could write what you think is the greatest cue you've ever written and it turns out that it just doesn't work.

You know, that's another thing that's exciting about scoring films in reference to your other question; you can go along just complaining, "I don't have any work and the movies I'm doing are horrible," and then one phone call and everything has changed. I think that's what is fun about it because you can rise up quickly. If a movie makes money, you are along for the ride.

Do you have a favorite film that you've scored?

I like *Galaxy Quest* and *Bowfinger*. I also like a movie that no one saw called *Broke Down Palace,* which is a drama. They get put in a prison in Thailand. I like *Serenity*. There are certain cues I like and identify with in certain movies. I did a movie called *My Father the Hero;* I wrote a little lullaby groove piece at the beginning of that movie that I really liked. I think my best experiences have been with Danny DeVito. *Matilda* and *Hoffa* were highlights for me, but all his films were wonderful to work on. It was great because I just dealt with him—no studio or anyone else.

How many cues do you typically write in a single film?

Probably thirty to fifty, depending on the length of the film.

Multiplying that by one hundred films . . . that's a lot of music! If I was an exceptionally talented aspiring film composer, what advice would you give me that might help me get there a little bit quicker?

That's the hardest question to answer and the one that everyone wants to know.

I think that number one is that you *never give up*. There is no clear path to film scoring, but I would say you first have to have an agent. That's probably the single most important thing. The catch-22 is that you won't find an agent without getting a job. So you'll want to research the agencies and where you'd want to go and who might take you, as well as who you might like to work with.

Next, you want to get as much of your music as you can to music editors, because music editors provide the temp scores for movies. If your music is temped in a movie, and you have any go-get-it-ness in your nature, you can probably get a meeting with the director. Otherwise it's next to impossible to get that meeting. You can also try the film editor. . . . Obviously you want to get your music to anyone you can, but the film editor and the music editor might cut your music into a temp score. That's one of the only ways you're going to get a movie—*get your music in a temp score.*

Let me throw out a couple of other ideas and see what you think. What about the idea of interning with an established composer?

I think it could be a good thing, but for many it's not, so you need to be careful.

There used to be a stigma that if you did television, you couldn't do films, and people that did films couldn't do television. I think it's much more open now, though. Even orchestrating, which used to be a stigma (if you're an orchestrator, you'd never be able to score a film] has disappeared to some extent.

So if you're a young person, and approach it the right way and *not say,* " I'm only doing this as a stepping-stone or something," and you're putting your entire heart and soul into the internship, I think it may work for you and you can move on from that starting point.

You have to be very careful and smart about how you do this. Do as much political research and information research as you can, and if you're going to intern for somebody, you should find out as much as you can about him or her. If you're going to one of the music schools that have a film scoring program, you probably will have the resources to perform your due diligence.

Take the time to figure out what all the agencies are about, who's doing what, who is really taking interns and how they treat their interns. You can also get a job doing music prep. Of course, you have to be trained and that's potentially a different career starting point.

What is music prep?

Essentially music copying. But they call it music prep, because it's much more than copying now. A lot of people work this way: They come from a pop music world and maybe don't even turn a click on when they are writing. Nothing is in a grid, so there are no bars and beats. They're just playing what comes to mind without worrying about the tempo or meter. Then they'll send a MIDI file with the audio to a music prep house and somebody has to transcribe it. I don't know how much of a stepping-stone it is to composing film music, but there are a lot of people doing music prep and making a lot of money doing it!

What have you not done in music that you would still like to accomplish?

I want to write an opera, which I'm actually in the process of doing. Maybe not a grand opera, but I want to write an opera. I can't discuss it at the moment—check back with me [*laughs*]. Opera is my passion.

WHEN MY PARTNER, ALAIN, AND I SHUT DOWN OUR LITTLE MUSIC COMPANY, I had to make a very important decision: Should I go back to work as a recording engineer for a guy I didn't respect or strike out on my own as a composer? It proved to be the hardest decision of my life at the time. I could go back and do something I knew how to do, that was comfortable but not moving forward, or jump into what looked like the abyss and become a full-time composer. I've always been one to take a risk, and as scary as it was I took the leap. I didn't have any idea where to start, but I did know I needed a reel, so I gathered up my best tracks and put them on a CD. (I didn't have any video to show.)

Next, I sat and made a list of all of the production companies, advertising agencies, and corporations that probably had marketing departments in the area. I was really nervous, so I wrote out my little pitch like telemarketers do. Then I picked up the phone and started with the lowest level companies so I could hone my nonexistent phone skills. After a couple of days and maybe twenty calls, I started to gain a little confidence and could get through my pitch without feeling stupid and stumbling all over myself.

My first appointment was with Florida Film and Tape, a great local film company run by a very capable director/cinematographer, Brad Fuller. Brad specialized in outdoor marine film work, and I remember very clearly going to his office, sitting on a little wooden chair in front of his desk, and saying, "Hi, Brad, I'm Michael Redman. I write music. Do you need any?" Not the best sales pitch, but I at least got it out. Sales didn't come naturally to me, but Brad gave me my first job and I was on my way.

A few months later, I got an appointment with the Bozell agency that handled the huge lottery account for Florida. I attended a short meeting at their office, feeling pretty confident, and met with Leslie Tharpe and her team of producers, and they listened very politely but didn't say much. I was a bit confused because I knew the music was very good, but they didn't comment; they just said, "Hey, Michael, thanks for stopping by."

Days later, Leslie called me, "Mike, you seem like a nice enough guy, so I thought I'd give you a little heads-up. The issue everyone had with your reel was that the spots were so bad they couldn't even listen to your music!" I was shocked; I'd never considered the video part of the commercials.

One week later, another friend, Ron McQueen, suggested an unusual tactic. "Michael, get on a plane to NYC and take a video recorder with you. When you arrive, check into a nice hotel and record a bunch of great commercials, then come back here and write new music for them; problem solved!" After some begging, I was able to get another meeting at Bozell and showed them my new reel. The response was 180 degrees from my first meeting and they loved my music; the lottery business and Bozell became one of my biggest clients for the next several years.

Composing for advertising is an art form that's very unique and has its own special set of rules. Writing music for a defined time, typically thirty seconds, can be challenging for some, but for me it was natural. I would write little thirty-second songs for most of my clients, but in the case of Disney it was primarily post-scoring TV spots and changing tempo, key, and style, sometimes every second.

Breaking into Disney as a composer was not the easiest thing to accomplish either. I lived in Orlando and every few weeks I'd call the broadcast department of Disney and attempt to get an appointment with the head of broadcast, Jim Derusha, a transplant from a big New York agency. Finally, after a few months and twenty-five calls, he agreed to see me, and once through the Secret Service–type Disney security, I made my way to his office.

I was really intimidated when Jim introduced himself, mostly because I knew he was the gatekeeper to the Magic Kingdom, so to speak. With his help I could be introduced to all of his producers and start what I hoped would be a long, prosperous relationship with Disney.

The first thing out of Jim's mouth was, "I was hoping you would be a great-looking young lady! When I was in New York, I would have five or six beautiful music house reps stop by each week to see me, but I've been here in Florida over a year and have yet to see the first one. So I guess you're it? What can I do for you? Are you any good?"

I responded, "I'm okay, I guess," and Jim said, "Well, maybe you should come back when you're great, because I only work with people who are great at what they do." I showed him my reel and he was mildly impressed. "Okay, I like your music. I'll give you a call if something comes up." That was it, end of meeting.

Andrew Sherman

ADVERTISING

Andrew Sherman is an awarding-winning advertising composer who has written and scored thousands of commercials. He is also the owner of Butter, a notable music house in NYC.

What is your daily work routine?

My two main responsibilities as a commercial composer are to listen to as many different kinds of music as I can so I know what people are talking about when they call, and being able to translate their words/direction into music.

You need to stay inspired when your skills are tested constantly; your chops get old quicker in this business than any other. Most people's point of reference when communicating about music is not musical at all; it has a lot more to do with "Did you hear this band? Do you know this song by this band? Or, there is this sound . . ."

One of my to-dos is keeping abreast of not only what is popular now, but also what is up and coming or going to be cool. The thing that can be a badge on someone's lapel in this business is if they can identify the next hottest thing before it's the next hottest thing.

In your opinion, what is the toughest part of your job?

For me, I think it's revisions. The initial writing phase is always fun because you have new projects daily, and it's not a movie that takes months to finish. The commercial world is a little more of a revolving door.

You have a thirty-second spot and you're going to write two, maybe three versions in one day. If you're lucky and win the job (they are almost always competitive, or demos), that's when the revisions start. If you thought it was hard to understand the initial creative brief, in non-musical terms, the changes can even be worse. Occasionally they improve things, but usually your demo will get scaled down to accommodate voice-overs and the like.

And compensation?

If you're playing on your own composition, you're going to get lines on a contract; if you're singing on your composition, you're going to get SAG lines on your contract, the residuals from which can be exponentially larger than a musician's contract. There are also publishing residuals. Until recently, I was unaware how lucrative they are for commercials. There is an organization here called AMP, the Association of Music Producers, and they were apparently instrumental in electing a guy to the board of ASCAP who started lobbying for greater monitoring and greater tracking of music residuals on commercials.

The Wojahn Brothers out in LA [successful commercial ~~composers~~] ~~referred~~ us to the Windfall Agency, ~~whose specialty is tracking~~ publishing residuals. They take 10 percent commission for it, but they go and find money that you would never, ever have the time to worry about. I think our checks tripled or quadrupled when they took over.

Knowing what you've learned, what advice would you give someone who wants to compose for advertising?

I get resumes and reels, and I believe your reel is what gets you in the door. The advice I would give somebody who's just starting out in this business is to be self-sufficient and become a great composer-engineer combination. Then start pulling spots off the web and scoring them if you don't have any final spots for your reel.

Being a producer, engineer, and composer in one package? Is that common these days, with the lower price of high-tech gear and sample libraries?

Yes, and being a bit of a programmer helps too! There are ways to make bad strings sound good, and there are lots of ways to make great string libraries sound horrible; you have to know what you're doing in that department. What I look for in people that I hire is a synthesis or a production background, where they've had exposure to more than just compositional skills because the definition of "composer" has changed greatly in this world.

MY BAND, HEADLINES, played this great bar, Brassy's, in Cocoa Beach, Florida. Brassy's was just the coolest. It was over 10,000 square feet, had a huge stage, beautiful people, and they paid us well. We played mostly original music, but threw in the occasional Clapton song. On slow nights we would huddle in the corners on breaks and play Pac-Man or Asteroids. I probably spent thousands of dollars trying to become an expert at something that meant absolutely nothing, but oh well, it was a lot of fun.

Today, gaming is a way of life for anyone under twenty-five, and I enjoy the 360 Kinect with my girls, and even though they kick my butt on a regular basis, it's a blast. I've heard that writing music for games is also a blast, and as Chuck Carr tells me, it requires some special talents.

Chuck Carr

GAMING

Chuck Carr has numerous high-profile video game credits, including various NBA and MLB games, Twisted Metal *games, and* Gran Turismo 5.

Chuck, I know you've spent considerable time as sound designer for many successful and well-known gaming franchises. How did you make the transition from sound design into composing for games?

Well, when I was first hired at Sony PlayStation in San Diego, it was as a sound designer, but my first choice was writing music. I saw the need to have music composed internally and started writing music for some of the internally created games. I worked mostly on the sports titles, which were well suited to my writing style, and it just blossomed from there. I basically formed the creative music department at the San Diego campus.

How does composing and writing songs for games differ from writing for film, advertising, or even for the general commercial market?

Well, the biggest difference is that it's not linear like film and television. With film, advertising, and TV, what you see and hear on-screen while scoring is how it's going to be seen and heard when the public views it. There's only one version. But with games you may have many different outcomes that occur based on the player's actions. Because of this, often times interactive or adaptive music is used. Here, you can have various game scenarios play out while having music seamlessly move from one game state to another.

The majority of interactive games will have an ambient layer of music where there's not a whole lot of action going on, a medium-action layer, and then there might be a fighting layer, which is very energetic. You've got varying scenarios on-screen that pull you in and out of those layers for game interactivity. There are also some games like racing games and sports titles that usually don't require interactivity, and it's just a straight linear track that plays back.

Given that film scoring is different from game scoring, what are some of the things you should consider when writing game music?

My goal is to underscore what is happening on the screen, just like in film, but in games what is happening on the screen differs just about every time you play it. For example, let's say I'm going to write music for a sports game front end, which is game production terminology for the menu music.

In most cases, it's not desirable to have lyrics for many reasons—in a basketball game because if you're licensing a track, often times the lyrics are going to have language that doesn't fit an E [everyone] rating. If you need to meet E-rating requirements, you'll often need to edit most of the lyrics out. In that case, I would just decide to do instrumental hip-hop tracks.

If we're going to use interactivity, the music would begin very basic and would get more intense the deeper you moved into the menu options, like when in the settings and modifying your character screens.

At the first screen, I might have a simple hip-hop beat with a bass line that's just filling space and fits the mood that you're seeing on the screen. If you're going to modify your character, which could be quite meticulous and time-consuming, I'd probably add some elements to the music and slow the tempo a bit, essentially designing music for that particular place in the game.

Now if we wanted interactivity within a role-playing game, it can be quite different, but in concept it works the same. The ambient layers might have a nice light mood with some strings that set the tone of environment we're in during game play.

With our sword not drawn yet and looking around exploring and figuring out what we need to do, and then all of the sudden someone jumps out of the bushes and, "Oh, I need to draw my sword." I'm not really fighting at this point, so we're just going to add some percussion elements, maybe some light sixteenth notes on top, or a few timpani hits, to establish that something important is about to happen.

Next we're walking around and—*bam*—someone else appears and we're going to be fighting. So I'll add some urgency by adding some more parts—maybe some staccato strings, some brass and bigger percussion, then we're full-on fighting.

So you've got all these layers to play with and you can do whatever you like with them based on the various game states.

How are composers for video games compensated?

Most of the deals are work for hire. This means they hire you to compose the music and then they own it outright. But this also depends on how big the company is you're working with. For instance, if it's a start-up, they may offer you a royalty deal, which could end up being a nice payday or a freebie. I know Sony is good with helping composers keep their writer's share when releasing game soundtracks. Depending on the status of the composer, they may be offered some kind of royalty share, but the good chunk of money will be upfront and the company will still own it.

Chuck, you've moved to Michigan. Are you still working on games remotely?

Yes, I am still working in games. I just finished some music tracks for a Sony title and also just finished a Wii title I acted as audio director on. I've been doing a lot of sound design for games and I've realized how much I enjoy working on the SFX side. Starting out as a sound designer and working alongside sound designers my whole career has kept my sound-design chops up. I prefer to do the music, but it's also satisfying to make a world come alive with sound design.

Several people I've talked to have said that the gaming industry is still growing and a viable place for composers to look for work. What's your take?

I agree. Mobile and online games are stealing the show right now and there are lots of opportunities out there. It's amazing how fast things are moving. Just last year, it was the consoles owning the game space, now they are hurting. Getting in is a bit tougher these days if you're looking to get in with an established game title.

So you believe someone should be considering the gaming industry if they possess the right skill set?

If you compose and write music, design sound, understand programming (not that you have to be a programmer), understand networks, and online gaming, I would say it's as good a market as any because of the growth.

Would you talk to me about your educational experience at Full Sail and how it's contributed to your success?

When I went to Full Sail, I had a pretty good idea of how unlikely it would be that I was going to get a job after I graduated. What school was for me was basically an engineering program that taught me how to use the consoles, how to be a good runner, and all of that kind of studio engineering stuff. And if you were lucky, you'd land an intern position at a studio.

When I started school, my first goal was to see how I could parlay this into being a rock star. But as the rock star thing wasn't happening, I started thinking, "What am I going to do?" I thought, "Well, I love gaming; I love computers . . . how about music for games?" Just as I made that decision, I was walking around some supermarket looking in the magazine section and saw one of the first game developer magazines. I immediately bought that magazine and focused on an interview with one of the composers, Bobby Prince, who did all of the music for the first *Doom* games. He put his phone number in at the end of the article.

I looked him up, and low and behold, he was in Florida but on the west side of the state. I prepared a bunch of questions and then called him up. We talked for three hours. He was very helpful and kind. So my story worked out just the way I was hoping. I went to Full Sail to get exposure and hopefully make something happen, and it did.

After working for Bobby as a contractor on a couple of games, he introduced me to Sony through a headhunter that contacted him. A couple of weeks after that, I moved to San Diego and started my job with Sony.

Though you are predominantly focused in the gaming industry, what do you think the future of the music industry holds?

It's in trouble until we find a way to compensate artists for the art they create and compensate industry people who help an artist get exposure and succeed. But as long as people can steal music easily, they aren't going to pay for it. Music back in the days of borrowing a buddy's CD and ripping it onto a computer didn't make as big of a dent as going to a torrent site and downloading an album the same day it comes out. Also, the landscape has changed. As of today, there really isn't a perceived value for music.

But there's also the bright side. I'm confident that there will be a streaming system in place where one can place tags in music streams that makes the music trackable, similar to a UPC. Artists could plug into the system, get our own code, and when people play the music, we'll get paid for it. YouTube and other streaming sites are the beginnings of these types of revenue. There will always be a music industry; it's just going to be different than what we've been used to. And I hope that's a good thing for the artists and the artists' enablers.

EARLIER, I TALKED WITH DAVID NEWMAN, who has a name that most film composers recognize and is at the top of his career. The path to this place of recognition, where you receive unsolicited phone calls offering composing gigs, can be long. For some, it's an adventure and an enjoyable ride, learning to multitask and juggle different types of work while you rise to the top.

I'd like to say there are thousands of great film composers, but the fact is that there are only hundreds that make it, so to speak. It's a competitive field, but if you are talented, you *can* move into a full-time career as a film composer like Ted Masur. Ted is an up-and-coming film composer who understands firsthand what it takes to climb the many rungs of the film-composer ladder. Hardworking and multitalented is how I would describe Ted. Not to mention he is quite a gardener!

Ted Masur

FILM

Ted, would you tell me a little bit about what you do as a film composer?

Well, that varies depending on the moment. But the basic idea is to support the project on an emotional level—dramatically, comedically, or whatever—with music, in alignment with the director and/or producer's vision. So to me, it's really about collaboration—being part of a team and doing whatever I can to make the project as strong as it can possibly be.

It ends up being a wide variety of projects—features, additional music for television shows, the occasional short film or arranging gig. I supplement that work by writing music for a custom library that provides music for several network TV shows.

That's very interesting! So you're filling space with other revenue opportunities between film composing gigs?

Exactly. I have friends who have been doing the library work for several years and they're making a decent living from that royalty stream. This particular situation is very flexible, so when a project comes up, I can take it and know that the library gig will still be there after the project is done. Between projects, it keeps my chops sharp and forces me to write in a variety of styles at a high level.

You mentioned that you write additional music for films and TV shows. What is additional music?

Composers have to balance many tasks in addition to the artistic job of composing. Sometimes they have too much work to do all of it themselves. They might say, "I have two or three shows here and there's no way I can write all of this music. I need someone to write some cues for me." They call this "additional music." Some composers keep a book of themes for a project, and I compose the extra cues based upon their established themes and direction. They will typically give me detailed spotting notes and tell me exactly what they are trying to achieve.

And the ghostwriting is where someone calls you and says, "Hey, Ted, would you write some music for me and I'll pay you X."

Yes. I've had friends who have ghosted for composers and actually been in the room when the music is being presented to the producer, who is giving praise to the composer while the person who wrote the music watches and can't take any credit. With an additional-music credit, your role is known—it's out in the open. Also, there usually is some kind of cue-sheet [royalty] split for the writer's share, which cannot happen in a ghosting situation.

How about your equipment, what's your current rig?

Well, I've simplified my setup in the last six months. I used to offload my orchestral samples to a couple of dedicated PCs slaved to a Mac Pro. These days, I use a pretty powerful eight-core Mac with twenty-four gigs of ram, and for most situations, I can do what I need to do on that machine. When I am doing larger orchestral scores, I use the dedicated PCs to do some of the heavy lifting. I have a wide variety of orchestral and cinematic sample libraries, including LA Scoring Strings, Symphobia, Albion Orchestra, SAM Brass, CineBrass, Westgate Studio Modular Winds, and various percussion libraries. I'm a big fan of Spectrasonics products—especially Stylus RMX and Omnisphere. Then add in lots of textural soft synths, effects plug-ins. It's an ongoing investment process, always having to be mindful of the difference between want and need.

How do you marry all the technology together?

I do all of my composing work in Digital Performer (DP). Sometimes I'll host samples in Vienna Ensemble Pro, sometimes I'll use the Kontakt Memory Server. If the end result is all samples, I'll mix in DP and deliver according to the editor's specs. If there are live players involved, I will record stems and export them for my scoring mixer to use in Pro Tools (PT). He'll record and mix the session in PT and make the final delivery. So it really depends on the final deliverables.

Could you tell me about the members of a composer's team and their responsibilities?

There are certain things that always need to be done—budgeting and general planning, spotting notes, music editing, composing, orchestrating, mixing, and delivery. The number of people doing those tasks depends on the size and scope of the project; if the budget allows for live players, there's also MIDI translation, generation of written score and parts, contracting of musicians, conducting, and recording.

On *The Best and the Brightest*, I had an assistant who covered MIDI translation, score prep, and music copying. Ideally, a music editor would prepare the spotting notes, but in this case, I did that and he came along late in the game, helping only with final preparations and the recording session. A contractor hired the musicians, and my scoring mixer recorded, mixed, and delivered the music. I composed, orchestrated, conducted the recording sessions, and oversaw the entire process—including budgeting and general planning.

Bigger teams come into play with bigger budgets, tighter deadlines, and simultaneous projects. In those situations, it's about choosing parts of the process that make sense to farm out. Hans Zimmer has the manpower to turn around a project in a couple of weeks. At the opposite end of the spectrum is a one-man team. Most composers are somewhere in between those two extremes.

Was there a time for you when it was like, "Oh my god, it's all falling apart, my life is over"?

Yes. I had the good fortune of interning one summer for Steve Bartek, who is Danny Elfman's orchestrator and a prince of a guy. At the time he was still working with pencil and paper. Each day, cues came in from Elfman, I would set up Steve's score paper, and he would orchestrate. Steve had his own project; I think it was *Another Goofy Movie*. He was using some hot young band with a brass section, and I had to prepare parts for the recording session.

I was so hyper-vigilant about getting every detail that instead of doing a regular drum chart, I was transcribing exactly what he had played on the MIDI track—which is an insane thing to do. The night before the session, Steve called me every hour to see how it was going, and finally at 2 a.m. he said, "Okay, you need to come over." So I did. He was very nice, even though he wasn't happy. He got it done very quickly as I sat there hanging my head. That was not fun!

You've been able to put together a good living for yourself. Would you talk about how the financial side works?

First and foremost, the music is being contracted within the context of a project. So that's always the reference point. The bigger the overall budget, the more money you can realistically expect to be allocated towards music. Somewhere in the planning process, decisions have to be made about what kind of music will be needed: Will it involve live players? Is it an orchestra? Is it a smaller ensemble? Is it all synth? Etc.

Sometimes this is clear from the start—they're looking for a particular sound and that clarifies certain parameters, or there's very little money, so some of those choices are already made. Sometimes you can lobby the producer—with the director's blessing—for money to cover the ensemble you think is right for the needs of the film. That's the big thing to remember: the score is there to support the film, and any financial proposals must be rooted in that understanding.

These days, you often have a package deal—the production company allocates a lump sum that you, as the manager of the scoring process, distribute to members of your team to get the job done. Ideally, I like to separate those two things—a creative fee for my work as composer and a production budget for all other costs. A good resource on this subject is Richard Bellis's *The Emerging Film Composer,* which is a must-read for anyone interested in exploring a career in film music.

In terms of how you get paid, there are two basic categories: upfront fees—what you're paid to do the creative work—and the backend, meaning the royalty stream, which is money collected by your performing rights organization. If you're lucky enough to have a network TV show, you're getting a decent upfront payment for doing the work, and a healthy royalty stream on the backend.

If you're working on a low-budget independent film, one thing that you really have to do is find additional ways to value your music beyond what they can afford in payment. You should be able to retain the publisher's share of the royalty stream, keeping the ownership of the masters and having the ability to license the music for some other usage.

I had one situation where I wrote music for a great little independent film that didn't go anywhere. A producer heard this music on my website and began to temp his film with my tracks. They didn't have the money to hire me outright, so I licensed these tracks to them for use in the film for a few thousand dollars. The only reason I could do this was because I had retained all the rights.

Compensation in the music business is really changing. Upfront fees are shrinking, and the royalty situation is also unclear as content delivery shifts more to the Internet. Nobody knows exactly where that's going at this point.

What advice would you give somebody that's an aspiring film composer?

Write a lot of music. Keep writing, even when you don't have a project. Deeply learn your gear, to the point where you can create and deliver quickly. Listen to lots of music and refine your networking skills. Develop relationships with directors who are at similar stages in their career—hopefully they'll take you with them as they move forward. Talk with a lot of people and get opinions that challenge you. Generate opportunities to continue learning, and find a good mentor or two. Relationships are huge. The biggest projects I've worked on have come from my long-term relationships.

Beyond that, it's important to cultivate a larger view. The path is long and it's unpredictable. Learn from every opportunity that comes your way and then re-calibrate. Move forward, find new opportunities, and continue to grow.

ONE MORNING ABOUT A YEAR AGO, my friend Helene suggested I meet a young fellow, Ryan Lott, to see if we might have some common ground regarding a music project I was working on. I called and we met for lunch. From the moment he opened the door and welcomed me into his home, I could feel his special energy and charisma. We talked about music, and life, and music. He reminded me of myself at twenty-five, totally engaged and enthralled with music every second of every day.

After a time, he confided that he'd been asked to move to New York City to join a team at one of the leading commercial music houses. He was excited and I was excited for him. It was in many ways the key that would open many doors for him. Ryan has a composing style that is unique, and fast . . . really fast. In the time it takes most of us to compose a thirty-second underscore, he has in fact finished five or six.

Ryan just sent me an update about what he is doing, and the doors are opening fast:

- Scoring the film *Looper* staring Bruce Willis
- Scoring seven short films for Coke
- Wrapping up a new Son Lux release

You should check out his work as Son Lux the artist.

Ryan Lott

Ryan, how did you get to where you are today?

It all started when I met my wife, a dancer and choreographer. She turned me on to the idea of writing music for dance, which is something I had never thought about, and my professors at IU looked down upon. [*laughs*] To me, there's something profound about marrying music to another art form.

I started writing music for her dance projects when we were fresh out of college, basically living out of our Subaru. I started cranking out all kinds of music for her dance company.

During that time, I was living in Cleveland, Ohio, and I was doing tons of production work for people long-distance. When I traveled to New York, I always stayed with a friend who worked at Fluid Music, and I didn't know anything about writing music for advertising. I would bring copies of my Son Lux music and periodically leave tracks with him. At one point he brought my CD to work as a Calvin Klein ad came through the house. They gathered all the submissions and included two of my tracks. He didn't tell me; he just did it and then I landed a really high-profile job for Absolut vodka.

The owner of Fluid called and asked me to consider moving to New York. It was a no-brainer because we had a goal to live in New York.

Would you take me through a day at your office composing music?

I get in at 9:30 and get out at about 8:00 p.m., but sometimes I'm here until midnight. I purposely live close to the studio so I can come to work on the weekends.

At any given point we might have ten to twenty jobs in-house at various stages of production. They require everything from an adaptation of an existing music track in our library to sound design to original music to a re-record [parody] of an existing piece of music.

Today, I got in and started work on a track for Ole; it's a new campaign and I did a retread of an old track of mine that they'd responded positively to. Usually we do internal library searches first and make a playlist to see what kind of tracks they respond best to.

This time the one they responded positively to was mine, so I will have three versions to complete today, two of which I haven't started. [*laughs*]

Do you find yourself working alone a lot or as part of a writing team?

My projects are mostly solo, but we definitely attack certain jobs as a team. We will always have multiple options for the creative approach and all of our composers have different strong suits. I am primarily a pianist, but also play guitar and percussion. So my drum programming comes in handy for some of the other composers. Judd's guitar playing helps us a lot and so does Drew's piano playing. We also hire a lot of outside talent as well.

Aside from your team, do you work with live musicians in the studio?

A couple of times a week we'll have live musicians come through our studio. It totally depends on the style of the job. If we do a track that is supposed to sound like a big band or a string quartet, you just have to bring in real players to get the sound just right. You can't mock up that stuff up on Logic; it doesn't matter how good your sample libraries are. You aren't going to communicate the music the way it's supposed to be heard without those people sitting in the studio and expressing the music. We have a really impressive roster of talent; for example, we have five clarinetists, and each one has their particular super strength.

It sounds like you have an abundance of great talent around you, Ryan. Even so, I'm sure you run into roadblocks on some projects. What would you consider the trickiest part of your job?

Translation! We, as composers and music producers, have a high level of understanding about music and how it's constructed. We also have a very good understanding of context, musical culture, and its lineage. The people that hire us, and are ultimately judging us, don't usually have that understanding. We're technically the "pros"; so it's a catch-22. Translating what they say into what they mean and what they really want is always a challenge. Everything from highly technical discourse to "It should be more inspirational" is what we deal with on a regular basis. It's like, "Okay, do you mean inspirational like Coldplay? Or like Phoenix?" Music is subjective, so trying to find exactly what a client is looking for can sometimes be challenging.

I can imagine the headaches. How does it feel when you hear your music on the web or TV?

It's very cool. The coolest thing is, I know I just got paid. Cha-ching! [*laughs*]

On that note, how do you get paid?

It depends on each person's arrangement. What makes it a good living for me is the multiple streams of income; I'm on base salary here, upon which commissions are added. If I win a job, then I get an additional percentage of the commission, which is variable based upon whether it's competitive with other music houses and things like that. If it's higher stakes, it's a bigger commission.

Also, if I don't win the job but play on someone else's spot, then I get a spot rate as if I was called in to do a recording session. If you're lucky enough to land your voice on a spot maybe singing background, that adds to the bottom line.

And then there are AFM and SAG union wages. American Federation of Musicians and

Screen Actors Guild are unions, and they collect recording wages and benefits on behalf of their members.

Finally, there are publishing royalties. As a composer, if you maintain a portion of publishing for whatever you write, then you are entitled to publishing royalties. That's where ASCAP, BMI, or SESAC come in. They track collect publishing royalties for their members, though it's a very sloppy process, and a lot gets lost in the mix. Also, it's impossible to track everything, so they don't try. Some people find it worth it to pay a third party to assist in the effort, for a percentage of reclaimed royalties.

My situation is unique because I also maintain 50 percent of my publishing [the composer's share]. So I also earn ASCAP too.

Ryan, you have a very unique approach to composing. Would you elaborate on your technique?

Outside of the advertising world, the way I make music depends on the job. For my own personal music, I love to let the sound itself speak to me. Often, rather than listening to my inner ear, I often make a sound and explore the potential of that specific sound for hours. I'll sit there and listen to the same sound and manipulate it and contextualize it in different harmonies, rhythmic structures. I'm a collagist. I love to take disparate sounds and re-contextualize them into something new. That's something hip-hop taught me.

Now that I have more resources, there's the added dimension of pre-composing, composing small pieces that I then re-sample and then re-contextualize. For example, if I have a track at 120 bpm, I might think, "What I if I wrote something at a mathematically proportional tempo for a little string trio, an eight-bar thing." Next I'll write and record that section and then experiment with how it sits against my track at 120. If that doesn't work, maybe it wasn't supposed to. Maybe the resultant chemistry is supposed to change in a fundamental way than what I initially conceived. It takes a crazy amount of time.

I also have a light-speed mode for the ad tracks, and then my traditional Son Lux mode. I have been working on my second full-length record for over two years now. That's why the NPR thing was particularly insane. Son Lux doesn't do that. I have fragments of audio that I recorded two years ago that I'm only now starting to explore.

What does the future hold for you professionally?

Well . . . I've just started to get into music for film. I know I could absolutely kill it. I've already written music for pictures and worked on arrangements for feature films, so I would love to head in that direction. I just finished doing 95 percent of the arrangements for a French film and that was really cool!

I think I would also like to catch up on my sleep because I don't get enough!

The first time I heard the band Toto, I was a young musician and the song was "Hold the Line," which is still one of my favorite tracks of all time. You may ask why, because it wasn't one of the stand-out songs of the past thirty years. For me, it was the introduction of the era of musician's music, a time when we as musicians were excited that other talented musicians could in fact produce hit songs for themselves. Toto was a musicians' band comprised of some of the best musicians of our time, not to mention they were the wrecking crew of the '80s, a studio band unmatched by any other and to be heard on hundreds of hit songs.

I was playing in a cover band at that time and we would sit for hours trying to figure out the intricately woven fabric of Toto's music, the mystical nature of Steve Lukather's guitar solos and tight groove they produced seemingly without even working at it. If you listened closely, you could hear a thick molasses-like underscoring texture, a blanket of beautiful but complex sound that enveloped the wide stereo field, and the magic glue that held it all together. All of that magic was created by Steve Porcaro, master synthesis of the band, and for that matter everybody else in the LA music scene too. It was an honor to speak with Steve as he prepared to score an episode of the hit TV series *Justified*.

Steve Porcaro

TV AND FILM

Steve Porcaro was a founding member of the Grammy-winning, platinum-selling rock band Toto. In addition to his work with Toto, Porcaro also topped the charts with Michael Jackson, Don Henley, Elton John, Boz Scaggs, and Barbra Streisand.

Steve, how did you break into the film-music world?

James Newton Howard turned to me one day while we were working in the studio and asked, "Do you want to try this?"

How long have you been scoring for film and TV?

It's been about fifteen years. I started with a TV show and then I did a couple features, and now I'm settling into a great cable show called *Justified*. The times I'm not doing film work I've gone back to working on my own songs.

I think we may be kindred spirits because when I was composing music for a living, I was either working sixteen-hour days or sitting around thinking, "Oh my god, I'm going to starve to death." It took several years before I could say to myself, "Okay, this is normal, Mike."

You know, I never get used to it. I have a thick skin in a lot of other areas, but you have to find things to keep yourself busy in the downtime.

Could you take us through an abbreviated version of what your personal process is for scoring for TV or film?

Sure. Often I'll get the script first and then meet with the producer if it's TV or the director if it's a film. Next, I get a rough cut of the picture that might hopefully be locked,' meaning they've officially finished editing.

Then we go in the studio and *spot* the picture. This is when you sit with the producer or director and decide exactly where the music will start and stop for different scenes. At this session you usually have a music editor making notes about the scene in question, what the producers like or dislike about the temporary music, and the SMPTE start and stop times of the cues. Every frame of a film is embedded with a time code, which is a time stamp.

After the spotting session I go off and start writing. On a TV show I only have a few days to send in my rough ideas, so I'll do all of my cues as QuickTime movies and marry my music with sound effects and the rough dialog. I then post them on the web for review by the team.

My roughs will hopefully get approved and sometimes with directional notes, like, "Can you give us more here, can you give us less here," and then you finish the recording, mix it, and deliver the cue or track. This all happens in the course of a week with a TV show. A movie's timeline may run to six weeks or more just to compose the score.

Another thing to note is the temp score that you usually hear at the spotting session, which was created by the music editor or video editor, depending on the budget. Most composers hate the temp score because the team gets married to it. It's a real drag when they fall in love with John Williams's ninety-piece orchestra, and all you have is your synths, $8,000, and a week to deliver. [*laughs*]

Lately I've been lucky in that the producers have been digging my music on *Justified* to the point that they've started temping with my music! Once you're at that comfort level, it's pretty sweet sailing because you know they like what you're writing. Getting there, though, can be a bitch.

Do you usually work to a budget or an allotment of money for each episode?

I get what's called a package, which is a set amount of money and the producers expect me to deliver the score for that package number. In other words, I get a flat rate to compose, record, and deliver the music.

What types of issues complicate a project?

It can be difficult when a producer hears it one way, his partner hears it another, the studio wants it done like a horror movie, and the network wants a love theme. I've truly walked into situations where everyone has a different idea of how the score should sound. The process can be prickly. As a composer you need to be the problem solver, keep from freaking out, and hopefully make everybody happy. That's the plan, anyway. [*laughs*] The best way to get them to agree is to write something that really works.

On a show like *Justified*, which I think is a wonderful mix of Cajun blues and a folk thing with synths mixed in, how did you go about creating the sound canvas?

When I got the gig, they had been working on the pilot for a long time with a temp score, which can be very tricky. Many times they've been living with it for a couple of months and anything you write just sounds wrong to them because it's not what they are used to hearing.

When I walked into *Justified*, they had already put a lot of thought into the temp score, so it gave me a good idea of what they liked and expected from me as a composer.

On *Justified*, the score is often guitar-driven, but I'm not a guitar player, I know like three chords, so I compose and Marc Bonilla plays all of the guitars on the show. We also sneak in a cue of Marc's every now and then. We all agreed that we wanted a unique guitar sound, so he plays a National and really makes it his own. It gives the show a backwoods sound. Then when there is a chase or action, or someone is sneaking around, my synth chops kick in. We also use Charlie Bisharat quite a bit. He is a wonderful fiddle player and improvises on many of the cues. I think this particular mix of instruments allows the listener to hear the geography.

Let's talk about dollars for a moment. You obviously can make a pretty good living composing for TV.

Well, there's upfront money, which is essentially your creative fee. I often get half my payment when I spot and the other half when I deliver the score. There are also backend payments. Backend payments have to do with what time your show airs on TV. If it's in prime time, every minute of music is worth more, and in the United States, ASCAP and other performing rights organizations keep track of every second of music that's performed on TV.

Our music editor creates a cue sheet that lists all of the music in the show. Every bit of needle drop and score is listed with the writer's name, duration, and what type—foreground, background, etc. You'll also receive money if the show goes into syndication and viewed in different countries. All of this backend money is the reason you sometimes see very small upfront fees paid to the composer or to license a commercial track. The producers know you'll do very well financially on the backend if the show is successful.

Do you have some advice for an aspiring young composer?

Get a job with a composer as an assistant or an orchestrator. Try to find a job where you're around people who are doing it every day at a very high level. If you've got the goods, most leading composers will give you a shot writing a couple of cues when they get busy. It happens every day.

Grab any gigs you can, like student films, etc. The real cream will always rise to the top, and if you are a truly gifted composer, you won't have all of the struggles that 90 to 95 percent of us have. I see it all of the time; people talk about how competitive it is and how horrible it is, and then you'll see a guy who just seems to sail right to the top, and deserves to do so because he's so talented.

Any last words of wisdom, Steve?

I'd want to tell people who are reading this and just starting out, whether they're jazz or classical musicians, want to get into film, or rock and rollers, Find what's unique about yourself and go for the balls towards it. Don't try to be something you're not. Just be the best at being you. That's where true success is found.

Well said!

WHEN I HAD MY RECORD DEAL, we recorded at Criteria in Miami. My band was made up of the best musicians I had ever heard, thanks to some seed money from an angel investor and some good friendly connections. One musician in particular, Lloyd Landesman, was a phenomenal keyboardist. During the stresses and pressures of recording our album, we clashed. I was young and eager to be in control of my own universe and a bit intimidated by Lloyd's talent. He was a master, and to this day I still listen to our jam sessions and marvel at his talent. Through the years I have often wondered what went wrong and can only chalk it up to the above-mentioned youth. Lloyd and I have since reconciled and both agreed that youth had its challenges, but we somehow got though it and prospered.

Lloyd went on to do great work in the advertising business and wrote some of the most memorable jingles in the industry, including "Sweet Dreams," and "Proud to Be Your Bud." He also never stopped playing, and you can hear his fusion band, Meridian Voice, in New York City.

Lloyd Landesman

ADVERTISING

Lloyd Landesman is also an award-winning composer, who has written some of the most memorable commercial themes in recent history for Budweiser, Coke, and Nestlé.

Lloyd, tell me how you chose to write commercial music—fell into it or planned it?

It kind of chose me. I was pursuing the recording star dream for years in my early thirties and I decided to become more of a session player, so I moved to Manhattan in NYC. One thing led to another. I was doing a lot of session dates, and many of them were jingle dates as a synthesizer player.

I ran into an old friend who happened to be working at a jingle company and did some arrangements for him. The arrangement I did was liked so much by the owners of the company that they decided to throw me some commercial work. For me, it was a windfall financially because after a couple of jobs I had doubled my savings.

The first big jingle I wrote was Nestlé's "Sweet Dreams" commercial and then I was invited to become a staff writer. At that point I decided to commit myself and everything unfolded from there. So it kind of chose me in that sense. I saw that it was lucrative and fun and I got to work with great musicians, singers, great top-shelf studios, and be on the front lines.

You had an incredible start to your career. How does one make money in the commercial music business? For instance, when you sing on a jingle and it's a union job. Do you continue to make money for years to come?

A singer is held under the Screen Actors Guild (SAG) union and paid a rate very similar but not as much as an on-camera actor. Actually, a solo performance is the same as an on-camera actor, so there's a residual income based on the SAG agreements with the AAAA, which is the group that represents the advertisement agency.

It's all very legitimate in the sense that everybody works through the unions, and on each network airing the commercial you get paid as an individual and it gradually diminishes over a thirteen-week period. If it runs again after a thirteen-week period, it starts all over again.

It can range anywhere from $250 a play down to $50 a play. When I started, cable was in its budding state; it didn't have nearly as many stations as it does today. There was also radio. Radio was another medium where commercials ran. Yes, I did get money as a singer, and in many ways it's how the composers were rewarded for their work. Many times, if you wrote something but actually didn't sing the lead on it, you were in a background vocal group and would receive a slightly lower residual payment just by being called a group, group singers. I was very fortunate to be in the right place at the right time! [*laughs*]

You mentioned that writing advertising music is hard work. What's the most challenging part?

There was tremendous competition, albeit it was a small group of people who are competing. You basically were trying to translate the advertising creative concepts for the music from people who weren't really articulate in that area. Occasionally you would get someone who knew what he was talking about musically and was very specific, but most of the time it was very nebulous and you had to make it up as you went along.

There is a lot of stress because the turnaround times can be as short as twenty-four hours, and we needed to hand in fully produced demos. Prior to that point, people were just doing piano demos and would then record it with all live musicians. First hour was the rhythm section, second hour was the horns and strings, third hour would be the singers, and the fourth hour would be the mixing, so after four hours the commercial was done.

There was also stress of going into a high-end studio and dealing with very high-end budgets. You were in the spotlight and responsible for all the music, not only as the composer but also as the arranger; I was writing the charts, which at the time was not my strong suit.

One time I got in at four in the afternoon to write out a whole chart for a rhythm section, a horn section, and vocals. It was a group of five spots, all the same music but edited in different fashions. This was one of the first big sessions I had ever done. I'm sitting there with the score paper and calling my friends, asking questions like, "How low does a baritone sax go?" I had the Don Sebesky's arranging book and was obsessing over it for hours. I finally finished at 3 a.m.

At 10 a.m. I was in what today is Avatar Studio, but then it was called the Power Station, just sitting there with all these top-shelf players. I'm this new kid and in walk the horn players and they're like, "Who is this guy?" And of course the person I worked with at the time always ran late.

Would you say that some of the most exciting parts of your job are stress related?

Certainly! I can give you a perfect example of something that happened where I was working with this creative director at BBDO ad agency. I liked him a lot, but he had a particularly volatile personality and could explode at any moment. We were in doing this Visa spot and he said something, wondering what we needed at the end of the spot to accentuate it more. I immediately came back with, "But you said you wanted it like this!" which is sort of like an arrangers thing. [*laughs*]

He said, "Well, I was just thinking about it." Then I realized, he was just being creative. Of course that happened to me many times in the future and I learned to say, "Okay, let's try that," and I would go make the change, figure it out, and tell the musicians what to play.

After many years of those stressors, I realized they are also the most creative part of my job.

Lloyd, I know you play several instruments, but I've never known you as a guitarist. What instruments do you play when you're composing?

I'm mainly a keyboard player, as you well know, and I wrote a lot of my earlier work on keyboard, but about fifteen years ago I decided to pick up the guitar, because my joke is, "I'm a guitar player trapped inside a keyboard player's body." I bought an acoustic guitar and told myself that I'm going to learn how to play this instrument. I did and I love it.

Playing guitar gave me that element of naïveté. I was able to backtrack a little and my music became a bit simpler. I would devote a lot of my more sophisticated techniques to actually producing the tracks.

What would you say are the essential skills for a composer in advertising music today?

It wouldn't matter what year it is, but: perseverance, sticking with it past failure and moving on. Try not to take failure personally. I know it's very difficult because you're putting your heart into a piece of music. More likely than not, it can or will be rejected, for something that has nothing to do with your talent or ability.

It's really just continuing to show up, dealing with your emotions, and your stressors and developing coping skills for them. When I was younger, I took everything very personally and got upset when I didn't win a job.

Woody Allen said, "Ninety percent of success is just showing up." If you're there and work hard and stay at it, you'll learn. You'll learn how to use the gear; you'll learn tricks. If you're in an environment with other composers, you'll see what they do and some of it will filter into your work and vice versa.

When I went to work at Crushing Music, they had just created "Heartbeat of America," which was one of the biggest jingles of all time. Most people haven't heard of it now, but when you're writing jingles for Chevrolet, it's a major financial windfall because there are so many spots attached to the campaign.

I also had Budweiser for ten years with my good friend Steve McCabe. Crushing Music also did Coke, Diet Coke, and Dr. Pepper. I had Dr. Pepper for many years.

Those are some incredibly high-profile clients. What would a normal day look like for you?

Most days started in my studio with a phone call followed by a script. We would all go into the owner's office, which was Joey Levine, of bubble gum fame—he wrote "Yummy Yummy" and "Chewy Chewy" and a bunch of other big bubble gum hits in the '70s.

All of the composers would sit there, sometimes with the client (the "creatives" from the ad agency)—and say, "We want a track that's modern and contemporary," which were always the words they would use, and maybe they would say something like, "We're really into Tom Waits. We would love to hear something like he would do." Then we'd all think about it, leave, and go into our little studios and program up tracks. After that the creative would come by and choose the ones they liked the best and wanted to produce.

If my song was chosen, I would book the talent, book an engineer, and maybe a guitar player to start. Everything else was programmed. Then we might hire a singer and get a couple of guys to come sing in the group that worked at Crushing because most everybody could sing.

Somewhere in the next three to six hours, that track would be completely finished. Then it would be submitted to the agency, and if it got picked, then they would go to their client, and if their client liked it, it would eventually go on the air. Quite a few steps that sometimes happened in twenty-four hours!

I'm really simplifying the process because I've had situations, like with Budweiser, where they liked the music very much, and then they would subject the creative to a six-month exploratory and testing. Over that six-month period, I wrote fifteen or sixteen demos while everybody else in the company was doing demos and people around the country were doing demos. Eventually they had a meeting with the CEO, August Busch, and he said, "What happened to that first music you brought me? What's was wrong with that one? I really liked it. I listened to that track in my helicopter, and I love that one. Let's put it on the TV. Let's use that one." That just shows how unstable it is sometimes! [*laughs*]

Lloyd, you've written some incredibly memorable themes, like "Sweet Dreams" and "Proud to Be Your Bud." Was there one that stands out as a personal favorite?

It's hard to say I had a favorite because what always happens is you start working on a track and it's fresh, and by the time you finally turn it in weeks, months, or maybe even a year later, you're ready to choke and don't ever want to hear it again! [*laughs*]

But I would say the "Proud to Be Your Bud" thing you mentioned actually was very interesting. The whole company was writing for it and I was working literally ten hours straight obsessing over this music because it could be embarrassing internally if I didn't win this job—because it was *my* job.

I was working all day and I brought Joey in to hear it and he says, "I don't know, Lloyd, it sounds a little dated," and I just felt like I wasn't really writing with my mind and heart; I was just putting together pieces of what I thought sounded good. There was no great song in there, which can happen a lot. I had a session booked for the next day, with players and singers, and what am I gonna do? I don't have anything . . . and I just said, "Geez, you know what? I'm going home."

As I was walking down the street, I literally wrote the song in the time it took to actually sing it from beginning to end, in about thirty seconds. I knew exactly what I was going to do. I came in very early the next morning, programmed the whole track with all the percussion stuff, got a guitar player, and got the singers in. It went through about six months of panel analysis and I happened to win it in the same week as I won the Dr. Pepper campaign. I was like, "Oh my god, I can breathe for a few months." You see, part of the gig is you don't have a steady paycheck.

Given that a steady paycheck can be hard to come by, what do you think the realistic lifespan might be for a composer in the advertising world?

As long as you want it to be, but you have to do a lot of homework, stay current, not get jaded, which to a certain extent I have to fight. "Oh I can't believe I'm working for this kind of money." You have to think about what's more important: the actual work, keeping your brain rocking, and feeling a sense of self while you're doing it. Okay, so you're making 60 percent less than what you used to, but you're making something.

Also, you need to be constantly open to new music. Look, there's a bunch of the new music that leaves a lot to be desired for me personally, but the other side of that is, things are always changing. When the Beatles came out, our seniors, who were our age now, were saying, "Aw, the Beatles suck. What is that crap?!" So you have to really be open new ideas and you don't have to always like it. You have to be open to constantly reinvent yourself!

4

Digital Distribution

Rapid Fire

Skill Set—You should love technology, and it doesn't hurt to be an early adopter. Change should come naturally to you and you never, ever fear it. You must have the ability to foresee the future and have vision. It wouldn't hurt to have at least a minor in business either and like all styles of music. And you need to be better than average on a computer, iPad, mobile devices, etc.

Hours—There are so many jobs in this category that the hours are hard to identify. Programmers like to drink Mountain Dew and work all night, whereas the office folks usually work 9 to 5. It will be your call depending on the job you do. Just remember that companies *are* companies, and if you work for one, you will need to conform to its culture and hours.

Upside—This is the future of the music industry and given that it's in flux and continually changing, *in my book it's a great place to be*. If I were staring out in the music business again, I would look very closely at this area of the music business because the potential for making connections and growth is unparalleled. This translates into more options and financial security in the future.

Downside—Hmmm, I don't really think there is much of a downside. I suppose it might be the development of an intracranial music distribution system, where the music comes from the artist's head directly into yours and eliminating this business segment. But then again it will take someone to create it and that person might be you!

Financial—$$$ to $$$$ and beyond. The type of job you pick in digital distribution will likely dictate the money chain and how much you will make long term. In general this job will pay well and have good long-term upside potential.

Location—Most large markets have a significant lead in the area of digital distribution because they are close to the industry players. San Francisco, Seattle, LA, Boston, Oakland, and other places are easy to find and track down on Google.

Future—It should be obvious that the future is blindingly bright. As we move fully into the digital age, people that understand technology and are adept at leveraging that technology will become valuable assets and probably run the entire music business.

WE ARE ON THE CUSP OF A NEW REVOLUTION IN THE MUSIC INDUSTRY. It is the era of digital distribution and the short story is this: it's the fastest growing segment of the entire music industry, and will continue to be for the foreseeable future. I won't endeavor to enlighten you to the fact that records have lived and died, followed by CDs, and now we live in the digital realm, where one day soon we will most certainly rent music and no longer own it—or for that matter *want* to own it.

I recently met with a young man whom I was trying to help with school and gave him my used MacBook. I upgrade my computers about once a year, so it wasn't a dinosaur and he was very pleased to receive the gift. Prior to giving him the computer, I reformatted the hard drive and reinstalled the programs I thought he might need for school. There was only one thing missing, and it was a big thing. Music . . . there was no music, or video.

The next morning, he brought the computer over and plugged in his headset and started doing some work. I asked, "Did you put some of your music on the Mac last night?"

He replied, "Oh yeah, maybe a couple thousand tracks and some new movies,"

"I thought you left them in Florida," I said.

"I did, but I just found a few torrents and downloaded everything."

This was my introduction to BitTorrent, a peer-to-peer file sharing system for moving large pools of data over the Internet. This young man in the course of one evening had downloaded about $3,500 worth of music and video content illegally and for free! Torrents are the download system of choice among young people, and of course it only stands to reason that *if* torrents become the mainstay of downloading music for the general public, there may not be a music business at all, because nobody will pay for content.

If you download music using torrents and don't pay for it, you may say, "Why should I even care?" But I would challenge you with a single question: What *if* . . . torrents disappear and you can no longer download your music for free? You will still want to listen to music, but you'll need a different digital delivery system.

This is just one example of the world of digital distribution, albeit detrimental to the current music business model. I should also mention that many bands are starting to harness the power of torrents to promote their bands, leveraging huge networks of users to help spread their music. (Innovation—wow, cool and scary.)

You see, we are at the very beginning of the Next Big Thing, so to speak, and as you read this book, you'll find that most of the contributors agree that the industry is changing so fast no one knows exactly where we are going. I would make the observation that with innovation happening at an incalculable rate, the distribution of music in the very near future will likely happen in a way we can't even imagine today. This is an exciting time for sure. Having said this, I talked to a couple of guys who know where we are today and can talk a bit about the current state of digital distribution.

Adam Parness

EVP RHAPSODY

Rhapsody is the number-one subscription music service in the United States, which, as of January 2013, has well over one million subscribers and a catalog of more than 20 million songs. Rhapsody also now owns and operates the Napster service in Germany and the United Kingdom.

Would you tell me a little bit about what you do at Rhapsody?

I'm the senior director of music licensing, which essentially boils down to content licensing and business development. Primarily what I do day to day at Rhapsody is anything in the area of music licensing that touches the Rhapsody business. For publishing, that could include dealing with performance rights organizations, such as ASCAP, BMI, and SESAC, to the Harry Fox Agency and thousands of independent music publishers for the rights required to operate our service.

Adam, can you talk about your path and how you ended up in the digital distribution industry?

Like many people in the business, I started out as a music lover and musician. When I got my hands on a guitar at ten years old, I knew my path would include music.

I attended New York University for music technology, where I was exposed to music publishing, which is an important and often overlooked segment of the music industry. I had a professor who mentored me and hired me before my senior year to work on the publishers' litigation against the original Napster service.

Fast-forward a couple of years and Rhapsody was looking to hire an expert music publishing person in the wake of the launch of Rhapsody to Go, which was its first portable subscription service. So I was brought on board to be the publishing guru, which is still one of my responsibilities at the company.

As a musician, does your job at Rhapsody fill that place in you that loves music?

The good thing about Rhapsody is that it's the perfect job for a musician because you're surrounded by music all day long and working with people who are fanatical about music. My officemate grew up with indie punk music, most of which I had never heard of, and he just runs his stereo all day. I'm an old-school guitar player who was raised on classic rock, so I hear new music coming from his side of the office and every two seconds I'm asking, "Who's that, who's that?" Music surrounds my business life.

What are some of the other jobs in your business segment, the types of jobs that musicians might be thinking about?

Being in a digital music and distribution company, there are a bunch of technology-oriented jobs, particularly for developers. When you think of a service like Rhapsody, you have a downloadable client, a website, all kinds of access points like set-top boxes, Tivo, or Sonos, and most importantly smartphones. Mobile applications for iPhone, Android, Blackberry, and any Windows device are driving our sector of the business, so there is a huge amount of work and opportunity.

We have a reporting staff that creates royalty payment systems for the labels and publishers, and there are all types of finance jobs. We also have extensive staff engaged in business development and marketing.

Could you talk a little bit about how you see the digital distribution model changing the music industry?

Well, generally I think digital distribution is very quickly *becoming* the recording music industry. The biggest thing I see within the subset of digital distribution is this access-verses-ownership idea.

Access to our service wasn't as wide as it should have been over the past ten years, and that was because services like Rhapsody couldn't get on Apple devices. But when Apple launched the iPhone and the App Store, that changed the game not just for us but for the entire subscription-music industry and validated our model.

Therefore, it proved the concept that access to music is better than ownership. You don't need to own the music, and if your hard drive crashes, you won't lose the music you love. So if you pay $10 a month for a service and always have access to your music, it's worth it. People who sign up have access to the huge Rhapsody library that they could never possibly ever afford.

Adam, it sounds like you really love your job. What's the toughest part for you?

We have over 20 million tracks and I don't always get good music publishing data, which makes it challenging to ensure all the music publishers get paid. Despite our best efforts and being a good corporate citizen and respecting copyright, sometimes you just can't find every single music publisher. We work with a company called RightsFlow to identify them, which is a big help.

What haven't you done that you would still like to do in the future as it relates to the music business?

It's not necessarily a career goal, but the one thing that I've never done is tour. As a musician, I've never jumped on a bus and toured our country for two or three months. As many cool highlights as I've enjoyed in my career as a player and a producer in the studio, I've never toured.

Do you have a band?

I play guitar in a hard-rock band called the Border Cops out of NYC. I also am a student of classical guitar and play in a really fun '70s funk cover band.

With your job, your wife, and all of your other personal endeavors, how do you find time to practice with a band?

I don't sleep much. The cool thing about Rhapsody is that it's not like working at a soulless company where you're putting in eighty, ninety hours a week. I work even harder than I normally do leading up to product launches, but it leaves me the flexibility to pursue my personal musical interests. Even on the roughest days, I come home and put in a good hour of practicing. You have to be dedicated, like I am with the classical guitar. I take weekly lessons and have found that not wanting to make an ass out of myself in front of my teacher is a huge motivator [*laughs*].

Brian Felsen

PRESIDENT, CD BABY

CD Baby is the leading digital distributor of the works of independent artists, authors, and publishers.

Brian, would you describe what CD Baby does and what your role involves?

CD Baby helps make the little artist look big and helps them get their music to the masses. In the old days, you needed gatekeepers; if you were to record, you would then need to send it out to radio stations and have your music formatted in a certain way so it could play well for radio. You would have to get distribution and the record labels would take all of your money, or they would front you lots of money and you would have to pay them back. At the end of the day, you would end up with very little for all of your efforts.

CD Baby was started by Derek Sivers about twelve years ago, and he was a musician who did it as a hobby. He was like, "Hey, the Internet is kind of new. Let's sell people's music on it," and he started selling music on his website.

CD Baby allows you to upload your music, or you can send us CDs to warehouse for you.

We'll give you a web page with samples of your music. Then people can go to your page, buy a CD, and we'll ship it anywhere in the world.

We only take $4, so if an artist has a CD that sells for $14, the artist makes $10. We ship it out same day, tell you who bought it, and it's all good. Currently, we're the largest aggregator of independent music on the Internet, with over 3.5 million tracks and 250,000-plus artists.

How is digital distribution changing the music industry right now?

It's changing it in the way that you don't have to get thousands of CDs or millions of records pressed and then snail-mail them, or go to a place and buy them, and have all these middlemen take money from you.

You can distribute your music free anywhere and anybody can hear it. I can discover music much more easily. On the downside, music is becoming commoditized, people are less willing to pay for it, and also attention spans have changed so that people are channel surfing much more.

In the old days—five years ago—[*laughs*] someone would really listen to a concept album, sit and focus, and digest it through repeated plays. Now music has become much more social. People look at each other's playlists, discover music through YouTube, Facebook, and MySpace.

Can you tell me, as the president of a large company, what your typical workday looks like?

There is no typical day, of course, because we have over one hundred people here, and there's always something going on. We're constantly developing new features for our artists and dealing with millions of dollars in accounting, because we pay out every Tuesday, every single week. We've distributed almost $200 million to our artists.

We have to bring in discs and ship them out the same day. Then there are all of our other divisions and services, like the credit-card swipers for musicians to sell stuff at shows, download cards, web hosting for musicians, as well as for artists and filmmakers and authors; and then BookBaby, which distributes eBooks. There's an exhilarating amount of development happening in terms of new products. There is a constant stream of developing new partnerships to work on, so you can see there's enough to keep a person pretty busy.

If somebody was considering a job in digital distribution, what are some of the types of jobs they might find?

Boy, that's a tough one . . . the digital distribution space is in a very interesting place right now. As music becomes more commoditized, as record labels are falling, and as the tools of production and distribution are becoming more democratized for musicians to accomplish and produce, it's becoming cheaper and easier than ever for musicians to produce and get their music out there.

Careers in this space are changing. Many of my friends at major record labels are finding themselves out of a job now that record labels are consolidating, and everything is sort of moving towards technology. At South by Southwest (SXSW), the technology division is up 20 percent and now has surpassed the music division in terms of size. As far as jobs, CD Baby is in a different position than record companies because our job array includes everything from warehouse management to customer service, IT, and development, but they often involve activities, which help the music industry but also would be practical to work in a company like Zappos.

We do digital delivery of music and music assets, so there are many new positions opening up in the tech side of our business, as well as in the industry in general. There are also a lot of careers in marketing and A & R, but they are certainly harder to come by now.

So, Brian, how personally satisfying is working in a business like CD Baby?

The correct answer for this book would be for me to say, "This is the most incredibly fulfilling thing in the entire world, and everybody should be glad to be me." [*laughs*] In truth, like most jobs in this world, it's probably slightly less satisfying than working for Doctors Without Borders and much more satisfying than building war machines. We're definitely on the side of the angels—I'm proud to work at CD Baby. It's a wonderful company in the music industry, which is hard to come by. I love our artists, and to work with independent artists is a noble mission.

I think that if you can make money from your art, you're lucky, you're blessed, talented, and hardworking and all that other stuff. What's great about CD Baby and fulfilling to me is that it helps artists do that. We help them get their work out to an audience so they can keep creating.

That's great. Do you still play or write music yourself?

I write and produce secular gospel music right now. It's gospel music for atheists, agnostics, and humanists. I'm working with some gospel musicians, and a choir in LA, and recording. That's what I'm working on right now. . . . I write all kinds of music, but that's my current project.

And where will I hear your music?

On CD Baby, of course! [*laughs*]

Do you have any thoughts on how the music industry might monetize this whole new world? Most people say, "If I knew the answer to that question, I wouldn't be working anymore." [*laughs*]

As far as how the industry could monetize it, honestly I hate to say it, but my passion is not industry; my passion is independent artists. Apple's been able to monetize because they've released delightful hardware, and Google and Facebook have been able to monopolize with delightful products, and then monetize. And we've done a great job providing a splendid service and taking a modest cut.

But on the bright side for the industry, it's also possible that the commoditization of music is a fad. That's quite possible . . . that with cloud storage, like the new Google Music beta, and the convenience of being able to access your music anywhere, companies such as Apple, Google, or Amazon will be always able to monetize, and artists will need CD Baby to be able to handle distribution to all of them.

For me, I want artists to make money and, if possible, make a living off of music, but to me, the end goal is creation and distribution, above everything else.

What gets you up in the morning?

The people that I work with, both inside and outside of the company. At Rhapsody, we get to set and drive the marketplace as opposed to reacting to it. That's a great part of my job, as well a key differentiator between working at a traditional label or publisher. I love this place and I love this job.

5

Entrepreneur
(Starting Your Own Music Business)

Rapid Fire

Skill Set—Education is a plus because entrepreneurs develop new businesses. You must be good with people, as you will spend much of your time on business development, raising capital, and presenting your ideas. Therefore, presentation skills are a plus, being unaffected by jet lag, feeling comfortable with risk, understanding multiple technologies, being a fast thinker, having a thick skin, and . . . coming up with an idea a minute doesn't hurt either. It also is nice if you know people with money that believe in you, want you to do well, and can provide some financial assistance in the start-up phase. They are what we call angel investors. They provide the seed money that brings ideas to life.

Hours—There are no typical hours for an entrepreneur, but you probably should know they are long. It's not unusual to work seven days a week for a year to get your idea off the ground. I should say, however, that you will most likely love every minute of this process. *Not a good job for new parents*!

Upside—Everything—*if* you are successful. A real entrepreneur will take failure in stride and keep moving forward, always looking for the next opportunity.

Downside—Everything—but it will likely be a lack of adoption for your idea or company. There can also be significant financial risk because most investors will also want you to have some skin in the game; that way, they know you will work hard and if the venture fails you will also lose money.

Financial—The sky is the limit, but your own pockets and bank account will shrink during the start-up process and there is always the possibility of financial ruin. As I said—the greater the reward, the greater the risk.

Location—Anywhere, as long as you are willing to travel and have the funding to do so. Otherwise NYC, San Francisco, or LA are good bets, especially if you have a family, because the travel can be a real strain on your personal relationships.

Future—For the right person with the right attitude and commitment to your ideas, it is very promising. Music tech start-ups are popping up every day. Remember that only 20 percent of these start-ups will make it past the first year, and even fewer will still be in business in the critical fifth year, when most tech companies move in the black and start making money. The upside of a tech start-up is that you can be quite successful with the right group of people and without breaking the bank.

FOR THE PAST TWENTY OR SO YEARS, I HAVE BEEN AN ENTREPRENEUR. What that means is that I don't like holding a regular job, have too many ideas at any one time bouncing around my cerebrum, and that I'm not very good at doing the same thing for any extended period of time. It also means that I'm not risk averse, I don't mind taking chances, I'm ready to work incredibly stupid hours while making little to nothing, and with no guarantee that I ever will. I do what I do because I believe in the projects I work on.

Entrepreneurs share a love of moving life, business, and the world forward, sometimes with little regard to their own livelihood. They also thrive on making things happen and are charged up by new ideas. I believe we live in the best of times to become a music entrepreneur, given the changing music industry and the potentially endless possibilities leveraging technology.

In the past ten years, I have started eight technology-driven companies, ranging from advertising software to personalized endurance-race videos to founding the Hard Rock Academy, Reeltracs, and MyMusicSource. Every one of these companies had relevance and a reason for being (at least I thought so), delivered a great service, or automated a complex process. Some have done well while others have failed for a variety of reasons.

If you are the type of person who wakes up in the morning with a new idea that you believe will change the world, and understand enough about business to make a good business case for your idea, then you might think about the entrepreneur route. You'll need the ability to sum up your idea and value proposition in a couple of sentences, and also have the stick-to-it-ness to persevere even when things are not working out the way you expected, because they rarely do.

Experience has taught me that before I get too excited about my idea, I need to spend some time in concentrated and focused thought, perform the due diligence, and make sure I believe my own press, so to speak. Many times we have ideas that seem like the best thing since sliced bread, only to find out that nobody else cares about our great idea and won't support or adopt it. You may find that there is no real market for your idea or product, so beware your self-proclaimed genius and do your homework. It is well worth it.

I have a close friend, Fritz Lehman, and together we founded the Hard Rock Academy a few years back with the Hard Rock Corporation. The business is what School of Rock is today but supercharged by the Hard Rock brand name. The mission was to give kids a chance to experience playing an instrument, playing in a band, and generally feeling like a rock star. The short story is that a few Hard Rock executives made corporate changes and the academy was dumped as part of a new corporate mandate. The reason I tell you this is to make one simple point: To be successful in music, or any business for that matter, you need to put yourself out there, try things, and take chances. Some will rock and some will not.

Hard Rock was one that should have been wildly successful, but because of changes beyond our control and another insane partner (not Fritz), it fell flat on its face; there's another lesson here: Pick your friends and partners well. Today's best friend and partner could well become tomorrow's mortal enemy. So hang out with them for a while and understand their character before going into business together.

Entrepreneurial endeavors make for an exciting life, but it's not for the faint of heart. My brother-in-law, who has been very successful in business, once asked me, "Mike, why are you always doing start-ups? They are so hard. Just buy a little business that's making a few bucks, tweak it a little bit, and generate more money." I do believe that's some of the best advice I have ever been given, but after trying to find a business for a year, I slipped right back into my ideas. It just isn't as easy as Richard said because we are all wired differently.

A good friend of mine, Jeff McElnea, told me about a young man who was doing a start-up and asked if I would meet with him over dinner one night and possibly give him some advice. That guy was Dan Zaccagnino, the founder of Indaba Music. All I can say is that he didn't need any of my advice. He rocks! Forward thinking, smart, quick, and a gentleman.

Dan Zaccagnino

CEO AND FOUNDER, INDABA MUSIC

Dan is one of the founders of Indaba. Their office in located in New York, where they share space with other innovative companies, one of which is Foursquare. It seems appropriate because Indaba is all about new thinking and helping musicians find industry access while they hone their craft.

I recently visited Dan's starkly decorated office, which looks a bit like the early incarnations of the Facebook workspace; empty walls waiting for inspired murals, and rows of computers lining foldable tables with wires in what you might think are meaningless tangles but with purpose. Dan and I sat in a makeshift meeting room with a huge flowchart of the first version of the Indaba website mounted on the wall. We talked about life and business and of course what it's like to be an entrepreneur.

What inspired you to start the widely successful Indaba Music company?

Throughout college I had interned at major record labels—specifically for (one of my future

Indaba business partners) Mantis Evar at Blue Note Records and later for the CEO of Virgin Records. Simultaneously, I had also been working on creating a student-run record label to record and promote bands on campus with Matt Siegel, another soon-to-be Indaba co-founder.

There were really two things that inspired us to start Indaba Music. The first was the fact that digital production technology had become so inexpensive that anyone could produce studio-quality music in their own bedroom with tools like Pro Tools, Logic, Audacity, and GarageBand. There's no question there were more people making and recording music than at any other point in history.

The second thing was that the web was connecting musicians and fans in ways never before possible. One of the major problems facing musicians was, *"How do I get these 800 CDs I just printed into the hands of fans beyond handing them out at local shows?"*

The distribution issue had evaporated on the web because you could e-mail a five megabyte song to a person in China just as fast as you could get it to your next-door neighbor—that level of connectivity was very exciting to us, but everyone was still focused on the distribution, consumption, and promotion part of the value chain. No one was applying the power of the web to musicians' creative process in a meaningful way.

So we envisioned this idea of creating a platform that took these concepts and put them together specifically for musicians and their creative process. It would be a social and professional network where you could meet other musicians, exchange files, write music together, and produce music for fun and commercial release.

Can you tell me exactly what Indaba Music does?

It's evolved quite a bit. The original concept was to create a social network so that people could actually collaborate online. For example, a bass player in LA could record a bass track and a guitarist in New York record a guitar track, and then you could mix and edit them together either using any of the tools that we've already talked about (Pro Tools, Audacity, Logic) or using our web-based digital-audio workstation.

One of the things that was so encouraging was as people started to make more and more music on our site, we attracted a lot of attention from the more established music industry. Record labels, managers, publishers, even consumer brands who saw all this creative activity wanted to tap in to us—either to draw on the community's creative power as a promotional tool for their brand, or to source new content via our songwriters and producers.

As we grew, we started to run contests and other opportunities where you could remix a Mariah Carey song or write a virtual duet with Yo-Yo Ma or write an original fight song for your favorite NFL team. Many of these compositions and recordings have been released by established labels (over one hundred records have been released commercially) and licensed for film and TV, and have received other forms of exciting exposure.

Because of all this activity, Indaba has become much more of a marketplace—connecting our community of over 675,000 musicians with opportunities to create new music for brands, major artists, publishing companies, and so on.

This is a one-of-a-kind service, and has tremendous potential to expand and further change the way music is created. How did you finance this business, Dan?

To finance the business, originally we didn't go straight out into the venture community, but instead chose to go the route of talking with angel investors and friends and family to try to raise seed capital. We really wanted to have a product, and not just vaporware, before we had started to talk to any institutional investors.

Some people would say, "I'm not interested in investing, but I know this person in the music industry that you should really talk to." Through those types of conversations, we met some really incredible people, one of which was the woman who ultimately became our lead investor and has been the chair of our board for the last five years.

Martha Crowninshield is a general partner emerita at Boston Ventures and most well known for her work in the entertainment business—she bought and sold Motown Records in the one of the biggest turnaround deals the music industry has ever seen, and also sold *Billboard* magazine to Nielson. We were very fortunate that she stepped in to finance Indaba personally, but also because she has been incredibly valuable as a mentor.

Can I put you on the spot here and ask you: Is Indaba Music in the black and profitable?

No. We're not, by design. We are following our business plan, which calls for us to establish a critical mass of our community, which is our most valuable asset. We took a very deliberate strategy to offer a lot of free features, and at a certain point, which we thought was about 500,000 musicians, we would launch a subscription service, which is the core of our business model.

We reached that goal at the end of last year and are now offering additional services: for example, you can network and record for free, but if you want to sell your music on iTunes, you have to be a pro member. That's the first level of our premium subscription. It is working very well for us, but we are just at the beginning of that now.

Can you tell me some of the challenges you've faced with millions of other music-related sites saturating the web?

One of things that is always challenging is the recorded music industry. They still have this huge asset [all of the songs that have ever been recorded] and four companies primarily own them, but they don't know how to leverage them online. It can be a challenge to work with them because they are very cautious. They're afraid to do something online that might change their business model and open a door that can't be closed.

Another challenge is the artist trust factor. When we worked with John Legend or the Roots or Mariah Carey or Peter Gabriel, we had to win their trust and prove that what we offer has value to them, wouldn't damage the asset they work so hard to protect.

And then there are challenges that are more intrinsic to just running a business online, which is that a lot of people expect a lot on the web for free, and when you don't give it to them, they look somewhere else. So striking that balance is tough. It's hard to say at some point, "You know, you're getting so much value out of this, you should be paying $50 a year." Defining that point and what you put on each side of that line is always a challenge and something that we're just now addressing.

Was there a moment when you realized, "Oh my gosh, Indaba Music, we're going to be successful"?

One of the things I've found as an entrepreneur is that you never really feel like your business is successful, meaning that it's reached its end point, but it is important along the way to celebrate your smaller victories. Early on, I felt like Indaba was successful when there were 1,000 users, then had that same feeling when we hit 100,000 users.

Every time we've done something technologically challenging, like the digital-audio workstation that's in-browser and provides all these high-quality recording tools for people, it was a very significant technological achievement for us. All along the way, we try to feel like we're doing things that are successful, but that doesn't mean that that there isn't so much, much more we aspire to accomplish.

So now we know the abridged history and current status of Indaba, but what about you? I know you're a musician. Can you talk a little bit about that? Your love of music.

I started playing acoustic guitar when I was around ten and spent every free minute after school playing. That really got me into listening to music a lot more than I ever had before, so I started collecting CDs, and now I have a big vinyl collection and a digital collection.

I turned my bedroom into a recording studio with a mattress, which my parents were not thrilled about, but I did anyway. By the time I got to high school, I played in a couple bands and would record for other bands in the area all through college. I still play music, write a little bit, and collect acoustic guitars, but certainly after starting Indaba, it's been much harder to find the time to make music.

If you were to give *yourself* some advice and just starting out, what might that advice be?

I think there are important business issues that really don't matter whether you're starting a law firm or a music company. You have to understand everything about the business structure so that you set yourself up to be successful and so you can focus on the creative aspect of our endeavor. You should think about how you can set up the control of the company so that you never find yourself in a position where your company isn't yours anymore.

In terms of things like equity and ownership, it's great to own 100 percent of your company, but if you own a very big piece of a very small pie, it is never going to be as good as owning a small piece of an enormous pie. We have people who feel a real sense of ownership, and we're all working for something more than just a paycheck.

Where do you see yourself, or your company, in five years?

I would like to continue to see Indaba grow as there are so many different directions that we could go. We are extremely focused on progress, but it's very hard to predict our path.

There have been some big music-industry shifts since we started Indaba and there will undoubtedly be more. That could result in our merging with another company, being acquired, or even Indaba acquiring other companies.

I would also like to get more involved in finding my creative energy to get back to making and producing music. I'd like to see a recording project through from start to finish and do that with friends for fun—for our passion around recording.

What does the future of the music industry look like from where you're sitting today?

That's a really good question, obviously, one that a lot of us think and talk about. I definitely think that music publishing is going to continue to play a huge role in the monetization of music because you have so many more musicians that are creating and owning their own masters or working outside of the label system. So there's a huge opportunity in music publishing through placements, including commercials, films, live events, etc.

The real value of music is as great as ever, and corporations, companies, and brands are going to license that music and pay for it. I think that that's important for emerging artists.

Beyond that, I think that entrepreneurial artists will continue to find new ways to take over more of their own business responsibilities. There have been a lot of great web-based tools to help them manage their fan list and digital distribution. It's a relatively fragmented space to date and it's frustrating that you have to sign up for ten different accounts to do all these different things.

Ultimately, there will be a consolidation of all these services, with a few key companies that will help an artist or manager work the entire process from production to merchandise to CD printing and distribution.

Sounds like the future of Indaba Music.

You know, it certainly could be!

Michael Redman

ENTREPRENEUR AND AUTHOR

I guess this would be me! There several places in this book where I choose to interview myself, as I have held these particular jobs at one time or another. The interview format is much more direct than the narrative and I can address some of the important points not covered by my contributors.

What are some of the pitfalls of entrepreneurship?

I would say the biggest issue to think about is your idea, and how you are going to pull it off. Most of us believe our ideas are just great, but if everybody thinks that, well, get my point. I have a little folder on my desktop called Mike's Ideas because I have so many. The problem with most entrepreneurs is focus. We tend to have short attention spans and it oftentimes becomes our downfall. To be a successful entrepreneur requires razor-sharp focus for an extended period of time.

Why do you like being an entrepreneur?

For me it has always been exciting to build something new and see if there is a market for what I build. Did you read that last sentence? One of the lessons to be learned is to find a market and *then* build your product or service!

How would I get started?

First you need a great idea or problem to be solved; do you have one? Well, if you do, then a good starting point would be to ask some people you respect to help you evaluate your idea and see what they think of it, how you might market it, and so forth. Be honest and ask them what they "*don't*" like about your idea too, so you don't spend your time and money chasing a nonexistent market.

What are some of the best areas of growth for the music entrepreneur?

The obvious answer would be technology because there are so many exciting things going on today. I still think the social-music-system market is wide open because no one has figured out what the real potential is. I would also recommend looking at areas that others are not. Tristan Jehan and his partner did just this when they developed their data-collection system, The Echo Nest. Now they are the only game in town and the market leader. They found a terrific niche.

What do you do on a typical day?

I work like a dog, because no one believes in your idea as much as you do. I spend a lot of time educating potential investors, friends, and clients. I also need to work on my idea. In the case of Reeltracs, which I am currently marketing, I am always trying to put myself in the shoes of the people I would like to use our system and make it easier for them to both adopt and use it.

What is the biggest challenge for an entrepreneur?

I would probably say it is adoption of your idea or service. You see, most great ideas are innovations, and innovation requires people to change processes and habits, which is hard to accomplish. It's called the legacy syndrome. Typically people won't change the way they do things until the pain of change is less than the pain of continuing to do things the same old way. It's just human nature.

Is it hard to raise money for your ideas?

In simple terms—yes. The process can happen fast if your idea does not require too much capital and you have family and friends that are willing invest in you. Notice I said "you," that's because most of the time your money will come from people that believe in you and not so much your idea.

Now if your idea is a big one, you can expect to spend a great deal of time creating a business case and plan before even venturing out to look for money. You may need the assistance of a professional to raise your capital and give up a significant part of your company before you even start your business. You also need to understand that there are millions of other people developing great new ideas every day and yours is just one of them. A big company with lots of resources can come along and blow you out of the water in the blink of an eye, and they may have never known you or your idea existed!

Do you have some advice for me if I have a great idea for a product or service for the music industry?

Again, just check out your idea with as many people as you can get to listen to gain some thoughtful insights and feedback. If you still feel like it's the bomb, then go for it with everything you've got.

EVER WONDER HOW THAT COOL LITTLE APP SPOTIFY can build intuitive playlists of music you like from a single artist's name? Well, it's all about the data that's been collected, identified, interpreted, and manipulated to deliver what we perceive as musical intelligence. How can a computer understand this stuff? Well, this was just what two MIT graduates talked about for several years while in school before finally deciding to take the risk and make the jump into entrepreneurship and start a business. The Echo Nest is a music business that you've probably never heard of, but you experience the results of their efforts on a daily basis.

Tristan Jehan

FOUNDER, THE ECHO NEST

Could you tell me where the idea came from for The Echo Nest?

Brian Whitman and I were both students at the MIT media lab in Boston, working on our PhDs, both trying to describe music, and we had two different approaches. I was representing music by using machines to listen to the waveform and extracting perceptual information from it. Brian was describing music through text, using crawlers and natural language processing to extract information out of reviews, news, and blog posts.

We sometimes argued about the best way of understanding music. I was like, "You get it from the signal, that's really what you hear," and he was like, "Nah, it doesn't really matter, you can learn it from what people are saying." The discussion went on for a couple of years, and as we were finishing our PhDs we wondered what we would do next. At the time, there were only about two companies that were in the music discovery arena, Pandora and Last.fm.

Pandora was at the very beginning of their service then and were using a manual process (they still do). As scientists, we were like, "No, that's not the way we're going to do this." Last. fm was better in that they were gathering a lot of data from listeners and were making sense out of it.

All of this happened about the time Napster had exploded and people had access to a lot of music. . . . *So how do we help people find music they like? How do we help them discover new music?* We thought by combining automatic machine listening and crawling the Internet to find out what people are saying about music, we had a good shot at fixing that problem.

We turned down good job offers when we graduated and decided to go into business. Our goal was to "fix" music, understand it, and turn our technology into an engine able to help people discover and experience music in new ways. We decided to create The Echo Nest and built the service we generally call music intelligence. We basically turn a huge amount of data that we have collected into useful information and tools, and provide them to large media companies and independent developers of music applications.

So you decide to go into business. How did you fund The Echo Nest?

We had in our mind that we had the right technology to fix the problems but no idea how to build a business. We were going into this totally blind.

When we finished our PhDs, we were very lucky. Brian's advisor, Barry Vercoe, who also was on my committee, said, "I'd like to help you." He knew us and liked what we were doing. That was great because right from the beginning we were able to afford an office and machines to start building the technology at scale.

So you turned down a good job to follow your passion. What are some of the risks you took starting your own business?

In our case, the big challenge was that our idea was completely new: nothing like it existed. We decided, "Let's put all this new technology out there and bring it to people."

It was risky in a sense because the companies we talked to weren't quite ready for Echo Nest. It was very hard to convince people that it was something important and that what we were doing was better. Today nobody is asking that question. [*laughs*]

For you personally, what's the best part of owning your business?

For me, it's really seeing the amazing growth we've experienced, and how excited our people are to work on this. Ultimately, it's about helping the end user find more of the music they love.

There's also another side of our company that works on content manipulation, remix stuff. That's the next step. I think there is a lot of potential for creators and listeners to personalize the way they experience music and have a more interactive connection with their music.

What do you think that the business climate is for music-related innovation? Do you think that a lot of young people should jump in and start a business?

Yes I do, I think actually that it's the perfect time to get into this side of the music business. The MIDEM music conference in Cannes, France, is one of the biggest music industry conferences and there was a very positive feeling. In previous years everyone was quite pessimistic. I think it's turning around now, and there's a lot of optimism for the future.

People are complaining a lot about the record industry, but they are only one part of the business. The web is growing like crazy, and I think the music industry will actually be saved by the web. It's not going to be about selling albums but services around music that's going to make it all happen.

So can I ask you how the business is doing financially?

It's always a challenge when we're young and growing fast. But if you were to see our list of our customers, it's definitely doing well and moving at a healthy rate. We're now a fairly big team and everyone is really excited and optimistic right now.

You're in a great space without a lot of formidable competition.

We're the only real big music-data platform in the industry. Anybody from the developer in his garage to the big media company can access our billions of data points of information around music for 30 million songs and 2 million artists. It's a lot of data!

Having been through this, and developing your own start-up, what advice would you give to somebody who's sitting at MIT or another school when they say, "I'm not the greatest guitar player, I love music, I really love technology," and they have a good idea?

Honestly, I think you should do what you really love doing. In a way, I'm a musician, but I'm more of a scientist and engineer. That's really what I'm really good at and what I really like to do. It made sense for me to do this because it's a very technical company. It's really engineer and technology focused.

If you were a musician, I'd say play music, if that's really what you like to do. But if you want to go beyond or do something else, I'd encourage you first to find the right people and do your research to know what you're getting into. I wouldn't advise doing it alone. Brian and I had ups and downs, and being alone in the fog can be very stressful, so it helps to have someone to share with and bounce ideas off.

COLD-CALLING AND CONNECTING WITH PEOPLE online was a long and tedious process that swallowed up the first six months of writing this book. Thinking about and finding the right people to interview was tough going. The ones I wanted to speak to were successful and therefore busy. I did, however, tap into a gem now and then that was quick to understand why I was writing this book and saw a bit of themselves in it.

Paul DeGooyer impressed me from the moment he said, "Hi, Michael," into his Skype headset. Very articulate and ever the gentleman, we talked for a long time about the gaming industry in which he is something of a superstar dealmaker. Since our first interview, Paul has started his own company, Relative Comfort (cool name), that helps other companies realize their goals.

We have also become personal friends through our high-tech introduction and are working on a couple projects together. I love to listen to him talk! I love a brain and thought process that integrates all parties and appreciates the value of a win-win. Very refreshing—thanks, Paul!

Paul DeGooyer

FOUNDER, RELATIVE COMFORT

Paul, how did you get into the music business?

Long story, but probably similar to others you've heard in connection with this book, in that music has always been the central passion in my life. As a teenager, I was an experimental guitarist in the rather straight-ahead punk rock scene in Washington, DC. I definitely did not fit in musically, and perhaps as a result, I learned how to record and mix my own music and then started recording other bands. Eventually I moved to Boston, where I became an A & R scout for the indie arm of Virgin Records and produced a couple of records for them. At some point, they hired me to be a product manager and A & R rep and moved me to New York. I got a crash course in the nuts and bolts of releasing music, working on Peter Gabriel's Real World label.

I then went on to work at Sony Music, where I co-founded their artist development operation, called Red Independent Network, or RED Ink, and worked with artists like Aimee Mann, Train, John Mayer, and DJ Krush. Chris Blackwell, the founder of Island Records, hired me to be general manager of his multimedia company, called Palm Pictures, where I learned about film production and releasing and was involved with early digital video-streaming site Sputnik 7. From there, I went to work for the venerable Rhino label in Los Angeles, where I managed Warner Music Group's video releasing operation.

Let's talk a bit about your past job at MTV. How did you become the lead executive behind the wildly successful Rock Band games?

In 2005, MTV hired me to run their home entertainment operations and at some point that year, the original publisher and developer for the Guitar Hero video game approached us. They had been to every major game publisher with their idea and had been turned down. They were prepared to go it alone and release the game directly but needed a media and marketing partner. We loved the game, so we did a deal with them to market Guitar Hero on MTV, and it exploded.

In the wake of Guitar Hero's success, MTV purchased Harmonix and we turned our attention to making the first full-band game, Rock Band. MTV decided to publish the game, and I was tasked with leading that team.

How involved were you in the selection and production of the music for the games that you were involved with?

I was the nominal music supervisor in addition to my other responsibilities, so in theory I was in charge of picking every song. In reality, my job was to set creative direction and acquisition strategy, and then make sure that my teams had a good process and were left alone to do their jobs. I'm very proud of the results. Rock Band leads the entire video game industry in downloads sold. There are over 3,000 songs available for purchase, and we've sold more than 100 million of them. Harmonix still profitably releases new music for Rock Band every week—as it has for the past five years.

How do you see the game industry shifting?

The big shift is the transition from physical media to digital distribution, and from a console-driven experience to more casual games on mobile and tablet devices. It's currently putting the entire console business under tremendous pressure. That said, all the major console manufacturers have very robust delivery systems that are now delivering music and video content as much as interactive content, and game consoles are set to play a leading role in the coming multiscreen entertainment era.

What does your new company, Relative Comfort, offer, and how does it relate to your past job at MTV?

As I mentioned earlier, my job at MTV was initially quite broad. It was only after my team helped launch Guitar Hero and MTV acquired Harmonix that my entire focus became video games.

So with Relative Comfort, I'm going back to a broader approach. We help media and technology companies optimize their products, distribution platforms, and branding. We are currently working on five apps, of which only one is a game, three console video games, a digital platform strategy project, and a digital service re-branding research exercise.

What was the most uncomfortable part of leaving a secure job with MTV and going it alone as an entrepreneur?

I was lucky in that I immediately had clients willing to hire my firm, so finances for the new company were not an issue. My biggest concern then and now is ensuring that I can provide world-class service as my company grows. I am very aware of our bandwidth constraints, deliverables, and deadlines and want to make sure we're planning properly to exceed our clients' expectations every time they call on us.

I know there are times where you look back and think, "Why did I do this?" What is the goal of your entrepreneurial venture, say, five years out?

I would like to have a portfolio of projects where I helped my clients change the world to benefit both their customers and their business goals. It's a very exciting time for digital media, and my company is right in the thick of the struggle to figure out what's next.

You were guided down the entrepreneurship path by life's experience and you probably cannot give advice as to how to do this, but would you share something you've learned along the way that was an epiphany or not to be forgotten in deal making?

Absolutely. The best advice I can give is this: Be fastidiously straightforward in your communications with the parties to any deal, and always keep the core value proposition in sight. The deal is not an end in itself; that core value proposition is. If that starts to erode, be very crisp about cutting your losses and moving on. Don't close a bad deal just because it seems to have momentum, or your ego appears to be at stake.

**Paul, that's some of the best advice I've received while writing this book!
What role has your education played in the progression of your career?**

Learning to think critically, process information from disparate sources, and to write reasonably well has been essential. My concentration on English literature has served me very well in the business world, and in unexpected ways. Beyond that, I really believe that it's important to be engaged and have a point of view on the world, which can certainly happen outside of the context of formal education.

Mentorship has been very important to my career. I have been very lucky to have the opportunity to work for, or alongside, truly great creative, finance, and marketing executives who took the time to really help me learn what they do. Working for Chris Blackwell and seeing how he speaks to artists and puts deals together was a highlight for me.

I make time to play guitar every day and listen to massive amounts of new music every week. I own a console and recording rig, so I stay very close to that side of it. Music is my passion—hearing new recordings and trying to figure out how they got all those sounds is very exciting to me.

Understanding the process of music creation through direct experience and being able to speak that language has been very valuable. If you can talk to any musician about their creative process or even their gear of choice—real talk—they'll light up, whether it's a newly signed artist or Sir Paul McCartney. You're much more likely to have real, meaningful interactions if you can establish this foundation. Plus it's a lot more fun to talk about than their advertising and marketing plans! [*laughs*]

**I know what you mean! You have got a pretty intense job, Paul.
What is a typical day like for you?**

Well, today I had a series of scheduled calls and then a call list that I never seem to get through [*laughs*]. On any given day I might have a couple of dozen people I need to call, and can usually get to about fifteen of them. Then there may be three to four hours of scheduled meetings.

In an average week, I plan for meaningful face time or mealtime with eight to ten people, and I'm generally traveling a week or so out of each month. I also spend about two hours each day, more or less unwired, focusing on writing: deal memos, proposals, reports, or marketing plans. It's busy but fun.

So you're somehow still playing guitar and finding holes in your schedule whenever

you can even with all of that going on? That's amazing! Would you say that your job fills that place in you that loves music and keeps you close to it?

Well, first and foremost, I want to make sure that I'm pleasing my clients. Fortunately, I find that if I'm listening to music, I'm much more productive in general. I always have new music running in the background, and I'll tag tracks and make notes when I hear something good. I really live for those moments, when I hear something brand-new and it's just truly great. So to answer your question—yes!

6

Educator

Rapid Fire

Skill Set—If you can remember your best teachers growing up, think about why you liked them. Those are the qualities you will want to have as an educator in the music business. Beyond knowing your subject content, which I assume you do, you also need the ability to creatively communicate those ideas and concepts. Not everyone possesses these qualities, but if you do, they will make you cool and ensure job security. Also, on my "must" list is patience, without which you don't stand a chance. This alone was the reason I didn't do so well as a teacher.

Education—Depending on the type of school and your personal goals, a higher education is super important because this is the gauge in many cases by which your pay scale is determined.

Hours—Normally school hours and several evenings during the week for planning. One-on-one private lessons can take place at any time depending on how you arrange your schedule. If you work in a store, obviously you will work store hours, but if you teach at home or on site, you can set your own hours. Also remember that there are lots of school holidays!

Upside—Fulfillment in knowing that you are making a difference in our world. I have been told that having a flexible schedule is a big plus too because it leaves time to play music part-time or explore other personal opportunities.

Downside—Again, depending on the area of education you decide upon, you may need an additional job to live the lifestyle you would like and finding a teaching job might take some time.

Financial—$$ to $$$$ There are people teaching in music stores making $25,000 to $45,000 annually and there are professors in large universities who are paid $150,000-plus. If you are shooting for the upper-level jobs, you'll need to be in demand as a successful musician or industry executive, or have worked your way up gaining tenure and expertise along the way. These jobs are not offered too often, and when they become available the competition is usually significant.

Location—Any large metropolitan area that has these two components: a substantial population and culture. A quick Google search will help you here. The USA has over 5,000 colleges and universities not including specialized education.

Future—My contributors tell me that the future looks good in all areas of music education and will for as long as there are students.

BEFORE YOU TURN THE PAGE TO FIND A SEEMINGLY MORE EXCITING CAREER, READ ON. Think again about what you like to do. Does it include playing your instrument on a regular basis and being part of the performing community? If your answer is yes, then being involved in the music education field might be just the right job for you.

Several months ago while traveling, I met a young woman at the Dallas airport who had recently graduated from Eastman and wanted to be a concert pianist, and I asked her, "So what will you do now that you have this degree?" She replied, "Probably perform." And I thought to myself: How many concert pianists have I seen lately? How many concerts and opportunities are there for an unknown pianist? Her chances of living that part of her dream are pretty slim. She could have such a fulfilling career in the music business if she was just aware of the industry as a whole. I said, "You know there are many, many ways for you to work in the educational field while playing on the side and making a great living!" We talked for over an hour about the world of music education.

Most people think that education, teaching private lessons, or being a professor is a dead end. Remember the old saying, "Those who can, do, and those who can't, teach"? It's just not the case. As I sit here writing this book, I am in a way trying to teach you—teach you to view the music industry through a macro scope.

Musicians have many wonderful reasons for teaching, though I have to say that I tried to teach and fired myself. Teaching wasn't for me, I didn't have the patience required to be successful, and frankly couldn't bring myself down to a level that was engaging to my students.

There is a great school you have probably heard of called Full Sail, and when they were in their infancy I was the chief engineer at the recording studio where they would conduct classes. They asked me to teach a class that was something like Audio Engineering 101, and I agreed. My first class had eleven students from different backgrounds and we spent ten hours a day following the curriculum developed by some engineering guy somewhere, and it just didn't make any sense to me in the real world where I worked every day. To make a long story short, I just couldn't to stick to the teacher's manual, and after struggling for a time and not doing as good a job as I should with my students, I stepped down.

A good teacher needs confidence in his or her own ability, patience, charisma, and the ability to deliver a focused message to the awaiting student. A good sense of humor doesn't hurt either! You need that elusive Zen-like thing that the monk had from the *Kung Fu* TV series about 100 years ago starring the late David Carradine.

I should also mention that education is one of my favorite subjects, in large part because I turned my back on it for a time. I have many musician friends, and as a group, I would say they are a bright bunch. I'm talking about common sense—just plain smarts—not necessarily academic, political, or religiously motivated intelligence. Most people I know in this group have very little business acuity or experience. That said, I applaud *you* for reading this book early on in your career, because in the end you will in fact be smarter, or at least have a better idea of the possible impact of your early music career decisions.

BEFORE YOU READ ANY FURTHER, I WANT YOU TO GO TO YOUTUBE and type in "Jaco Pastorius." If you don't know who he is, you should, and if you do, then you will understand what I'm talking about here. Most people don't typically associate academic musicianship with drummers or bass players. They have always received less respect than Rodney Dangerfield, yet it's the bass and drum combination that creates the foundation for all popular music . . . period. As a matter of fact, if it weren't for my drummer friend Lloyd Hanson, who had a degree in music composition, I would have failed miserably when Disney called me for the first time to write music for a commercial that required an orchestra.

Dan O'Loane, a friend who worked at Disney as a producer, often used my studio to record voice-overs and sweeten his TV spots. One day he called to offer me my first chance to break into the wonderful world of composing for Disney. It was a commercial with Mickey Mouse standing on the top of Cinderella's castle conducting an orchestra. Well, of course I jumped at the chance to prove myself, but I had never formally written anything for an orchestra, which you probably know by now didn't stop me from saying yes. I called on longtime friend Lloyd Hanson to help me pull it off so I didn't look like an idiot. I sat in the front of the room with my clients writing with Performer synced to picture, while Lloyd quietly transcribed what I was writing for the orchestra on a couch in the back of my studio. Nobody really noticed and nothing seemed out of the ordinary.

My secretary called a bunch of musicians who played with the local symphony, and by morning we had the finished soundtrack that was just beautiful. I have often wondered where I'd be today if Lloyd wasn't there with his degree to make it all happen. I couldn't have done it by myself.

A few years after this harrowing experience, I landed a great job with Universal writing the music for a live show that I lovingly called the "Dead Celebrity Christmas Special." The cast was made up of a number of celebrities that have long since passed and the theme was *Ricky Ricardo's Latin Jazz Christmas*. If you are old enough, you will remember Ricky from the *I*

Love Lucy show. There was only one problem, which was that I had no experience writing jazz and even less with Latin music. Fortunately, I knew this great bass player, Chuck Archard, who was an expert in all styles of world music, so I hired Chuck and another friend (and soon to become my partner), Greg Sims, to write all the arrangements for the show. They did an amazing job, the show was a hit, and once again I looked great pulling it off.

Chuck is one of those extraordinary musicians who would have excelled no matter what instrument he played, but he fell in love at an early age with the bass guitar. He is very well-schooled and over time gravitated toward education, and in particular Rollins College in Orlando, where he is allowed to flex his creative muscle and pass on his extensive knowledge and experience to the current crop of upcoming musicians.

Chuck Archard

PROFESSOR AT ROLLINS COLLEGE

Chuck Archard is an accomplished bassist, composer, and educator whose original works have aired on Fox, HBO, Showtime, and in over thirty international markets.

Chuck, did you ever think that you'd end up where you are today when you started playing bass guitar?

No, but I knew I was going to play music and be involved with music. I started playing bass at the age of twelve and I've never stopped! My mom has often said, "Well, Chuck, you were lucky because you always knew what you wanted to do."

How did a formal education play into your decision to become an educator?

Oh, it was huge! Having the pieces of paper are very important in the academic world. You just have to have the degree. But I should say that there are also some great musicians without degrees that have gigs at colleges. If you're Gary Burton and you're teaching at Berklee and you're on a thousand recordings, I don't think they say, "Well, he doesn't have a doctorate"!

Formal training is very important, but I believe practical playing experience to be equally important because what you're doing when you're teaching is trying to help people with a profession, be it teaching or performing or both. My high school band director said, "You can always perform on a teaching degree, but you can't teach on a performance degree," great words of wisdom I've never forgotten.

You are well known as an encyclopedia of music! I thought at one point you would be a music historian . . . a rock historian. Do you have an incredible memory?

Well, my dad has a great memory and is really into all kinds of trivia, but mine is more limited to music. I don't read much fiction, but I love biographies, autobiographies, and nonfiction. Now I am in a school where I'm teaching history of rock and history of jazz and world music, and all of my trivia has a new home. I wasn't like, "Man, if I could learn about the Grateful Dead, Cachao Lopez, and Jaco because someday I'll teach it!" It just happened.

Tell me, what is a typical day or week like as Professor Archard?

For years I've been teaching 8 a.m. classes, not very typical for a musician, so that tells you something right there!

Luckily kids will get up for my 8:00 a.m. History of Rock class and maybe not so much for an 8:00 a.m. History of the Renaissance Lute class. [*laughs*] So I usually teach two classes a day, one in the morning and one in the afternoon. Then I also have lessons, various meetings, jazz ensemble, and then class prep.

When you teach history classes, especially continuing history classes, you have to stay on top of what's happening in 2013, not just 1913. So I do a lot of reading and a lot of research. It's a great way to stay relevant with your students without pandering. To be an effective teacher, I believe you have to find some common ground with your students. Knowing who Lady Gaga and Lil' Wayne are can sometimes get some interesting dialogue started.

Are you involved in the actual curriculum development?

Yes. Rollins, being a liberal arts school and a private college, is a wonderful place to teach, because if you have an idea for a new class it's possible to get it added to the curriculum. There are still forms and procedures that have to go through committee, but if the idea is substantial, it is seriously considered. Awhile back I started a music business class and an improvisation class, and currently I'm working on a roots and Americana music class.

Along the same line, what is the most rewarding part of your job?

If I can inspire kids to stay in the arts, promote the arts, and actually make a living at the same time, it's perfect. It's also pretty cool when you get e-mails years later. . . . I recently got one from a girl who said, "My boyfriend thinks he knows everything about rock, and they had a question on *Jeopardy!* about '60s rock and I knew every answer and I kicked his ass."

And your biggest challenge?

It's the double-edged sword, really. I absolutely love technology, but kids bring computers and cell phones to class now and they're tweeting and ~~posting on Facebook~~, so it's tough trying to disseminate ~~information so it~~ connects with the student and keeps them engaged. ~~We now~~ have smart classrooms that are totally wireless with drop-down screens, so I just bring my laptop and display all of my PowerPoints right there. It's not a bad thing and it's not a good thing, it's just a different generation that likes different visual stimulation. They also have a shorter attention span, so as an instructor you have to keep it moving and interesting.

The other issue is the sheer number of hours I put in to find new points of views and make sure what I'm teaching is factual.

I remember when you started at Rollins and was teaching a class about MIDI. I would definitely agree that you've always been into technology! Can one make a good living being an educator of music?

Yes, you can! There is opportunity at every level, from elementary through college. Financially it is the most lucrative if you've been on the job for a long time, especially in the public school sector where you get rewarded every year for staying on.

In college it depends on your status. I have a master's degree, and with a doctorate there is an upward pay scale move. I'm what is called an artist in residence, so my whole contract is a yearly lease, and if I'm doing my job, then they re-up for another year.

Can you change to a tenure track? If so, how would you go about that?

Not unless I get a doctorate. In many colleges tenure is harder to get anyway because of the current economy. I always remember that people work twenty years for a company and then get a pink slip. So any job is tenuous at best, so what I would say is yes, you can make a good living, and it all depends on what you consider quality.

I supplement my income as a musician as well, which I believe is important because I bring back a lot of that knowledge from the stage to the classroom. If all I knew was Renaissance-era music . . . well . . . good luck! [*laughs*] You have to teach a lot of different subjects and have depth in my classroom to keep my student's attention.

I was lucky to hook up with you, Michael, to learn about the commercial side of the music business, so I use that too!

What's the job market and competition like?

It's tough. If you were to go online and pick a few colleges at random, or some of the heavies, you'll see that many of those teachers have been there twenty-five–thirty years, because it's a good gig. It's like a symphony gig; the principle trumpet player ain't leaving, ever!

But with that said, there are more colleges being built, and lately I've been looking at Internet colleges. I've started to notice some are offering music history and arts because they're trying to offer a complete degree program and not just a two-year thing.

What sort of advice would you give somebody who is interested in becoming a professional educator?

Most importantly you have to want to teach. It is an incredibly worthwhile profession, but it is also very demanding and time intensive.

The best thing to do would be to get advanced degrees, because regardless of where you end up, you'll get paid more if you have a master's and a doctorate. The other thing is tedious, but you really need to learn a wide range of subject matter to be relevant.

If you play more than one instrument, can arrange or compose, know technology, or [are] a good public speaker, these are all factors in the hiring process today.

I had one teacher tell me, "Figure out what you want to do, and then find that person who's doing the job that you want to do." I had a teacher at Morehead State University and he played B3 with Wilson Pickett in the '60s, had a gigging band, wrote arrangements, played studio sessions, and he taught school. He put it all together and had a nice career. I would constantly ask him, "What're you doing this week? I emulated his model and now I pretty much do the same things he did!

Some schools are looking for people with experience, and others might take someone who has a doctorate straight out of Julliard over, say, somebody with ten years teaching and gigging experience at a smaller school. Be prepared and have as many diverse skill sets as possible.

I would tell anybody that being an educator is absolutely a rewarding profession. It's just a wonderful feeling to know you are truly having a positive impact on your students' lives.

IF YOU ARE LOOKING FOR WHAT COULD BE SUBSTANTIAL SUPPLEMENTARY INCOME, you might want to check into private music lessons. A multitude of working musicians turn to this profitable job and do very well over the long haul. The benefits are not limited to income alone, because there's nothing quite like passing your knowledge and experience on to others. Teaching is not for everyone, because you will inevitably encounter those who love music but have little to no feel or talent. You will also find the rather rare protégé that will make you think about putting your instrument in the closet forever. In mere weeks, they learn what took you years of practice; they devour everything about music on a level that most of us could only dream of. How cool is that!

Forest Rodgers teaches guitar and has seen both types of student.

Forest Rodgers

MUSICIAN, INSTRUCTOR

Forest Rodgers plays guitar, banjo, Dobro, and mandolin. He is also the author of the bestselling Pedal Steel Licks for Guitar, *distributed by Hal Leonard.*

Forest, you are an incredibly talented and well-established guitarist. What made you shift your focus from performing to one-on-one guitar lessons?

It was a little bit of necessity, but I genuinely like it as well!

I knew guys who wanted to learn some country hot licks and had done some one-on-ones. Some of these folks were advanced players, but I would still show them a few tricks I knew.

The actual teaching became interesting because I couldn't believe there were players who could dazzle me with jazz riffs and chord construction but just couldn't get the hot licks and the bends on a Telecaster. Sitting there watching them, I thought, "This is really cool," because they could blow me away, yet there I was showing them some of these licks and they'd beam at me. Some of these folks went on to do pretty well in Nashville.

I understand that you play music by ear. Since you've been teaching, have you learned to read music, or is it possible for you to get by without having to read?

When I started teaching I had to learn to read, and I will admit that I kind of bluffed my way there for a while; eventually I did my homework.

It's important because I have a couple of ear players that just don't get reading music and they don't understand tablature either. I tell them, "Okay, I can show you where to put your fingers and you can memorize this, but it's not the best way to learn." If a student can't read, I can't explain the rhythm, etc.

Forest, do you feel that teaching has helped you become a better player?

I think so. . . . It's almost uncanny. If I had known what I know now twenty years ago, I could have communicated so much better with other musicians. I'm not positive it would have helped my career, but the communication part has become so much clearer.

How many hours do you teach each week?

I teach four days a week. Generally I start around 1 or 2 p.m. and go till 8. The evenings are when most students are out of school, so I'm busy between 3 and 8. During the week I probably teach between thirty, thirty-five students. In past years it has been as high as forty-five, fifty, but there's been a little bit of decline with the economy.

Can you talk to me a little bit about the advantages or disadvantages of working with a music school or a store?

I have some friends that teach at home, and while it would be nice to be my own boss and completely in control, I would also say that working with a music school or a store that also provides lessons is a great combination. They get their split to maintain the schedule, payments, and deal with all the operational stuff while all I do is teach.

So your employer does all of the scheduling and bookkeeping for you?

Yes, and they provide the building! [*laughs*] Honestly, it's a pretty good trade-off because if I had to do all that out of my home, it just wouldn't work for me. Some people can do it, but I'm not set up for it.

Is the school's split negotiated or 50/50? How does that work?

I guess everybody is a little different. At our school, the teacher's split is 50/50, and I don't have a problem with it. Some schools are negotiable depending on your experience, or how many students you may bring in with you, but generally, that's the deal.

So you can make a good living just teaching full-time?

Yes! Especially if you're in an area like we are, where there are a lot of homeschooled students. That's the business of running the school, which I'm not involved in too much, though it is a cooperative effort. If you really can get with your owners and management and focus and target, it will be bigger than you could ever do by yourself.

Do you still play in bands and work as a session player?

I don't think I could do just job in music and make a living. I play several live venues here as well as do recording sessions. Between teaching, recording, and live performance, I make a very comfortable living; on top of that, I have the royalty money that comes from music libraries and instructional videos.

It sounds like teaching is something you really love. Is this a job you can see yourself doing for many years to come?

Actually, I can't see doing anything else at this point in my life. Now that I've been teaching for a long time, it's really who I am. I could do other things and I have done other things, but yes, I love teaching.

Assuming that someone has experience playing an instrument and is accomplished, the teaching process almost becomes natural once you get the ball rolling.

I get very prepared for my students, so when they walk through the door I can give them the best I've got. It's almost like, "Okay, show's on!" I don't take teaching lessons any less seriously than when I perform onstage, and the same goes for preparing for a live show compared to comparing for a lesson. I have to focus and give my students some parameters so they stay focused on the material too! The students know we will still learn "Smoke on the Water," but in the process we're going to work out of the method book and learn how to read and play.

I keep my students a long time and I think that says a lot . . . if I can brag a little! [*laughs*]

Forest, I can't imagine anybody not wanting to hang out with you. You truly are the consummate modern-day musician, a jack-of-all-trades, and a master of your instrument.

IN MY SEARCH TO FIND INDIVIDUALS with enough experience and expertise to impart their wisdom to you, I came across the next gentleman I interviewed. He is currently teaching film scoring to students at the USC Thornton School of Music. His name you may not know, but the body of work he has in some way participated in is astounding. Many years ago, Daniel Carlin's father took his music editing skills and moved them to his LA garage, where he hired his children, the people across the street, and probably the milkman to support the growth of his quickly expanding business, revolutionizing music editing along the way.

Daniel is wonderful to talk with and has enough stories about the music industry to write his own book.

Daniel Carlin

USC THORNTON SCHOOL OF MUSIC PROFESSOR

Daniel Carlin has worked as an Emmy-winning music editor (Under Siege), *Emmy-nominated music director* (the Temptations)*; conductor, music supervisor, soundtrack producer, and consultant on such multiple award-winning films, including* An Officer and a Gentleman, The Black Stallion, Steel Magnolias, *and* The Last of the Mohicans.

Dan, up until recently you were the chairman of the film-scoring department at the prestigious Berklee College of Music in Boston. Why did you choose higher education?

During the technological revolution of the '90s, our company, Segue Music, was the first to beta-test Pro Tools, the digital-audio workstation that has become the industry standard. That came about because two of our best employees, former Berklee students Chris Brooks and Curtis Roush, told me, "There is going to be a huge technological change, and we need to get in front of it." So we started collaborating with Digidesign on Pro Tools, which led to our being the first company to download a film score into a digital-editing machine, prepare the tracks, and then take that machine to a dubbing stage to place the music into the film soundtrack. (This was in 1993, and the move was *Last Action Hero*, starring the Governor, Arnold Schwarzenegger.)

It was the start of a revolutionary change that was very expensive. We had twelve or thirteen music editors, and we had to switch from gear that hadn't changed in half a century to gear that was changing every six months. So Jeff Carson and I looked for a financial partner, and we wound up selling our business to Zomba, the parent company of Jive Records, and taking long-term contracts to keep running the business. They eventually sold their entire corporation to BMG, who didn't want to be in the music-editing and music-supervision business and cut us loose to go back on our own.

By then, I had become involved with the Recording Academy (the Grammy organization), where I was elected chair for two terms. I found that work to be very gratifying, especially the part that involved working in music education. And with our children out of college and our daughters already married, my wife and I now longer felt the financial pressure to keep the money rolling in. So I started thinking about a career change.

About that time, I received a breakfast invitation from Patrick Williams, with whom I had broken into the television business as his music editor and sometime substitute conductor. While still scoring television and films, Pat also was the artistic director at the Henry Mancini Institute, and he asked if I would take on the position of executive director, which I did. The work was very gratifying, and I was terribly disappointed when the board decided to close down the institute a few years later. When that happened, I had the choice of retiring, going back into the entertainment industry, or pursuing music education. I was too young to retire, I had already done the music editing/supervision thing, and I really liked music education. In 2007, before the job market completely collapsed, there were still a few interesting opportunities available. After considering several, I settled on the Berklee College of Music because I respected their work, and I had gone to graduate school in New England, so I knew I could survive the winters. [*laughs*]

What's your inspiration? What gets you up and off to school these days?

The most fun that you have in Hollywood is on the scoring session because you get to hang out with musicians all day long. That's what I get to do at Berklee—collaborate all day long with musicians, whether they are administrators, faculty, or students. Everyone is here because we all share a life and love of music. Most of the faculty and administrators have enjoyed successful careers in some part of the music business. This gives them great credibility with the students, most of whom are absolutely thrilled to be here. Additionally,

25 percent of Berklee's student body is international, so that makes for an enriching cultural and artistic experience as well.

Berklee is the only institution anywhere to offer an undergraduate degree in film scoring. If that's your interest, and you get accepted, you become one of the 350 students at Berklee College of Music majoring in film scoring. Our students are intrigued and excited by the way music works in movies. So I get to help teach and mentor the most gifted and motivated among them; I get to work with a talented and inspiring faculty; I'm able to use my networking connections in Los Angeles to help students get internships and assistant composer jobs; and I get to host wonderful former collaborators who come in from LA and New York to speak and offer master classes. I am lucky, grateful, and happy to be working here. My wife says it's only because I finally found a pond that's small enough! [*laughs*]

7

Lawyer and Business Affairs

Rapid Fire

Skill Set—Higher education, relationships, focus, and a very accurate memory. A real love of music is a must or you're just not going to make it.

Hours—Most lawyers and business affairs people have office jobs, and office hours sometimes interrupted by travel.

Upside—Working in a creative industry with artists and their management teams. Conceptualizing and developing deals and contracts that are complex with many moving parts can be fun.

Downside—Not much of a downside except for the challenge of finding your first job. It can be difficult breaking into the entertainment business as an attorney because everybody wants these jobs. I have to assume that if you are thinking about this type of job, you are smart enough to figure out a way in.

Financial—$$$ to $$$$ Business affairs lawyers are in the upper echelon of the music industry, negotiating sometimes very big deals for very big dollars. They are paid well for their work. As you might expect, there is a ladder to be climbed. It may take you awhile to become adept at the music business.

Location—Where the business is done. NYC, LA, Nashville, and some international locations.

Future—Steady as she goes. As long as there is a music business, there will be lawyers and business affairs people running it.

ONE OF MY BEST FRIENDS IS AN ATTORNEY, and until the day I met him, I'd always wondered why anyone would want to practice law except for the obvious financial reward. He told me that beyond preparing the typical contracts, divorces, and run-of-the-mill legal work he performs on a regular basis, he considers the practice of law to be very creative. He loves negotiating both sides of the same argument and seeing the big picture for his clients. He told me how great he felt when he negotiated a deal for everyone, and he really believed in the win-win. He also told me that he still played his guitar every night for an hour before bed, "Just to clear my head."

When I had a record deal with Good Sounds, distributed by Atlantic records, we were recording at the famous Criteria recording facilities in north Miami. One morning, I was told that there would be a 1 p.m. meeting with the record company. I mentioned to our producer that I would be happy to attend, and he said, "That won't be necessary, Mike."

Slightly put off, I replied, "I'm the leader of the band and should be there if it's something the band will need to consider."

"Michael," he said, "this is business. You play the music and we'll do the business." Translated, he was saying that the lawyers like to talk to each other, and most artists just cause problems.

In the years that have followed, I've learned that most musicians have no business doing the negotiating, because the very thing that makes many musicians great—a deep emotional connection—is the same thing that will kill a complicated deal before it ever gets off the ground.

Lance Grode

USC Law School

Lance Grode was formerly the head of worldwide business affairs for the MCA Records Group (currently the Universal Record Group), where he oversaw the negotiation of thousands of contracts for artists, publishers, merchandisers, concerts, distribution, manufacture, and home video. Some of his clients included Bob Dylan, Michael Jackson, the Eagles, Neil Diamond, Jimmy Buffet, and Donna Summer.

Lance, would you tell me why you decided to focus on development strategies for artists and exactly what that means?

I had an opportunity when I was in San Francisco to work for one of only two lawyers living there who represented bands. We were not developing the artists or managing them per se, we were trying to get them record deals. Once they got the deals, we'd find them managers and agents.

After about a year, my best friend from high school was working for a boutique law firm in New York that had hired the top music lawyer in the world, a guy named David Braun. He had recently moved to Los Angeles, and I relocated from San Francisco to work with his firm. Among other people, we represented Bob Dylan, Neil Diamond, George Harrison, Donna Summers, Michael Jackson, the Eagles, Steely Dan, Kris Kristofferson, acts at that level. It was an amazing time.

Was there a specific reason you picked entertainment law over a general corporate practice?

I would love to tell you that it was a carefully planned strategy, but in my case it wasn't. I just had a music lawyer friend who said, "You know a lot about music and you're passionate about it. Why don't you come work for me." One of the reasons he offered me a job was that I could talk to musicians and artists. You just can't parachute into this business not knowing anything about the business; you can't just wake up one day and say, "I think I'll be a music lawyer," or, "I think I'll be a film lawyer." It doesn't work that way.

So as corporate counsel for MCA and 20th Century Fox, did you work closely with your artists?

One of the things I learned when representing musical artists is that they tend to come to you with every type of problem, and much of it falls into career advice or career management. "Should I do this? Should I do that? Should I do a movie? Should I go on television?" You can't just say, "That's not my area, I'm busy negotiating your copyright and royalty clauses," [*laughs*]

If your client asks for your opinion and you think they're making a huge mistake, you have to speak up. It's hard to maintain that line between what is legal advice and what is career advice, but ultimately you'll end up doing both or parts of both.

Is entertainment as a vertical market growing or shrinking, given the global uptick of media and music production?

We know that the revenue base of the music industry is definitely shrinking. The issue is that while people are listening to music more than ever, they aren't paying for it, or paying very little. That's difficult for the artists, record companies, publishers, and everyone involved. So the biggest challenge is to figure out how to capture the money. The fan base is getting bigger and bigger, but revenues are shrinking and shrinking. If anyone had an answer, they would be rich and famous in five minutes. [*laughs*]

When you were in private practice, what were the things that kept you up at night or ruined your day?

I would have to say this: in the five years I was in private practice, it was like a golden period for the music business, and therefore for entertainment lawyers. I was working for the top music firm in the world, making tons of huge deals, working with exciting stars, and honestly if the biggest problem in your day is, "Am I going to get $1 million for this album deal or $1.2 million," I would say that everybody wants to have that problem. [*laughs*]

One of the things that used to bother me was how our artists didn't look at the money tangibly; it was just like, "I'll spend it all today, and then I can just go out on another tour or put out another record and make my money back." Very few of our artists saved their money. We had big-selling artists that were broke, and there were some acts that went bankrupt. I didn't feel I had the right to go to world-famous people and tell them, "You don't have to rent a jet to go on tour; you can do what the country artists do and take a tour bus, so at the end of your tour you'll have made $1 million more," but they wanted to go on jets.

Yes, that still goes on today. I've been pretty fortunate myself, but still have musician friends that are struggling to make mortgage payments. You've worked with a lot of well-known artists. Did any of them become personal friends?

It's very hard to be friends with an artist if you start off as one of their support staff. Robbie Robertson from the Band and I were friendly. Some clients I was friendlier with than others, but someone like Bob Dylan is not looking for a friend, and in the five years that I worked there, he only came into the office twice. Big artists don't feel comfortable around non-creative people and like to keep their distance. I came to the conclusion that as big of a fan as I was of all these people as artists, for me to be effective it was better to keep my distance personally.

I did, however, have plenty of friends snorting coke and orgy-ing with clients (which I don't condemn or condone; I'm not making a moral judgment here). David Braun's style when I worked there was, "We are lawyers and we conduct ourselves as lawyers first. People want us to look like lawyers and act like lawyers." I think the lawyers who ended up smoking dope and partying with their clients also found themselves on the wrong side of things when they finally got a big-deal offer. The artists would then look at their lawyer and ironically say to themselves that they needed a serious lawyer, not some partying drug user, to get the most out of the deal. It bit them in the ass.

You obviously love music, Lance, and that's what this book is about. What would you say was the most rewarding part of your job?

Well, like anything else, we made a lot of breakthrough deals at different times. I remember when Neil Diamond made his record deal with CBS, it was the biggest record deal in history. Then when Michael Jackson was a client after *Off the Wall*, we were renegotiating his deal, and that ultimately became the biggest record deal ever made. We really enjoyed making huge, complex deals for important artists.

What advice might you give a young professional that has all the right skills. How might they get started on a career in entertainment and music law?

This is the area I'm fascinated with in the entertainment law field. We have to start with the fact that for every person that gets a job in entertainment, there are probably a hundred that are looking for a job in entertainment. These jobs are hard to land, and the first thing I tell young people is, "Never forget how incredibly competitive this industry is." That is number one!

Number two is this: *Never walk into a room and simply express how much you love the business.* The guy after you is going to say, "I love this business so much I'll clean the toilets after work if you give me this job." What you need is knowledge. You can't show up and say, "I want to get a job in the music industry," and not know who the players are. You don't know that EMI went bankrupt and is owned by Citibank, you don't know the names of the chairmen of the music groups, and don't know who Taylor Swift is, you don't know how many records Adele has sold, and that's just the music part of it.

When I lecture, Michael, I go around the room and ask these questions: "What was the biggest-selling record in the country last week? How much has *Black Swan* grossed worldwide to date? How many of you have seen *Winter's Bone*? Who is the chairman of the Universal Music Group? What happened to the person who used to be the chairman?" These questions are being posed to lawyers in the entertainment law societies of important law schools, and almost no one knows the answer to one single question. Do your homework!

When you go into an interview, other than saying, "I *really, really, really, really, really*, want to work in the music business," wouldn't it be better to actually know something, and be able to impress someone instead of telling them how passionate you are? Being able to say, "I'm amazed that Adele was able to have the bestselling record in the country," proves you know something. What I call it is being cross-examined about your resume instead of having an interesting dialogue in an interview.

Throughout the course of an interview you'll be asked standard, what I refer to as "stupid" interview questions, and if all you do is go through an interview process and answer those dopey questions with canned responses, you can't impress anybody. For example, let's say you were interviewing at a company like the Universal Music Group, I would find out who their big acts were, and then say, "Hey, did you work on the Taylor Swift renegotiation?" or something of the kind. I would want to show them that I know something about what they do. Again, do your homework.

What's the future of the music business look like to you?

The first thing I would say, and I believe this with every ounce of conviction that I have, is that anyone who tells you where the business is going to be in five years is just making it up. The fact is that *nobody really knows*. I think we can, however, look at certain things and say that they are more likely to happen than others. For instance, I think the era of the large music company is dead. We are down to four music groups, one of which changed ownership in the last year and another is currently for sale. The economics of having these gigantic music groups, signing and breaking new acts, is over; it was just a matter of time.

The question becomes: What replaces it? Are we going to have independent labels? Maybe.

Are we going to have artists that are going to function as their own record company? Maybe. You can do everything online. Recording is much cheaper than it used to be. You can have a website, sell merchandise online. You can make videos inexpensively. The only thing you can't do is tour online or play out. You can theoretically build up a fan base online, and then go on the road to support your online presence without any record company involvement at all.

The issue is how do you get people to know who you are? If you get your website up and sell 732 downloads, you're never going to become Lady Gaga or Taylor Swift or some internationally famous band. That's the real challenge! Marketing, promotion, and branding is the part that has yet to be figured out. That doesn't mean somebody won't figure it out, but until they do, we're going to have a rich and poor world. We're going to have a lot of bands that exist in cyberspace, and we'll have a handful of big stars and heritage acts like the Eagles, Aerosmith, and others that can tour until they are a hundred years old. [*laughs*]

LA IS A HOTBED OF ENTERTAINMENT of every conceivable form; just drive down Sunset Boulevard and you'll be amazed at the sheer number of billboards lining the hillside promoting current and upcoming films, TV shows, and emerging artists hitting the scene. This town also draws some of the best talent on planet Earth and not just actors and musicians. It's impossible *not* to know someone in the entertainment business as it makes up the very fabric of this city. For every actor in LA, there are another fifty people working in support roles of some sort, including makeup, stage construction, management, or legal representation.

Phil Cohen is one of these people, a musician *and* an executive at Universal. Music brought him to LA and music keeps him here. Phil and I hit it off right away, simply put, because he's a nice man, dedicated to his work at Universal, and willing to share some of his many years of experience with the next generation. Oh—and he's quite a drummer!

Phil is a drummer-turned-lawyer and his story may sound vaguely familiar, because many of us started down one path only to end up in another place, one we had never even considered. Check out his last thoughts regarding what he would like to do in the future. Those of us who love music never lose the passion.

Philip Cohen

UNIVERSAL STUDIOS FILM, TELEVISION, AND PRODUCTION

*Philip Cohen is an exceptional person and music attorney, who rose through the ranks
at Sony Pictures Entertainment before joining Universal Pictures.*

Phil, would you tell me a bit about what you do at Universal?

I am head of music business affairs and Universal Studios Film, Television, and Production.
We also have our home video division, theme park division, and of course NBC. All music deals
come through my office, so I'm involved in everything that might affect the studio.

**Tell me a little bit about your past and how you found yourself in your current
position at Universal.**

A lot of hard work and happenstance, I would say. I started playing drums when I was nine
years old and found myself in a swing band at twelve. I dropped out of college after a short time
and, long story short, wound up in California many years ago in a band that broke up almost
immediately. [*laughs*]

Over the years, I finally managed to get an undergraduate degree, although it was never
something I really worked at. I was concentrating on my music career, but circumstance pointed
me to a different life. Through some friends, I ended up at Columbia Pictures—that was a
separate entity at the time and not yet bought by Sony. I was basically a paralegal and it was my
first 9-to-5 job.

After working there for about six months, West Coast Legal came to me and said, "Phil,
you seem to be pretty good at this stuff. Have you ever thought about going to law school?" At
first my response was laughter because I thought he was kidding, but I went to law school the
next semester. I was working full-time and soon after stopped working as a musician because I
didn't have the time.

After law school, I landed my first position as an attorney for then Sony Pictures, and I've
been working in the music area at the studios ever since. I've been at Universal over fifteen years
now.

Was it hard for you to stop playing music?

Yes, it was very difficult to stop playing. Unfortunately I don't know it if was the stress of
the times, but I wound up developing asthma, which put a cramp in my playing because I'd
be playing and all the sudden have an asthma attack. I felt a really deep void in my life after I
stopped playing music, but I was so busy I didn't have time to think about it.

Is it different working for a large entertainment company than it might be in a different industry in business affairs?

Well, I'm sure it is. This is a unique business that is run by artists and very different from a manufacturing company or real estate. All businesses run on personalities and politics to one degree or another, but there's a different mentality here in the entertainment business, because you're on display and people who find their way into this industry want to stay here.

What's a day like for you at the office? What do you do on a daily basis?

After my e-mail work is done, I get on the phone and into the many deals that could be in any stage of completion.

I also have meetings almost every single day with department heads and business affairs. I'll speak to agents and managers, and then comes the paperwork [*laughs*]. Deal memos, contract drafts, and of course receiving paperwork from the other side with comments requiring phone calls that can go either very smoothly or be very difficult. I'm not one of those people who gets on the phone and starts yelling and threatening to break legs. You'll hear stories about the yellers and screamers in this business, and that has its place, it can even be used as another negotiating tactic, but most of the time I try not to go there. [*laughs*]

So as you can see, I have a very busy schedule!

Phil, what skill set should someone bring to the table who's interested in pursuing a job in the corporate side of the music and entertainment business?

First of all, having an advanced degree as a lawyer or MBA would be helpful. Lawyers have the upper hand and can get into this business easier. That being said, it's not easy to get in. Lawyers want to work in the entertainment business, so we have a large pool from which to hire. Typically you'll have to go to the best law schools, and then work for the best law firms, because when there *are* openings studios will typically look to those firms to hire.

However, if you're going to do production, it's a whole different story. Of course, you've got to graduate from a film school, but then you'll still need to start working in the mailroom or the equivalent and learn the business from the ground up. Production people and even a lot of the heads of production are attorneys, so it certainly doesn't hurt to work in the mailroom as an attorney.

How does executive pay work in the media industry . . . is there a range?

It's a difficult question to answer, but there's money to be made and good solid careers to be had. But just like any business, you've gotta love it. That's the key. If you get in at a fairly high level, you can make a very nice living either at a studio or at a viable record company.

So, Phil, you've been doing this job for a long time. What's the most rewarding part?

The most rewarding part for me is when we're working on composer deals, original recordings, and contract albums. The funny thing is that I can go through a whole project and not hear one note of music, until I go and see the film. "Oh, okay, that's what I've been working on for the last year and a half." So to hear that piece of music, be it a score or a great new song, is the most satisfying.

Is there something that you really want to do at this stage of your career?

Yeah, I'd like the move out of my current position and have my band become successful enough to make a living doing that for a while. That was my life's goal when I was nineteen, and it's come back to be my life goal once again.

Steve Winogradsky

INDEPENDENT LAWYER

Steve Winogradsky has held positions at Hanna-Barbera Productions, Inc., MCA Home Entertainment, Universal Pictures, and Universal Television. Win/So's current clients include the National Academy of Recording Arts and Sciences, MTV, CBS, Fox Sports, and Sony.

Steve, would you tell me about the types of services you provide as an independent entertainment attorney?

Well, our firm does many different things. Some of them are strictly legal work, some are creative, while others are more business oriented. We represent TV and film composers, artists, songwriters, music publishers, and perform publishing administration, as well as music licensing.

Your bio mentions that you're a guitarist, performer, and songwriter. Are you still playing?

I mostly play as a hobby, but unfortunately not as much as I'd like. In my heart of hearts, I think of myself as a musician, even though day to day I'm not.

Why did you select a career as an attorney as opposed to a performing musician?

I've been playing guitar since I was in grammar school and then all through college. I was in several bands, playing primarily original music, and tried to get a record deal. However, after a couple of years of beating my head against the wall, I realized that I like to eat on a regular basis and this wasn't doing it for me. It was a painful realization that although I was a good guitar player, I wasn't a great guitar player, so I thought that perhaps I shouldn't be pursuing performance as a career. After a lot of soul searching, I went back to law school, got my degree, and started practicing as an attorney, all the while still playing in bands as a hobby.

Did you go to law school knowing that you were going to be in the entertainment business?

Not really. It was something that I had hoped to do, but unlike college, where you major in a particular discipline, in law school you don't major in anything. Law school is broad-based education of fifteen to twenty subjects that are covered under the state bar exam. You're fortunate if you get one entertainment or copyright class while you're in law school. It took a couple of years before I landed my first job in the entertainment business, but I was lucky enough to combine what I loved in music and what I was starting to learn as an attorney.

Is there a reason you didn't go to work for one of the big entertainment firms?

Well, for a while I actually worked for Universal Pictures in their TV and film department as head of licensing, and then moved over to what's now called Universal Home, their DVD and Blue Ray division. It was a great learning experience.

So you got your feet wet in the corporate world and then worked your way backwards. Is there a particular area today where you see entertainment law growing?

The new media area is growing. The definition of new media is always changing and has even changed since we got on this phone call. Every day I read articles about some new development specifically with regards to music, new methods of distribution, and new methods of getting people to listen to music, or talk about music, or God forbid . . . pay for music [*laughs*].

Through our company website, Facebook page, or our Twitter page, we have postings every day, where we touch on some new development in the music space. It's a challenging path we are on at the present time.

I suspect you have a very tough road ahead of you.

That's why I make the big money, Mike. [*laughs*]

You obviously love what you do. What's your favorite part?

Well, in some ways the best thing for me personally is interacting with creative people. I deal with musicians on a daily basis, and every once in a while I get to exercise my creative instincts, either in talking to them about their music or suggesting some creative twist to a deal that benefits my clients in some way.

If I were starting out as a young guitarist, and understood that being a performer was not my path, what advice might you give me?

When I was in school, music business programs didn't exist, but now they do, and it's a great way for a musician to not only learn their craft but also about the business of music, which, as you know, are two very different things. Having the opportunity to learn about the business aspect of your trade and not just the trade alone is invaluable.

You may be an oboe player and want a job with the LA Philharmonic, but you better understand how the business works; otherwise, you're just going to get screwed. Also, if your career as an oboist doesn't pan out, you'll need a fallback plan so you can convert your love and passion for music into an actual job.

If there was one part of your job that you could do away with, what would it be?

Sometimes my clients will argue with me about the law or policy, and I tell them, "Look, my job is to advise you, give you options about what you can do, and explain to you what the document in front of you means. After that, it's your decision, it's your career, it's your money, it's your music, but please don't argue with me about what the law says. That's why you hired me."

That type of thing tends to get very frustrating, so if I could dump that part of the job, I wouldn't miss it for a second.

What skills are different for an entertainment attorney as opposed to, say, a corporate one? I'd include things like having to go out late at night to see your clients play.

Yeah, that gets less and less attractive the older I get, and I sometimes say to my clients, "If you don't start playing by 9:30, I'm home in bed." That's a little bit of an overstatement, but sometimes that's the God's honest truth because I'm sitting at my desk at 7 a.m.

One of the key differences from what I do and what a corporate attorney does is that I'm dealing with humans, human emotions and human finances, which all have a direct impact on their daily lives, rather than the corporate structure that says, "Oh well, if we don't close this deal, I guess we don't get to go to Aruba." If I don't close a deal, my client might not have money to pay the rent. It's very personal.

Along that same line, is the pay scale different in entertainment than the corporate world?

If you're working for a law firm, then you're either on salary or some kind of percentage of your billable time. When you're independent, you learn very quickly that you eat what you kill. When you're a younger attorney, you will do a lot of free work, so you have to suck it up and hope they turn into clients.

Steve, what does the future of the music business look like to you?

Well, in some ways it's already changed dramatically. The major record companies still believe that music is a product. I believe that music is a service. It's something people get access to, and don't necessarily need to own or hold in their hands. So I see the music business transforming from product-based to a service-based business. The challenge is to get people to understand and believe that a music service has value.

We are seeing services like Pandora or Rhapsody or Spotify, and on the horizon, Yahoo Music, Google Music, where there's a fee structure in place that is distributed to the creators of the music. If the creators don't get paid, music will become a hobby, not a profession, and if you can't make money at something, you won't do it as much or as often. Finding a way to monetize music and fairly compensate everybody then becomes the biggest challenge. If I had that answer, I'd be writing a book. [*laughs*]

8

Live Sound

Rapid Fire

Skill Set—You must be an excellent problem solver, have the ability to work on little sleep while still maintaining a smile. You'll need a basic technical understanding of electricity, the audio chain, lighting, and computer software. You may travel a lot in close quarters with others, so having good manners is required.

Hours—Long but you're always so busy you won't get bored. You're also the first people on a stage and the last people off. Enough said.

Upside—Exciting work environment. The satisfaction of creating a mix on the fly is just like playing jazz. If you are working with the right company, you'll see the world and not have to join the navy. I always loved this job. Good live sound techs are in demand.

Downside—Changing technology and stress. There are a lot of people counting on you to get it right and make them sound incredible, sometimes in less than ideal situations. The stress can be daunting, but you will get used to it if you have the right attitude.

Financial—$$ to $$$$ For the top jobs, live mixers do very well and some are under contract for $100,000-plus. For the rest of the industry, pay rates range from getting an equal band member cut to weekly salaries. As you get better and your name gets passed around within artist circles, your paycheck will grow.

Location—Large metropolitan markets with great performance venues and anywhere there are a lot of bands.

Future—From my own experience, I believe this job has longevity. There will be engineers setting up and mixing sound forever.

SOME OF THE MOST FUN I'VE EVER EXPERIENCED HAS BEEN MIXING LIVE SOUND. It's also one of the hardest jobs I've ever had. On the plus side, I always enjoyed the blank sound canvas in a new room, the challenge of trying to make a band sound as good as the managed sound we create in a recording studio, and the energy of a live audience giving their instant feedback on the action taking place on the stage.

The flip side can be harrowing. One time I was running the sound for a large conference in Orlando attended by some 5,000 business people who had traveled from all over the world, hoping to garner life-changing business guidance from the famous Tom Peters. I had rigged two wireless microphones that were nicely tucked under his vest and sounded great, until the moment he broke into his monologue about how he turned around the ailing Harley Davidson motorcycle company.

He said, "And the most important thing to remember is . . ." *The microphone went dead.* I quickly killed the mic and brought up my spare microphone that worked perfectly for five seconds, and then with an ear-shattering screech that shocked the entire audience and Tom himself *it also went dead.* This was bad, really bad. Tom waved his arms, pointed at me, and the entire audience of 5,000 turned in disgust and stared right through me. I sheepishly walked—then ran—to the stage to find a very frustrated Tom Peters whispering under his breath, "What the hell's wrong with you, kid? Don't you know how important this is?" On and on he went as I put a hardwired microphone on him, tested it, and crawled back to the console.

Live sound is for those of you who are first and foremost proficient problem solvers. Every gig has its own set of unique challenges that range from fixing the room acoustics to finding a clean, grounded power supply. It is also one of the most exciting jobs in the music and audio profession for the exact same reasons. Most of the time, no one knows who you are unless something sounds bad or the system goes down, like it recently did for the live Paul McCartney concert on Sirius broadcast from Central Park. Fortunately, since Paul is an experienced professional, he had a good sense of humor about the mishap, and the show went on after some quick problem solving by the sound crew.

I met this next guy many years ago at the Peabody Hotel in Orlando, when I was playing one of the Sunset Serenade series concerts. Our band was quite uneasy because one of the daily monster thunderstorms had just passed and there were puddles of water everywhere onstage. The concert was to start in the early evening—when the evaporating rain would raise the humidity to unbearable levels—and continue into the night.

I mentioned to the sound guy that we should get the water off the stage, and he sort of shrugged and said, "Hey, you'll be fine. Just don't stand in the water and kiss the microphone." I said, "So who are you?" with the hair standing up on the back of my neck. A simple, "Larry," came out of his mouth, and then he laughed. "I was just kidding about kissing the mic. We're grounded and you're protected, don't worry."

I was never concerned again when working with Larry, because he took great care of us, treated us like his family, and did his very best every time we worked together to make us sound better than we actually were.

Larry Epstein

PRESIDENT, PARADISE SHOW AND DESIGN

Larry Epstein runs a very successful full-service staging and production company headquartered in Orlando, Florida.

Larry, you've been in the business a long while and have a respected sound, lighting, video, and scenic company. Would you tell me exactly what a pro sound company does?

We make it louder—that's what we do. I have four full-time audio engineers and they play pretty nice together. Our business is primarily corporate in nature and we work with companies supporting conventions and produce a number of programs ourselves. What sets us apart from many of our competitors is the fact we can support name talent. Instead of moving the event to another room, we design the sound and lighting requirements of the talent into the business meeting.

We analyze the requirements of the presenters and the entertainment; we look at the equipment and then meld it all into a cohesive show. We try to select the equipment so it will work for music as well as have perfect high-fidelity audio for the meeting.

We also usually have some very exacting requirements from our entertainment artists. We aren't driven so much by the meeting as by what the entertainers want, which might include JBL speaker systems, Yamaha digital consoles, and all of the specialized processing equipment they require.

What made you decide to go into the sound, light, and show business?

I was attending college and between classes I worked as a sound tech. I was the guy in high school who could thread the movie projector, so I worked in the Resource Center helping with presentations and stuff like that. When I was growing up, a lot of my friends were musicians, so I helped them get little PA systems together and then make the sound work.

My dearest friend Richard Ruse asked me, "You want to be our sound man?" I answered, "I don't know how to do that." And he said, "Yeah you do, come on." And that's how I started. I was making $25 a week, working at various nightclubs with a Top 40 band; it was great fun. But it really took about six months for my lightbulb to really come on.

What's your favorite part of your job?

I'm always excited when I'm buying new equipment. Part of that is the wind beneath the wings. It's also very rewarding being appreciated for what we do by the artists we work with, like the Eagles, Phil Collins, Lady Antebellum, or Diana Ross. "Thanks for the great sound"—that's everything to us.

What would you say is the greatest challenge faced by a business like yours today?

Changing technology. We are asked to provide some pretty unique equipment, and it has to be the latest and the greatest. So even when the artist requests a Studer console, it doesn't mean we can operate it, and therein is the challenge—continuous education. I have to get my guys to school so they understand how all the equipment works. There's a ton of software for acoustical analysis, speaker enclosures, and it's very involved.

I know from my own experience that your business requires long hours. Tell me about a normal day when you are busy.

You know, it's different now than when I started. Today we almost have bankers' hours. For a meeting, you've got a day or two to load in all the sound, lighting, video, and scenery, and then we've got an 8-to-5 job until the entertainment. Our market is changing; often we will have as many as five or six shows running in the same week and dark the rest of the month. Many of these programs are booked years in advance. There are shows already booked in the Orange County Convention in 2020. Sometimes we have a year to plan and sometimes only days.

We mostly do two- to five-day shows, and the last night might be the awards program with a name act like Lady Antebellum or someone like James Taylor or even a local band or DJ.

What would you consider the state of the sound business these days? Is it still strong?

Yes and it's exciting. There are a gazillion new products released every day!

The problem is that nothing's cheap. The FCC banged us last year when they changed the law. We couldn't use our wireless microphones anymore. They took the frequencies we'd been using the last fifteen years and gave them to digital TV. I spent about $60,000 just in new wireless microphones. Now I am reading we many lose those frequencies in the next couple years.

So could I make a good living with a sound and lighting company?

Yes, but one thing that will make it or break it for you is that you've got to be proud of your product. If you're not proud of what you do, you're never going to get anywhere. If you are proud of what you're doing, you'll be successful. There is so much opportunity in live sound.

How would you recommend someone get started in the live sound field?

You have to start at the bottom. The guys that work for me came from the nightclubs and live theater. They understand everything about what it takes to pull off a great show—the motto really is "The show must go on!"

When there are problems, they have to solve them, because they've got a show to do. I always ask potential new hires one question: "Have you ever had your feet in the fire?" Because that's what it's all about; nobody wants to hear excuses. Go find a local band and help them. Go mix them for free if you have to.

We *are* the hot seat. Once you get some chops it's not too hard. You'll know what you're doing. You'll know how to plug a console in and make it sing, if you know what I mean. You'll know how to program everything—it's not brain surgery. But there is a methodical process. What you put in is what you'll get out; it is a commitment. I had one kid come in cold. His sell was to me was he was the soundman for a nightclub band. I loved his personality and energy. After a year or so of loading trucks and assisting on shows, we put him behind a console. He did a great job, both front of house and monitors. Some years later, I found out he wasn't the soundman for the band but the lead singer (ouch). He is a world-class engineer who can handle any situation.

What does the future look like for Larry Epstein? What do you see yourself doing the next few years?

I'll be doing this until I'm dead. [*laughs*] There was a time not too long ago that I was planning my retirement and getting my company positioned to sell. Then the economy tanked, a rough few years followed, and at the end of the day we were still standing. I really do love my job. I'm planning to spend almost half a million dollars this week on new gear and have a huge wish list for next year.

It's a tough business, but the toughness is the part that makes it great. It is what gets me up in the morning!

Michael Redman

LIVE SOUND MIXER

Yep, me again!

Is live sound physically hard work?

It can be. Especially for the crew! When I was mixing, I sometimes needed to help the crew get everything in place for a show because the tour economics didn't allow for enough stage crew. You will also be in charge (until you're a hot shot) of setting up the console and all other gear you run. Generally these days, the consoles are lighter!

What makes mixing sound such a cool job?

For me, it was always hitting the go button at the moment a show started, bringing up the show sound, and listening to the immediate results of the work I was doing.

There is a huge adrenaline rush and urgency associated with the beginning of the show and you are the one controlling what everyone in the audience hears.

Do you need special training?

You don't need a formal education to be a mixer, however, it wouldn't hurt and would help you up the ladder quicker. Many sound mixers learn on the job as an apprentice.

Are there jobs for sound mixers?

There are plenty of jobs out there for sound mixers. They vary from small bands and club gigs to worldwide tours for proven mixers. Some mixers even sit back at the console and add vocal parts or instruments to the live mix!

How about the pay scale, what's that like?

Again, it has to do with where you are in the food chain. Mixers' and live sound engineers' pay can run from a few hundred a week to thousands a week. I myself would work towards the big bucks, which will take a little planning on your end.

Will I travel?

If you are with a touring act, of course you will travel. Like the navy, you can see the world with some bands. There are acts that tour exclusively in the US and others that just play in Europe, for example. If you want to stay close to home, you will be limiting yourself, but there are a number of venues, like convention centers and arenas, that offer staff jobs.

Where should I live for this job?

One of the interesting things about live sound is that you can live anywhere you want, depending on what part of the live sound industry you like. Say, for example, that you are moving up pretty quick as a mixer and specialize in country music or are tied into that community. You would probably want to live in Nashville to make it convenient. But on the other hand, what if you were in a convention market and doing shows like Larry Epstein's. You would want to situate yourself in a market that was big into conventions. I'm sure you understand where I'm coming from.

Any advice for getting started?

Look at all your options to start. In other words, decide what type of sound mixer you might like to be. Then search out the largest companies you can find that do that type of work. Ask for a job as an intern, apprentice, or general helper. If you are a good student, you will move up in these organization pretty quickly.

9

Mastering Engineer

Rapid Fire

Skill Set—Love and appreciation for all kinds of music, computer skills, and great ears. You'll need a firm grasp on the current sound in all major styles of music. You should also know what makes today's pop, jazz, classical, blues, etc. sound popular.

Hours—Many mastering engineers work from home, so you can set your business hours depending on the situation you put yourself in. Obviously if you work in a large facility, you will be working their hours.

Upside—Listening to music every day. Working with talented artists and the satisfaction that accompanies your contribution to the artistic process. There is a freedom that comes with this job in the form of flexibility. You can master music part-time and combine it with many other music opportunities.

Downside—Listening to music every day, ha-ha. Starting out on your own can take some time as you build your clientele. As technology improves and mastering becomes more automated, many of your would-be clients may become your competition.

Financial—$$ to $$$ depending on how resourceful you are and where you work. If you work for yourself and are in demand even on a local level, you can do quite well, especially if you wrap mastering into an assortment of other services.

Location—LA, NY, Austin, Nashville, and other large music markets. You can set up shop in other markets if you are able to leverage the Internet effectively and work remotely.

Future—Changing but still solid, especially in light of the trend toward better fidelity in the digital delivery industry. As mentioned above, technology will no doubt have a big effect on the future of mastering. One day in Logic you may have a pull-down list of mastering options that include styles and your favorite artists . . . one click and you're done mastering. Hmmm . . . we'll have to wait and see how that shakes out.

THE UNSUNG HEROES OF THE PRODUCTION SIDE OF THE MUSIC BUSINESS are the mastering engineers, the folks who have been educating our ears throughout the years. They usually work by themselves in a room with excellent acoustics and wonderful speakers. They listen to music with a critical ear and a dedication to the sonic excellence we all hope to experience when listening to our favorite music.

Today's digital tools and Internet connectivity have made mastering a job that can be accomplished just about anywhere, since the delivery is digital and no longer requires the cutting lathe. A competent individual who is comfortable working on the Internet, who has great ears and the correct training, can start his or her own business and have a reasonable chance of success.

The fact is that most musicians and groups shouldn't have the last ears on their album before they release it to their fans, because they've been too close to the project for too long, and sometimes don't understand the sensitivities of what is called broadcast quality. The public is used to hearing music a certain way, and the chances of a song becoming a hit are enhanced when the music is void of distortion, the vocals cut through the guitars, and sonically, the music fills the frequency spectrum in the correct ratios.

Enter the mastering engineer, sporting ears the size of Mickey (just kidding), who is able to inject a little magic and help a song stand the test of time and take it to a whole new level. This is a cool job and mastering engineer Ron Boustead is leading the pack at Revolution Mastering.

Ron Boustead

REVOLUTION MASTERING

Ron, would you give me a little background on your decision to become a mastering engineer?

The how was sort of unintentional. I had recently moved to LA from Cincinnati, Ohio, and I came here as a jazz singer with a new record that was getting played all over the country, but when I got here, it was difficult to make a living as a jazz singer (to say the least) and I just started looking around for any kind of work I could get.

A friend of mine worked at a place that manufactured cassette tapes and said, "I can get you a job on the assembly line putting cassettes into cases," and I said, "Okay, I'll take it." I needed a job. To make a long story short, I ended up working in the mastering room at this facility and was able to parlay that into a job at Precision Mastering in Hollywood.

You've spent a large part of your career on the record side. Can you explain to someone reading this what a mastering engineer does?

Well, after someone has mixed all the songs for their project, and maybe they've done so over a period of a year or longer, and maybe they've done it in several studios with different engineers and producers, they would come to a mastering engineer. The job of the mastering engineer is to make all those songs work together to complete the artist's vision. The idea is to take all of the songs and make them sound as good as they can, make them all work together and seamlessly. At the end of that process, I create a production master that goes to the duplication facility, or whatever the delivery method might be.

So is this a creative partnership with the artist?

Yes, it can be, but a lot of artists just hand their project over to a mastering engineer and say, "I respect that you know what you're doing, so take it and run." But the other side of the spectrum is an artist who wants to sit in the room with you and "help" you make every little decision about their project. Usually it's somewhere in between, an artist may have notes about specific concerns he has . . . "Track three, I'm worried that the bass is too loud" or "I'm worried that you can't hear the vocal enough."

It sounds as if there are a lot of technical skills involved in mastering . . . is this something that takes years, and ears, to learn?

The thing about being a mastering engineer is that it's a very specialized skill set. If I go into a studio to record my own songs, I go to other people who are better at production, who are better at mixing. I haven't spent years and years honing those particular skill sets, but mastering is something I've done day in and day out for the past twenty years and it's a skill set that I'm very comfortable with. There is gear that is more specifically designed to do mastering work than to do recording or mixing work.

What might an example be?

If you think about it, when you're in a recording studio you might have a mixing board with twenty-four or forty-eight or ninety-six tracks and gear that's designed to work on individual tracks as you are recording or mixing them. In a mastering studio, I am dealing with stereo . . . everything is about stereo. What I'm trying to do is adjust the overall sonic palette, so my gear is designed just to enhance stereo files.

You said you didn't have a formal education when you started mastering. Do you think attending a school like Full Sail or Berklee might be a good place to learn the intricacies of what you do?

I do. I think there is some audio engineering coursework that would be very beneficial for a mastering engineer. I don't know of a specific mastering program, but to get a foundation in basic recording and mixing techniques and to get comfortable with DAWs and converters and processing gear, it's definitely an entry point. Beyond that, a person wanting to get into this career should find a mastering studio willing to take on an intern or a production engineer.

I've also heard it's all about the ears in mastering. Is it true?

I think it's fair to say that the ears are the most important piece in the mastering room's arsenal. One thing that the mastering engineer brings to the table that maybe a mixing or recording engineer doesn't is experience. Because I sit in a room all day doing this one thing, I have a pretty good perspective on what music is supposed to sound like in a lot of different genres. I know that if we're doing a pop dance song, I've got to get it somewhere in the realm of what Lady Gaga sounds like or it's not going to be competitive.

In your mind, what separates great mastering from so-so mastering? The reason I ask is that there are a lot of people that have home studios and advertise "I do mastering," but frankly all they're doing is raising the levels, compressing, and limiting, nothing special.

If a person has dedicated his entire career to mastering music recordings to the exclusion of everything else, chances are he's going to have a more refined sensibility about what good music should sound like.

Then there is the gear. I think a guy sitting in his converted garage with a Pro Tools rig and a bunch of plug-ins is going to be able to do a decent job, but if you have higher-end gear in a finely tuned room with a really great playback system, you're going to hear more detail and make better choices about the processing that you do.

Another important quality of a great mastering engineer is how they interact with the client. You should be able to give them a sense of comfort, so when they turn their baby over to you, you're going to elevate it to some new special place that they wouldn't have been able to achieve without you.

Is there a great project you've worked on that stands out?

Well, it was definitely very exciting to work on a Rolling Stones or Prince record. To be on the phone with Mick Jagger, playing him an edit and getting his approval! That's exciting because you're really *in* the business working at a very high level.

But then there is the other side of it, which is the music that's actually inspiring to me personally. If I think in those terms, I mastered an LA a-cappella group last year named Sonos that was just an outstanding musical experience.

Ron, let me ask you what were some of the hardest projects, either technically or personally, that you've worked on?

There are two kinds of challenging projects for a mastering engineer. One is when the client is difficult or has unreasonable expectations. They tell you, "I want my record to sound like the Black Eyed Peas," but they've sent you something completely different and poorly mixed, expecting miracles.

The other is when you don't personally connect to the music, but you have to plow through it anyway. I have a pretty varied appetite and palette for music, so that doesn't happen too often, but there are certainly occasions where this feels more like a job than other days.

Could you talk to me a little bit about how you charge for mastering? Is it per the job or song or hour?

Well, it's kind of all over the map. Most mastering houses have an hourly rate and then they make deals with people all the time to cut that rate, or to get people a flat rate for their project just to bring in more indie business or more budget projects to fill the spaces where they can't be charging their full rate.

I know, for example, at Precision we charged a fixed rate per hour, and even though we had that rate, oftentimes someone would come in and say, "I really only have $1,000 for my whole album," and we'd say, "Well, okay, we'll do that if we can fit it in between our other projects." When I started my own mastering company about a year ago when I left Precision, I decided to keep my rate very simple and to charge per song. That way people knew exactly what they were going to pay for their project, and I came up with a figure that felt comfortable to me that I hoped would be affordable to most of my clientele. It's turned out to work pretty well.

MANY YEARS AGO, I WAS AT THE FAMOUS CRITERIA STUDIOS in Florida, home to many famous recording artists and most of the gold records produced in the '70s and '80s. Everybody who was anybody recorded their albums at Criteria, including the likes of Eric Clapton, CSN&Y, Fleetwood Mac, James Brown, the Eagles, AC/DC . . . the list goes on. John Blanche was the staff mastering engineer and worked sixteen-hour days with his ears glued to the JBL studio monitors and one hand on the little knob of the cutting lathe. When the bass was too loud, John would turn it to the left so the lathe would not cut the vinyl so deep. If this happened, the record would skip when played and he'd have to start the entire process over. It was very tedious, but John was a master of mastering. He was the last person to hear the record before it went to press and finally to the record stores and a mass of waiting fans.

The first time I met John Blanche, he was in a little room adorned with one hundred gold and platinum records perfectly spaced and hung on the wall. He was soft spoken as he welcomed me to the mastering suite and asked what he could do for me. "I just wondered what you do in here," I replied.

"Well, I take the master tapes and make them into records," he said in a matter-of-fact way.

"Can you show me how it works?" I asked. "Sure," he said, and a long friendship began.

John went on to co-produce my album and meticulously helped us deliver our best performances, which at the time were pretty hard to drag out of us.

John Blanche

CRITERIA RECORDING

John, would you give me the brief history of how and why you became a mastering engineer?

I was a student at the University of Miami and we had an incredible concert jazz band, as they still do today. There was a studio in Miami, Florida, called Criteria, which was very famous at that time.

Ted Craiger and Dean Lee had a goal of trying to get into Criteria to record the jazz ensemble, so I took an intern job there. During that time we brought our band in twice to record. A gentleman there named Alex Stadkin was running their mastering department and about 60 percent of the mastering was Latin music. Alex was looking to further his own career and get more into audio engineering and producing, so I asked, "Why don't you teach me how to master so you'll have more time." That's how I got my foot in the door.

Would you explain in laymen's terms what the role of a mastering engineer is?

The original process of mastering was to get the mixes the engineer provided on tape onto vinyl and have them work. There were certain rules concerning low frequencies because you couldn't have any low frequency panned to an extreme side or it would just cause the record to skip. It was a much more physical process than it is today.

What was unique about mastering in the past?

Probably one of the biggest pluses in my life, and every other person at Criteria, was the fact that we were all taught by a gentleman named Tommy Dowd. Tommy Dowd was making about twelve gold records a year at the time; he was the king, and would be still if he were alive.

We worked on some of the greatest recorded music of all time, so we are able to create within our own mindset what things *should* sound like.

People that learn mastering and constantly hear music created in GarageBand have a very tough time, because they've never had a chance to work on great final mixes. I was mastering for the Eagles, Bee Gees, and Crosby, Stills, and Nash, so I was hearing wonderful music day after day.

What special skills does someone need in today's world in order to be a successful mastering engineer?

It varies, depending how you work. There are guys like Bob Katz here in Orlando, and he's probably as technical as anybody can get. He created many of the algorithms used by TC Electronics, and he approaches mastering from a very technical point of view. Then on the other hand, you have guys like Alex or Carl Richardson that weren't necessarily that technical but really had the concept of what the finished record should sound like.

I've heard it's all about the ears . . . so is that not true?

Hmmm . . . I believe it's really about training your ear to listen to what's current. The guys back in the '70s listened to a real round, soft-bottom end and they wanted that; in fact, they always added some sixty to seventy cycles to everything, and a little 2K to make things a little more intelligible . . . but that was that era. You can't think of today's music the same way.

What would you be listening for today?

There's still one consistent concept that all popular music should leap out at you. It doesn't necessarily have more volume, but it does have more punch. More musical hook than other music, so I listen for that and try to accentuate it. You always try to make the best part of a song sound even better.

How long does it typically take to master a song?

If a guy was to listen to a four-minute song for the first time, I would expect them to take two to three good plays to understand what is there. I would hope in a half an hour that a guy could really do a song right and definitely inside of the hour.

You have worked on some of the biggest-selling albums of all time. How did that come about?

I was at Criteria at the right time. It couldn't have been a better situation for any engineer . . . to walk into a studio and say, "Gee, who do I get to work with today . . . the Eagles? The Bee Gees? Firefall? Eric Clapton?" The list went on and on and on.

Those were the days, weren't they? Do you think somebody can strike out and make a career mastering today?

Absolutely. If a guy has his craft figured out and knows what he is doing, hooks up with even a local act that hits it, he will hit it too. That's just going to start generating business.

Any stories that come to mind when you think back on your time at Criteria?

Maybe the most challenging one for me that also turned into the most interesting time was the music I mastered with Crosby, Stills, and Nash. It was a case of a record that needed extreme mastering help, and I believe it was an error in the monitoring system in the control room and the album came out extremely bottom heavy.

The mastering needed to be very, very corrective. I took the entire low end out and made it more intelligible. The band was so thrilled with it that they asked me to re-master the first Crosby, Stills, and Nash album and some of the original albums they had done back in the '60s. They sent us piles of tapes, and all the engineers and myself just stood around and touched them. [*laughs*]

The tapes were so old, we had to copy them immediately using DBX decoding back then and make new masters, because as we'd played them the metal oxide that holds the recording on the tapes just started falling on the floor.

Oh my gosh!

Yeah—we were playing "Four Way Street" and watching the oxide fall off the back of the tape and just pile up on the floor

So would you advise somebody to look at some of the mastering houses and try the intern route?

Absolutely. Mastering houses are always looking for people, and interning is still the best way to get your foot in the door. Then try and create a situation where they need you, but mastering is a great place to be.

I wouldn't have wanted to start any other place than mastering because it really taught me how to listen to music.

10

Music Editor

Rapid Fire

Skill Set—First and foremost, a great understanding of both film scores and popular music. Second on the list is the ability to quickly edit on a Pro Tools rig.

Hours—If you're working for a company, it's normal business hours. Many music editors work at home and make their own hours.

Upside—Editing music is a fantastic job. It's creative as can be, always changing, and fulfilling. Once your establish yourself, the money is not bad either.

Downside—Primarily you may consider living on the West Coast a downside, but I don't. There are not a lot of these jobs available either.

Financial—$$$ to $$$$ People in the industry tell me that you can make a lot of money as an music editor, especially if you expand into a shop with multiple editors and have additional skills as well.

Location—LA is where I would find an apartment . . . music editors need to be in close proximity to the people who hire them.

Future—Music editors are deeply ingrained into the process of film making, so they are not going away.

Daniel Carlin

Dan, would you explain in laymen's terms exactly what a music editor is and what they do in the world of film?

There has been, as you well know, a rapid industry evolution over the last fifteen or twenty years, so the music editor's job has changed quite a bit. The way all industry jobs generally work is that you start out either in low-budget films or television. If you're lucky, someone you work with (a composer, director, film editor, or producer) advances into higher budget films and takes you along. So it depends on where you start as to what your job might be as a music editor.

Sometimes you are hired by the director to create a temporary music track. When the editing of the film is in its early stages, the director will want to show a version to the producer, then the studio, then to a test audience, and in order to have those screenings, they need to have a temporary music score created and edited onto the soundtrack. They don't have a composer score and record yet because they would have to have the music editor hack it up as the film continues to be edited following the various test screenings. So they want to hold off adding the original music for as long as possible.

It therefore becomes the music editor's first duty to find some existing music out there (from previously recorded soundtracks) and adapt it to fit the movie. That can be a very difficult chore. Every movie is unique, so you'll never find the perfect old score to cut into a new movie, but you can rely on music from that genre, whether it's romantic comedy, horror, mystery, etc. So you'll go to existing scores that are successful, yank out parts, cut them up, and piece them into a temp score that will ultimately just be thrown away and replaced by a newly written and recorded soundtrack.

Music editing sounds like a very creative job. Do you also work with the music supervisor for popular tunes or other tracks that a film might need?

That depends on whether they've hired a music supervisor, and if they're going to have many popular tunes. If there are only a few minor source tunes in a movie, they may not hire a music supervisor and instead rely upon the music editor or someone else to find the few songs needed. If, on the other hand, several songs are needed, then a music supervisor is usually hired to find those songs and turn them over to the music editor, who then cuts them to fit well in the appropriate scenes.

Does someone with a higher education have a better chance as a music editor, or is this something that is done by feel, taste, and understanding of music?

That's an interesting question. There have been highly successful music editors with little college or formal musical training, such as my former business partner, Jeff Carson; and there have been successful music editors who've had a lot of training and advanced degrees.

One of the reasons that I think education is important is that it gives you confidence when speaking with composers in their language, which in turn gives them a certain level of confidence in you. Also, with an education, you are comfortable going to business lunches and dinners with producers, directors, and composers, who usually are well educated. For instance, you can talk about the fact that the story is really *The Iliad* all over again. That was one of the edges I felt education gave me, the confidence to move in those circles and not be intimidated by people who were educated.

I did a lot of work with Oscar-winning composer Georges Delerue. He always conducted his own scores, but he wanted someone in the booth reading the scores during the sessions who also could collaborate well with the director, the producer, the music editor, and the engineers, while also watching and listening for performance or copying anomalies. If you have musical training and good ears, you can use your music-editing success to segue into that kind of job.

Music editors often specialize in one genre or another. Some have a flare for comedy, which is very difficult to track. Most editors will tell you that comedy is the most difficult musical genre because it is so difficult to walk that line, to not "Mickey Mouse" the action, but also not be so subtle that it's not funny. You don't go to college and learn that, instead it's all about your feel.

Relationships are important in every business, especially the music business. How did they influence your becoming a music editor?

Well, I got started the old-fashioned way—nepotism! [*laughs*] Hollywood, in the old days, was about families and connections. My dad was the first male negative cutter at MGM. He got in the business because his uncle helped him into the union. He then worked his way up into apprenticing, assistant editing, and eventually working as a music editor in the studios.

In the 1970s, many filmmakers left the studios in order to make more culturally relevant films that reflected the ongoing changes in America. (The studios were conservative about such matters, and, as a rule, would not invest in these films.) The challenge this created for independent filmmakers (producers and directors) is that they lost access to the studio infrastructure (departments of art, music, editing, etc.).

In the meantime, my dad, without any intention of building a business, incorporated himself so he could work on these outside projects without losing his union-related health and welfare benefits. That's when I started working with him in our garage.

There were just the three of us at the start, including Michael Tronick, who has gone on to a successful career in film editing. Within five years, we had blossomed into a business with up to thirty people doing a slew of television shows and features.

Nepotism was the vehicle for me, my brother, my two sisters, three of our cousins, the neighbor's son, friends, friends of friends, the musically talented waiter who worked at the restaurant where we ate lunch, and on and on. My brother Tom was Alan Silvestri's music editor, my sister Kathy served as Elmer Bernstein and Randy Edelman's music editor, and my sister Patty was Bruce Broughton's music editor.

Is there a story that might illustrate that very special time in your life?

In 1978, Paramount hired me (apparently the only available music editor in town) to work at night re-editing the Ennio Morricone score for *Days of Heaven*. I was dubbing *The Magic of Lassie* during the daytime, and then commuting over to Paramount at night to work with Terry Malick, the extraordinary director of *Days of Heaven*.

We discovered during one of our discussions that, while he had been studying and teaching philosophy at MIT in the early to mid-1970s, I had been studying and teaching anthropology at UConn. We enjoyed fabulously naïve discussions about how the world was going to change.

One night at about 1 a.m., I was working on the music in my editing room and looked up to see Jane Fonda walk in and say, "Hi, I'm looking for Terry." I was completely star-struck, but I managed to safely escort the most famous actress of that era to the other editing room where Terry was working.

That entire project was a memorable experience because it was, again, my first major film, and it was one of the most beautifully shot movies of all time. It won an Academy Award for cinematography that year, and it starred Richard Gere (in his breakout role) along with the brilliant playwright Sam Shepard and the future Broadway star Brooke Adams.

Would you tell me how music editors are paid?

Music editors are members of the IATSE Motion Picture Editors Guild Local 700, which covers film and videotape editors, sound editors, music editors, and virtually all engineers and other related workers in post-production sound. The AMPTP/Union agreement stipulates minimum wages and benefits, but in actuality there is a very wide range in what music editors are paid.

The most successful music editors, working on major studio releases, earn up to $5,000 per week plus rental fees for their equipment. And there are editors who work on non-union projects for less than a $1,000 per week. If you are talented and lucky enough to have built a successful career working on major films, you are being paid double or triple scale.

It sounds as if good editors can make a very comfortable living. Would you say that music editing could be considered a stepping-stone into another music industry job?

Honestly? Hollywood tends to pigeonhole people. If you want to be a composer, for example, I would advise against working as a music editor, even though you're collaborating closely with a composer who might mentor you.

Once you become an accomplished music editor, most industry participants like to think of you as a music editor. Very, very few music editors have transitioned into successful careers as composers. The late and wonderful Richard Stone did so, but he had to refuse to take music editing jobs, and he went through a very rough financial time until he got a lucky break at Warner Bros., where he was hired to score cartoons. This was what Rich was really good at, and he became extremely successful.

But again, that is rare for a music editor. On the other hand, if you start as a copyist, orchestrator, programmer, or composer's assistant, your opportunities to move into composing increase dramatically.

Music editing is, however, a great stepping-stone into music supervision.

11

Production Music Libraries

Skill Set—Interpersonal skills, a firm grasp of a music customers needs, and the ability to interpret them. Business connections can't hurt. The production music business is a bit like a record company, so you should be entrepreneurial in your thinking.

Hours—If you're working for a company, it's normal business hours, but you may be in the recording studio at strange hours recording because many libraries pay for the recordings, which translates to finding deals, which translates to nighttime hours.

Upside—Working in this arena is much like being in the recording industry, as you are close to the music and involved in the creative and production. There is also money to be made if you stick to it and network like crazy. Everybody needs music for their productions.

Downside—The competitive landscape is broadening, and at the end of the day (five years from now) there will be a reckoning and only a few production music companies may remain standing. The big ones will gobble up the smaller libraries and copyright insurance will prohibit the networks from using a library without E & O insurance. Just my prediction.

Financial—$$$ to $$$$ The money in this segment can be all over the place. I know people making $40,000 a year and others making $300,000-plus. Obviously the more copyrights and publishing you control, the better you will do.

Location—NY, LA, Dallas, Nashville, or any virtual location if you understand how to leverage technology. There are a number of large conventions, like NAB, where most libraries make direct client contacts, so you can live anywhere. I recommend living in a place where there are TV networks, corporate headquarters, film production companies, etc.

Future—Bright and sunny as more networks move to production music as an affordable resource for their music shows. There are reasonable entrepreneurial opportunities in this field as well.

MUSIC LIBRARIES, WHICH ARE SOMETIMES CALLED PRODUCTION MUSIC COMPANIES, are responsible for an enormous collection of the music you hear on a daily basis: everything from a corporate marketing video to a TV show to answering machine messages. Almost all visual programming you watch has an audio track, and that audio track usually includes some music. That music has to come from somewhere, and is supposed to be licensed because music is not free for everyone to use for commercial purposes. When an ad agency produces a commercial, it either has the music composed, licenses a popular song, or it uses a track of production music. When a video editor is cutting a video for a McDonald's training film, he too needs music, and it usually comes from a music library.

Music libraries come in all flavors, ranging from large libraries like APM, with well over 350,000 tracks of music, to small boutiques specializing in Arabian funk music with 200 tracks. Today, there are about fifteen major libraries, and I fully expect that number to increase over the next few years. We are also likely to see tens of thousands of smaller libraries appear out of nowhere as every indie label and composer offers his or her music online for licensing.

Starting your own library, or writing for one, can be a very rewarding experience, and I've done both. My first experience in the library world was as an engineer, and my partner at the time, Alain Leroux, encouraged me to start my own library, as he had. A year later, Powerhouse Music was launched and we had a great time creating music with very few rules or guidelines other than to be true to whatever style we were writing. From a business perspective at that point in time, the production music industry was wide open.

Today, the library model—like everything else—is evolving and changing fast, so an entrepreneurial person with good business sense and a new twist on the market might do very well. You do need to be aware of the competition, though, because every band is starting to license its music catalog on its website, and there are music libraries popping up everywhere. It might look to you as if the market is saturated and there's no room for you, but production music is alive and well, as Adam Taylor tells us.

Adam Taylor

President, Associated Production Music (APM)

Adam Taylor helps companies extract value from their intellectual property. Prior to taking the helm at APM, Adam was the founding partner of Goldman/Taylor Entertainment, where he developed properties, including the television series Confessions of Crime *for Lifetime Network and the PBS series* Joseph Campbell—Mythos.

Adam, you run APM, the largest music production library in North America. Would you tell us what a music library is and how it fits into the music industry?

A production music library is a collection of music that has either been specifically commissioned for or gathered for the purpose of licensing the music into audio-visual and audio productions. That could include a radio spot, TV spot, television program, videos, movies, and video games, corporate videos, websites, etc. Any place where there is synchronization of music to audio or audio-visual works.

Music libraries, APM and others, can be thought of as one-stop shops, including both master and publishing rights. Every track is usually the same price and there's separate pricing depending on what you want to do with the music, but everything is pre-cleared. You can also audition the music and try it without paying, so it has a lot of advantages over custom original music where you hire a composer and have no idea what you're going to get. There are clear advantages to the value proposition of a library.

How many songs or tracks do you have in your library?

We currently have over 350,000 recordings. It's the largest collection in North America. There are libraries that have a few thousand tracks and then there are those that go up to the hundreds of thousands.

With all the new media that's being produced by everyone on the planet, is library music a good business to be in?

Today, it is. The business seems to be growing, and I think there are a number of courses that push people in our direction. One is the sheer number of media productions; secondly there is pressure to keep production costs down, and library music is a very good alternative to commercial music. Additionally, it is cheaper to produce music today than ever, and new styles in popular music demand new production in library offerings. When you combine that with the fact that the quality of library music has been going up over the years, you can get very good quality music for a relatively low price.

What would you consider the greatest challenge to the music library business?

There are a number of challenges that are facing our industry as a whole at the moment. With the downfall of the record company model, along with the associated ability to generate real meaningful income from record sales, many songwriters and composers have been looking for alternative income streams. Some of them write for libraries, such as ours, or they put out their own library; there is a glut of material hitting the marketplace.

There are also lot of people who are writing indie songs and making them available through aggregators who offer their music on a non-exclusive basis. In contrast, all our music is exclusively ours. Non-exclusivity has an wide array of legal and collection issues associated with it and also adds to the overall glut of product on the market.

With all the music being pushed to the market, it's all the more important to find a way to make yourself stick out, which is quite a challenge.

Downward price pressure from the studios and the networks and others is also a big issue. With the acquisition or merger of broadcast companies, networks, and cable networks, studios, etc., you've got fewer owners, which in turn forces prices down. Those are the biggest challenges—today anyhow [*laughs*].

Would you tell me why you picked the music business and APM as a career path? What brought you into this line of work?

I was given the opportunity to be interviewed for this job through a mutual friend who was on the board of directors. They were looking for some new thinking. In fact, I specifically remember asking, "Why don't you hire somebody from the music business?" And they replied, "We don't want somebody from the music business." So here I am, and it has been a wonderful and truly life-changing ten years!

That's certainly a unique way to start; it's clear that the APM board saw your forward thinking as an asset. Now that you've been running APM for a while and have had time to develop a greater understanding of the business, what's the most rewarding part of what you do?

First, we have an amazing staff and a collaborative environment with people who believe in what they do and believe in our company. That's very exciting, and the fact that I'm in this business because I love music.

Here at APM we have every different kind of music and you're exposed to a lot of it on a daily basis. Also, working with songwriters and composers is inspiring! To be a composer, especially a film score composer, you have to have a lot of varied and interesting training. Many of them are classically trained with influences from the United States, Europe, Asia, Africa, and from Latin America, which makes them interesting people to be around.

Then the list of clients that we have is so extraordinary . . . there are so many people that use music. We work with every network and studio, and most of the ad agencies, cable networks, and music supervisors, and thousands of different corporations and organizations. We also do a tremendous amount of work with Apple, Microsoft, and video game companies. And we work regularly with the White House, the CIA, but of course I can't tell you anything about that! My lips are sealed.

Your client base includes the US government, Apple, and Microsoft? I don't think I've talked to anyone with those types of customers! [*laughs*] Speaking of technology, how does the Internet and social media play into the role of production music these days?

On the surface, you would think that it doesn't, but it does. People use YouTube and iTunes to search for music, and then they try to find out who owns that music. We have tens of thousands of our tracks up on iTunes and make good money from them. We have over half a million videos on YouTube with our music in them. We're doing close to 100 million streams a month. It's a pretty interesting phenomenon. We try to drive traffic to those videos and try to get people to go to our website. It's a whole bunch of cross-pollenization, where you drive traffic in many different ways and you try to use Facebook and Twitter and other tools to do all of this; it actually works out pretty well.

That's absolutely fascinating, Adam. What advice would you give to somebody who was seriously looking at starting a music library, writing for or working for one?

Well, if you are a composer or songwriter and you want to work for a library, you really need to do your research into the different companies. Consider whether you want to go exclusive or non-exclusive because those are totally different kinds of things.

I think that most serious composers or songwriters go with the exclusive relationship because it's a much more mature part of the business and it gives more opportunity for composers, and ultimately more revenue. It also means that your tracks are important to the library and they will be managed in a consistent way over the years.

You have to think about the kind of music that you write: What's your specialty? What can you offer that's better than somebody else? You want to take what you can do uniquely and really find a marketplace for that.

I would highly recommend that composers *do not* walk into a library and say, "Well, I can write everything." No composer can compose everything equally well, but there are composers who will still say they can, which leaves me at a loss.

I don't even know what to say in those situations except, "So you're saying you can write hip-hop and classical equally as well? Wow, there are not many people who *can* do that . . . so you must be amazing!"

When I'm hiring, I have a list and a production schedule of what I need to produce. I wouldn't even know where someone like that would fit in . . . so that's a piece of advice there for songwriters out there.

If someone wants to start a library, they should. It can be a good business model, but don't underestimate the importance of quality, the importance and expense of the search engine, and the central importance of customer service. Also, don't underestimate the nature of relationships and how long it takes to build them, or the cost of sales. It costs money to produce music and it costs money to sell it.

One last question: what does the future of the music business look like?

Well, I don't know if anybody can call himself or herself an expert anymore, but I think that you have a number of different forces that are operating. You've got the top-down forces of companies buying each other, and in the end we will probably see three or four major record companies and three or four major publishers, and that's about it.

Then you've got the bottom-up thing that's happening with the independent artists who produce their own music without a record company, without a publisher, and sell through various sites like ReverbNation, MySpace, and others, trying to build a marketplace for themselves. Those are bottom-up self-organizing forces that have power and potential.

The question then becomes, where is the money to be made? If you're a very big company, should you only focus on the large acts? Or is there another sort of business entirely in using social media and building bottom-up economics, like micro transactions, that might have a long tail? And where do the two curves intersect? It will be interesting to see how these things shake out over time.

Music is part of the culture. It's always going to be produced in a big way and people have to find different models to get out there. I think that we're in a world now with a lot of bottom-up stuff. People are making their own independent decisions about things because of social media, and they are not relegated to only relying on the forces of the entertainment industry.

The future looks positive, but I don't want to discount the power of disruptive force. Obviously digital technology was the first disruptive force within the music industry and it's not going to be the last. There will be something that comes up that will change the paradigm again. Every change in technology changes the power structure in this business. If anything is certain, it's that this is an interesting time to be in the music business.

I started out in the music library revolution with John Parry and Alain LeRoux, and it was a great time for production music since there were very few players and lots of opportunity. Today, there is even more opportunity, given that advances in technology now allow everyone to create media, and most film and visual art needs music.

Personally, I think the music library business is a great place to be if you have some connections in the industry, access to music, and you control the publishing and rights.

Michael Redman

PRESIDENT, MYMUSICSOURCE

Guess who.

I just read Adam's answers above, but he runs a huge music library. How about a smaller boutique library, is there a market for them?

Absolutely! One of my music supervisor friends in the next section, Rudy Chung, has started a wonderful small music library called Pusher Music that specializes in movie trailers. They are doing very well, especially since they have made the right connections in the industry.

There are many areas in which to specialize in the production music arena, and even if you don't represent a specific genre or style, you can still do quite well. Traditional libraries aren't usually too versed in the creative use of technology and that leaves the door wide open to you if *you* are!

What kind of education would be beneficial for this job?

This question has an unusual answer. If I were starting out in this business again, I'd major in computer science and minor in business. I say this because like all businesses, music is largely quickly becoming a tech business. I would also plan on being successful and have a business background because a sizable part of a successful music library is contract related.

Where does the money come from in the production music business?

Generally, the money that's made in production music comes from licensing fees associated with music usage, music blankets (this is where a company pays a fee for either an entire show, or per year) as well as backend performance royalties. I am talking more here about the people that start libraries, and not the salespeople or producers, because these jobs, even though they are available in the larger libraries, pay according to their size like any business.

Where do I need to live to be in the music library business?

I would say that you should live in NY or LA, where the film, TV, and advertising business is conducted. The lion's share of the music used in commercial production comes from companies located in these areas. Even though there are other great libraries, like 615 in Nashville, they still have sales representation in these big markets.

What's the best thing about this business?

I love this business because I'm a composer, and if you are into production music, you can write as much music as you can stand. There was a time when we were in the start-up mode and I was writing about fifteen tracks a week in every style you can think of. There's nothing like it!

Another great thing about production music is that if you work hard at it, you will more than likely be rewarded for your efforts. It's not brain surgery!

Does this job have a solid future?

The future of the music library business is very good, from what I can tell. There will be a need for good, solid commercial and affordable production music for the foreseeable future. The music libraries that will flourish will most likely be smart marketers that understand the current music trends. They will be like the smart record labels of the past and have the ability to move quickly, embrace technology, and visualize where the market is going.

12

Music Supervisor

Rapid Fire

Skill Set—A genuine love of music, the ability to focus and do the paperwork; you also need to have your finger squarely on the pulse of today's—and yesterday's—music scene.

Hours—A music supervisor needs to be available when the director and/or producer need them, so the hours vary greatly. I know music supervisors that just work a couple of days a week and others that never get more that five hours of sleep a night.

Upside—It is fun! Discovering new music, negotiating licensing deals, going to film shoots, spotting sessions, recording sessions, and being part of a highly creative production team.

Downside—Independent music supervisors typically work job to job, and even episode to episode, so the stress can be quite high. A staff music supervisor at an ad agency has a bit more security, but that can change quickly. Career lengths can vary as well. Just think about the one-hit wonders, where you are "the man" one day and the next it's someone else.

Financial—$$$ to $$$$ Music supervisors working on one show at a time might find themselves as a contract employee for a network. In this case, the money is okay but not exactly retirement worthy. Those managing multiple shows concurrently and producing soundtracks can make a very nice living. Also, as of today, music supervisors do not share in any long tail revenue stream, split publishing, or royalties. This will hopefully change in the future.

Location—NYC or LA only, because that's where the bulk of production for film, TV, and advertising takes place. You need to be where the work is and network efficiently.

Future—Changing but pretty solid. Music supervisors have a challenge in that every publisher, record label, and music library now has people they call "music supervisors." They used to have the job title of account executive. This is confusing the title and role of the true music supervisor. There's a lot of media being produced, and true music supervisors are a talented breed with an unusual blend of creative guts and business savvy.

MUSIC SUPERVISION IS AN INTERESTING FIELD THESE DAYS. It is made up of people from all walks of life, who, for the most part, love music and love selecting the perfect song to marry with images on film, TV, and other electronic media. Music supervisors are responsible for finding music, sometimes recording it, negotiating the licensing rights, and doing a pile of supporting paperwork to create the paper trail that will follow a film: a film can have many iterations of licensed usage as it travels from theaters to pay-per-view, HBO, and then DVD and the web over a long period of time. However, this job is not exactly the romantic position most people think it is; it's hard work!

What many of you may not know is that many suppliers of music are now calling themselves music supervisors as well, which is confusing the title, the market, and the requirements for the position. I expect that over time, this will change as music supervisors are recognized for their expertise beyond selecting music for a production, including their negotiating skills and attention to the post-production details, all required to be successful in this position.

I generally don't watch very much TV, but I do regularly watch a few shows, in particular *Dexter* and *True Blood*. I suppose it's my dark side showing through, but, oh well, I find them very entertaining. One of the things I noticed early on in *Dexter* was the creative use of music, both popular songs and great underscores. So I decided to track down the music supervisor responsible for all that great music and interview him. The fellow I am referring to is Gary Calamar, a veteran DJ and highly sought-after music supervisor for several of the top current shows on TV.

Gary is a busy guy and agreed to our interview, but I have to tell you, he's not an easy man to pin down between spotting sessions and recording projects.

Gary Calamar

PRESIDENT, GO MUSIC SUPERVISION

Gary Calamar is a four-time Grammy-nominated producer and music supervisor for his work on HBO's True Blood *and* Six Feet Under.

Gary Calamar is without a doubt one of the most successful contemporary music supervisors of our time. His credits include top-line TV and cable shows like *True Blood*, *House*, *Dexter*, *Weeds*, *Swingtown*, and the list goes on. When I caught up with Gary, he was running between table reads and sessions, as he does most days. He is a confident but humble guy, who loves what he does for a living and willing to share his thoughts with us on what it means to be a music supervisor today and in the future.

Gary, you're the music supervisor for several of today's hottest TV properties, including House, True Blood, and Dexter. How do you juggle so many high-profile projects at the same time?

I have a small but great staff that help me. Unfortunately, some of these are cable shows, only broadcast twelve episodes a year, so they're not full-time gigs on their own. If they we're, I'd be living in a different part of town. [*laughs*] Fortunately, the shows are kind of scattered throughout the year, and so far I've been able to juggle them without dropping too many balls.

Music supervisors get a fair amount of glory, but we certainly don't get overpaid compared to some salaries in the entertainment business, so we don't like to turn projects down, especially when they're great projects like you just mentioned.

Music supervision takes on many different roles depending on the media you're working in. How's cable or TV unique? Does it require special skills?

With a TV show, it's like a runaway train; you'll go crazy trying to get all the tracks together for episode one, and then you have episode two, three, four, and five coming up at the same time. It's a lot of juggling the schedule, which can be scary, and lots of stakeholders always breathing down your neck. The good news is that you know the project is going to be over at a certain point and that you have a steady paycheck coming from every episode.

It doesn't seem like it gives you a whole lot of time to sit back and enjoy what you're doing.

No, it doesn't. There are certainly thrills along the way, though. We just had an episode of *House* a couple weeks ago where we had to do a lot of behind-the-scenes with Peter Gabriel covering this Arcade Fire song. It was on-again, off-again, as Arcade Fire, who wrote the songs, are very particular about how their songs are used, so we had to do a lot of convincing. Peter Gabriel . . . well [*laughs*] . . . this of course is Peter Gabriel we're talking about! We needed the right project for him to want to get involved. Fortunately, it all worked out in the end and things turned out great.

Yes, sometimes you've got to go digging in the dirt and be a sledgehammer, am I right? [*laughing*] Obviously music supervisors today work with popular songs. Where do you find your music?

Well, I find music all over. I'm always reading music magazines, UK music magazines, and I follow different music blogs. There's no single place, but I try and just keep my ears open all the time.

I also get a bunch of music sent to me, and listen to all my colleagues at KCRW who play a lot of great music; XM Sirius Radio plays great stuff too. I also try to surround myself with friends that are music lovers and they make suggestions to me.

I get sent so much music between the radio show and the television shows that it's just impossible for me to listen to everything that comes in.

Could you walk me through a day at the office?

A day could start off with a fairly clean to-do list, but then by 10:30 a.m. there are three fires on one show and a clearance that won't happen on another show and we need to find some "Indian Bakery" music for another show.

The things that we do every day may include trying to find music for a particular scene in *True Blood* or *House* and dissecting a show, trying different songs out against the rough cut. At the same time, we're negotiating deals with the record labels and publishers, or maybe trying to work out a soundtrack situation, because we might want to use a song in a show and then in a soundtrack down the line.

Tomorrow I'll be at some recording sessions doing new songs for one of the shows. Last season in *True Blood*, Beck had written a new song for us and we recorded it; Lucinda Williams wrote a new song for us too. There are situations where we'll reach out to artists who want to contribute to the show. Also, three or four times a week, a label rep or publisher will come to our office and play me their new stuff.

It sounds like a lot of fun!

It generally is. I converted my garage into an office, so I work out of my own place and I work with people that I like. No complaints there.

So that's the fun part, but what's the toughest part of your job?

The toughest part is dealing with the politics. Usually, I'm working closely with the creator and the producer(s) of the show, but often there's a studio involved and the network that's airing the show. They all have their two cents to put in, and the internal politics can get a little stressful and frustrating, but that's just part of the job and the rest is great.

Do you sometimes have to work with music selection by committee?

I would say yes, most of the time. Even if I am the filter for Alan Ball on *True Blood*, he's going to make the final decision, and usually the writer of the episode has a vote on what goes in . . . so yes, it's generally by committee, and also a collaboration. I'm bringing the music to the group and we'll decide what gets in by committee.

How does a music supervisor get paid in the cable and TV arena, and secondly, are there any residual dollar points?

Generally in TV, cable or network, you get paid by the episode. You sign on for the whole season, but you only get a check after an episode is done.

For a film, it kind of varies on the budget. Indie films, which pay the least, are the hardest to deal with because they don't have much money to write songs and require a lot of negotiation to get a soundtrack of music together. But depending on the budget for the film, you can get anywhere from $5,000 to $100,000 or more.

Unfortunately for us, there are no residuals. The composer gets residuals, and we're very happy for them, but it'd be nice, depending on how involved we are, to get some type of residual. There's usually a soundtrack album release, and there are some sort of points you might negotiate, but in most cases, it doesn't add up to much unless you get a *Twilight*, which would generate considerable money.

Gary, you're fortunate because you're very good at what you do, have lots of popular shows airing, and have been working at this for several years. At the end of the day, it's job to job for a music supervisor, isn't it?

Yes, it is. We're basically freelance guys and gals. It's job to job and there are no guarantees. I work on an HBO show and a Showtime show, but I don't work for the companies, so there's no job security there. I have an agent that helps me, but this business is largely built on personal connections and the employers you've worked for in the past. I've also worked on shows that have been canceled after one episode. You think you're set for at least one season, but all of a sudden you're out of a job!

If someone reading this is knowledgeable and loves music, what kind of advice might you give them?

First of all, I would say it's tough and very competitive. I would also say you probably need to be in Los Angeles or New York. That's where the action is, and where a lot of production is happening. Just put yourself in that world because there's a lot of networking that needs to be done; schmoozing, lunches, and hopefully you'll catch on. I got very lucky to work on a show, *Six Feet Under,* which was very popular and kind of announced me to the world at that time. I've also been fortunate to keep working since that time, but it can be very hard to get to that first gig and make a career out of music supervision.

A good way in is an internship because there's a lot to learn. If you can work free or close to it, that works. I got started that way and I think that, especially music supervisors, who are not making that much money anyway and can't afford a big staff, always appreciate someone who will come in and help for free, even if you come in and say, "I can be here two days a week to help out." I can tell you that I've had several interns that have gone on to bigger and better things, and I have someone with a master's degree interning now. She's learning a lot and learning well.

As someone with a great deal of insight into the industry, what does the future of the music industry look like from where you sit?

I'm kind of leaning in that Rhapsody direction. I think as far as creativity and music, now is a terrific time because there are so many great artists out there moving forward without having to be signed by a record label and having to deal with label politics.

I think it may be some time before we figure out how musicians will get paid properly and what the record labels' future role will be, or will there even be record labels? We also will have to figure out a distribution model that works. I know as much about that as anybody else, and I'm just watching from the sidelines and using all the music being produced today. I'm also very happy to be able to expose new artists and music on the radio and TV shows, so I'm very optimistic about the future of the industry.

What would you like to do in the music industry that you haven't done yet?

Good question, Michael. My ultimate goal, or dream, would be to write a hit song that a lot of people get to hear and would somehow move them in a positive way, just make them happy [*laughs*]. I'd also love to produce a film myself and call the shots. Especially musically!

Brian Black

PRESIDENT, ZOOPHORIA MUSIC

Brian Black is president of a music supervision and soundtrack production company. His feature film credits include Meet Me in Miami, Sam's Lake, A Dance for Bethany, Cupid's Arrow *and* American Flyer.

So, Brian, would you tell me how your education, and specifically your business studies at the University of California, influenced or helped you in your music career?

My undergraduate education at Indiana University was helpful. I took music history courses on the subjects of jazz and soul music and rock and roll. Having a musicology background is certainly valuable in my profession.

Regarding UCLA, the music publishing course I took was probably the most helpful in my current career, primarily because I learned about the basics of copyright law, which is important knowledge for a music supervisor to possess.

Would you tell me about your role as music supervisor?

The role of a music supervisor varies from project to project because it's scope is influenced by two things: the film and the filmmakers.

Some film genres tend to be more music-intensive than others. For example, a romantic comedy or action film normally requires more source music than a drama.

Some filmmakers are more hands-on with the music than others. Some give me the rough cut, tell me during the spotting session where the music cues should be, and I choose the songs. Other filmmakers choose the songs, then I work on the rights clearances and licensing.

What's the most challenging part of being a music supervisor for you personally?

Convincing filmmakers of the essential value of my services, especially in an era of shrinking film budgets and subsequently shrinking music budgets. I realize that some films don't contain source music and, therefore, my services would be deemed unnecessary, but those cases are the exception rather than the norm.

To hire an experienced music supervisor should be considered by filmmakers as a necessity rather than a luxury. On almost every project that I've worked on, without my involvement, incorrect decisions would have been made that could have led to legal ramifications detrimental to the film's outcome. A filmmaker can ill afford to be "penny wise but pound foolish" about music supervision.

DURING MY QUEST TO FIND SUCCESSFUL INDIVIDUALS willing to share their recipe for a relevant music career, I came upon Raphaella Lima and was immediately taken with her energy and candor as she told me her story, talked about her love of music, and why her job as a music supervisor in the gaming industry is so fulfilling. Raphi knew at an early age that music would be her path, and it was apparent from her positively magnetic personality there could be no way she would fail.

When I first spoke with Raphaella, it became apparent to me that her drive, passion, and zeal for her work had been, and will continue to be, a major factor in her success at EA and a benefit to all music enthusiasts.

Raphaella works very hard to bring new artists to the forefront of the music world and is always looking for the next big act. For those of you who listen to music for a living, you understand that it's both a blessing and a curse to be in a position like hers. It's a blessing when you discover new talent or a song that moves you in some new way; it may be a sensation you have never quite felt before. However, the job can be a curse as well because you become addicted to that first feeling and it's an endless search to repeat it, to reproduce the magic of finding the *next big thing*.

Raphaella Lima

EA GAMES

Raphaella, would you tell me exactly what a music supervisor in the gaming world does?

It's probably the most different out of all of the other mediums that I've worked in. Depending on the title, you're not just thinking "music to picture" because there are many elements that come into play, including implementation and interactivity.

What different types of music might you find yourself using, or pitching, for a game title?

Here at EA we release dozens of titles a year, and when picking music, it's a combination of looking at the game itself, who we are marketing it to, and the personality or musical strategy we have defined for that title.

We have different categories of games as well. There are the mission-based or first-person shooters, and most of them will be matched with an originally composed score. For those, we will work with the best music composers available to create an interactive score soundtrack. Medal of Honor, Dragon Age, Mass Effect, and Battlefield, are some examples.

Another large category is sports titles. Our philosophy here is to look ahead, predict the future. It's really about finding those new bands and new musical trends that are on their way up and will be happening around the time we release a title. We may also look for elements such as tempo and energy, depending on the title and the personality it has adopted.

NHL, for example, is a combination of new and established artists, leaning on rock with a very anthemic and arena-quality sound. There are a lot of new acts launched in the game that end up having songs become a staple in the arenas for the live sporting events.

FIFA, as another example, has the vision to represent as many different countries and cultures when building the soundtrack. Being Brazilian and a huge soccer fan, I also try to capture the soul of the sport and the emotional moments, so in that game you might hear something very up-tempo, but you might hear something pretty laid back. Sometimes you may think that a slower song wouldn't fit in a video game, *but it does*!

There are other titles, like The Sims, where it's a combination of composed and licensed music, but if it is licensed music, the vocalists are required to go back into the studio to re-cut their vocals in "Simlish." It's a very unique approach and the team has worked with everybody from the Black Eyed Peas to Depeche Mode, Howard Jones, Katy Perry, Lilly Allen, and the Pussycat Dolls . . . the list goes on . . . to re-create their hits in the game's language.

We also have the lifestyle titles, like Need for Speed or SSX (a snowboarding title) or SKATE, where the music approach is a little bit more about servicing the consumers that are going to be playing these games . . . combining original score and licensed music to create a more cinematic approach.

How involved are you personally in the actual creative process for music development?

Well, that is our primary role. The department here is headed by Steve Schnur, with myself and Cybele Pettus as Music Supervisors. My department works together with the producer, director, executive producer, or whoever might be at the other end of a game title and in charge of the game's vision. We sit and identify what the goals are for the title, what the target audience is, and how we might approach the music in that particular version or year. Our job is to define a music strategy and deliver it; my job is mostly creative.

That's great! Music supervision for video games sounds quite different from the music supervisor position in episodic TV programming or film.

Yes, it's very different. I'm working on an independent documentary right now and it's a *very* different experience. Most of the time, you're presenting them with creative ideas, but a lot of time is spent just going out and "clearing" what they want. At EA we have a licensing team of three people that focuses solely on music rights and clearance. Once a song is chosen for the game, they negotiate fees and contracts.

You wear a lot of different hats! Can you run down what your day is like?

Like most entertainment jobs, it changes day to day. Besides music supervision, we have a music company with about twelve artists that we look after and seek out opportunities for them. Managing that and interfacing with team members or artists is usually a small part of our day.

Because of the sheer number of original scores that we've created over the past twenty-five years, EA Recordings now also releases game scores digitally. We will release on average twenty-five to thirty digital scores a year, so we'll work with the composer or the audio director to build a sequence that is cohesive with the game's storyline, develop artwork that is in sync with game art, and finally sort out copyright information in order to properly publish and release the songs.

Another part of my day can be spent on supervising trailers for the different titles. When you are working with trailers, deadlines are very different, and usually you have anywhere between twenty-four hours to a week, if you're lucky, to find and lock creative. We recently did a great campaign with Crysis 2 and created four new versions of the Frank Sinatra classic "New York,

New York" with different artists. All of that had to be executed in less than a ~~month, and some~~ in a week.

~~So I guess I do a lot!~~ [*laughs*]

You have the job of twelve people! [*laughs*] I'm going to speed up this interview so you can get back to work! Tell me a about the culture at EA. What is it like to work there?

The video game culture can be very corporate in a company of this size and stature. There's a political chain of command to follow that changes with the size of a project. Sometimes there are many stakeholders, and if it's a new title, I'm not going to be the only one spearheading it. It's a real team effort.

I have an amazing boss who comes from the music industry, who says, "It's all about getting your job done; whichever way you need to." He's not that guy who says, "You've got to be here from 9 to 5." Our team has been together for ten years, and we all really enjoy what we do here, and we all work hard at what we love.

Sounds like a tight-knit group, which I'm sure is very helpful when dealing with the crazy hours you must put in. What's the biggest challenge of your job?

I think one of our biggest challenges is how the music industry is changing and being affected by technology. Artists now finish recording an album and can immediately put it out in the market, making it a bit harder to stay ahead of its curve. Still, our team manages to network our way into artists' studios and managers' early demos so that we can continue to deliver against the bar we have set for our soundtracks.

Another thing that I find difficult is trying to explain a new trend or creative approach to the corporate executive who has his mind set on AC/DC for the trailer to a game. You have to put on your marketing and sales hat in order to illustrate why your proposal is much more relevant to the culture and consumer of a particular game, and that by using the track we suggest, the product will gain that much more prominence in the marketplace.

That's pretty cool, though! I can see the challenge because you're pitting known artists against new, upcoming acts while you're trying to explain to somebody why the artist they have never heard of is what the product needs.

Exactly! When it comes to music, everyone thinks they are an expert! [*laughs*] You gotta deal with that too.

How could somebody prepare to do a job like yours?

I think that, first and foremost, you need a genuine love for music. People who are the most successful music supervisors aren't one-dimensional; it takes a broad knowledge of different musical genres and an understanding of the culture behind those genres, as well as the culture of consumers you are marketing to.

Aside from being organized and a multi-tasker, what skills do you think are the most important to a music supervisor in gaming?

Well, you do need to understand the world of rights and licensing. What it takes to clear a song, etc.

Like a rock track can be very different to license than a hip-hop track. You need to have an understanding of what things cost and the reality of getting specific songs for the budget that you have. You also need to know your artists and understand if they are willing to be associated with a violent game or certain type of content (some aren't willing to do that). Additionally, you need to master negotiation skills.

You need to have a real understanding of current and upcoming trends in music and also be very resourceful; you also must understand your audience and the product you are servicing.

I had a project come up this week that required a really quick turnaround, and I sent out a track I've had under my sleeve for four years, and all of the sudden it became the perfect track.

I started as a very young kid and would go to every show I could. Managers of local acts would see me all the time at their client's gigs. Ten years later, they are managing huge artists and they're like, "I remember when you were that kid always hanging out at the music clubs!" They know I love and respect music no matter how small or big an artist is, which makes our business dealings easier. Your network and your reputation are big influences in your success.

As someone who has been in this line of work for a long time, what do you think the future of the music industry holds?

I think it's very exciting, honestly. I know that the record business itself isn't thriving right now, but artists, who are real artists, have a chance to shine and own their ground.

Music is growing stronger ties with other mediums. Music has become, and is becoming, more of a multifaceted art form. I see us going back to complete artistry, to the days where you pick up an album with not just an amazing collection of songs but with unbelievable artwork and story behind it; videos and all of that. Of course, it may not be an album we will be picking up. Still, a complete experience that is led and inspired by music and immediately translated into different languages (mediums).

I WORKED AS A COMPOSER IN THE ADVERTISING WORLD for a good part of my career, and I'd have to say that it was the best and worst of times. The deadlines could be manic, and some of the client side, as we call it, could be challenging. There are big dollars in advertising and that can lead to a boatload of stress for everybody. You don't often find anyone over fifty in advertising unless they own the agency. The agency world is largely made up of twenty- to thirty-year-olds, so you obviously need to be creative, have a thick skin, and lots of energy just to be in the game. I take my hat off to those who can make a lasting career in the advertising industry, for they are truly special people.

One such guy is Mike Boris, who for the past nine years has headed up music production for the famous McCann Erickson advertising agency in New York City, which as you know, is a pretty competitive place to work. He is a producer, engineer, and a drummer with an incredible ear, and knows how to work both sides of the fence. Clients can be hard to understand ("Can you make it sound more red?") and when you add musicians and artists into the mix, great communication skills become paramount. Somehow Mike has mastered this position, which by the way he loves!

Mike Boris

DIRECTOR OF MUSIC, McCANN ADVERTISING

Mike, would you tell me what a music supervisor in an advertising agency does?

Well, my technical title is SVP Executive Music Producer, and essentially my job is to find and produce the music you hear on TV commercials. Basically advertising agencies create messages to make people aware of brands. For the most part, I've worked on TV and radio the majority of my career, but there are many other ways to get messages out today with the Internet, the evolving record industry, and social media.

Music can drive the idea, support the idea, or in some cases be the idea. Most jobs are handed to me and I work with a creative team. The traditional agency creative team is made up of an art director, who is responsible for anything you see, and a copywriter, who is responsible for everything you hear, which theoretically includes music. There is, however, a lot of teamwork within a project. Sometimes they say, "Mike, we want this music or this song, and we want to work with this person," but sometimes it's "Mike, we've got this spot . . . what do you think?" The position is 50 percent music supervisor and 50 percent music producer. There is a time to find music and a time to create it.

Do you have any special responsibilities in your day-to-day?

I sign off on everything, but I have people who do most of the paperwork for me. I am responsible for understanding music rights and taking care of our clients to assure they are protected. I also make sure that our artist suppliers are taken care of as well.

In my world, there are many moving parts that include the music rights [who owns the music] and the talent side [whether it's AFM or SAG]. Then there are the elements of the performing rights organization, ASCAP, BMI, and SESAC, which is a big question mark for everybody now, no matter how long they have been in this business. [*laughs*]

What type of work is done with BMI and ASCAP ?

Because commercials run in different places on various media, we are eligible to collect performance rights money (which can be significant) on behalf of our client and send it directly to them. My composers keep their writer's share of the publishing, and in order for them to collect, a usage report needs to be filed with the PRO [performing rights organization]. The PROs need to see airing charts, where things ran . . . etc.

It's nice to know that you actually handle that part. You mentioned unions; in your job do you have follow-up payments every time a track is re-sung or cut in a different way for a new spot?

Yes, we're responsible for that as well, but it's not my job [*laughs*]. Fragrances, for example, many times they do gift with purchase tags, so you'll have this new perfume: "This new handbag! Free at Bloomingdales," and then the next version is "Free at Sears!" next one "Free at Kohl's!" so for all of those different spots, the talent needs to be identified and paid properly. Spots are also re-edited and revised periodically. Those are things we police, but if the music is a buyout, we don't have to worry about it.

So do you typically try to acquire the music used in a spot as a buyout?

I'd like to say it's all creatively driven, but it's decided client to client and job to job. Sometimes they don't care and it's just about the best creative solution. Sometimes they are much more cost-conscience and we need to deal with it.

It is also important to distinguish between buying out the talent (musicians and singers) and the actual music itself.

How big does an agency have to be to afford a full-time music producer on staff like you?

I think you have to be a major, worldwide agency like McCann, JWT, Grey, Ogilvy, BBD&O, or McGarry to warrant one full-time person or department that just works on music.

It sounds like there might be a job opportunity for somebody that does what you do on behalf of multiple smaller agencies.

Yeah, I think so; I think every agency could use somebody like me! [*laughs*] It would be valuable for a smaller agency to be able to scale out when they need an expertise in the music space.

Let me ask you this, Mike. What do you like most about what you do?

I love what I do. I think the best part is seeing the finished product as a consumer on the air when you're watching TV with your kids! Or surfing around online and seeing a spot has gone viral with my music track. I also love that this job requires that I stay current with music because it's so easy as a musician and a music producer, to live in your own little world.

You mentioned that a lot of your work is producing music. So do you often participate in production as the main producer? Do you enjoy that aspect of your job?

Yes, I do that, and it takes me back to my roots. I love being in the studio with talented musicians. There is nothing quite like it.

Tell us a little bit about how that works and some of the challenges of being a producer.

I'm the liaison between musicians, composers, agency people [creatives and account people], and our clients. First of all, it is my job to make sure everything sounds great. I have a background as an engineer, so I push for sonic excellence. I'll push a supplier to use live musicians when we have the budget and it warrants it.

There are times to bring in a real string section and there are times to use real horns. There's nothing like a live section when you can do it, and saxes still sound horrible as samples, as far as I'm concerned. I also do all the little things in the session to make sure the end result is as good as it can be and everyone involved is happy. I'm the one who says, "Let me hear it on the small speakers" so we know it's going to sound good everywhere. I'll get some young engineer looking at me cross-eyed when I ask, "Can I hear it in mono?" [*laughs*]

What's mono? That's a disease, right? [*laughs*] The fact that you are able to work in a variety of music styles is unusual, and certainly impressive! How can you go from working in reggae or ska to an orchestral piece?

You need to listen to *everything* and be a sponge. I am not a classically trained musician and grew up as a drummer [*laughs*]. However, I understand music theory and have pretty discriminating ears.

I always tried to be diverse and play and understand every genre and find opportunities to play.

For example, after rocking out in high school, I got to play in a twenty-five-piece big band in college that taught me how to listen. I played in a rockabilly cover band that helped improve my time tremendously. Post-college I got into roots rock and learned about overplaying . . . ha-ha.

My first job was at the Edison Recording Studio assisting Gary Chester. Gary was demanding of his assistants. We'd be recording a string section in the morning, later a reggae band, then a big band at night. The next day a Broadway show would come in to do their cast record. The next day might be two or three jingle sessions. It was crazy, but I learned how to shift my thinking on the dime. As an assistant engineer in those days, I was rolling tape, so you were essential in running the session. You had to listen! That was unbelievable training.

Another important part for me is letting go of control, stepping back and looking at the big picture. I always try to remember the role the music needs to play. It's not music for music's sake; it exists to support a brand and/or a message.

One more thing is team work. I've got the people I use and trust when I am moving beyond my area of expertise. I am not well versed in opera, but there are great people I am not ashamed to call. Choosing the right resources is a big part of producing.

That kind of leads me to another thought. Do you ever work with a composer one on one?

Absolutely, all the time.

Direct communication is essential. I have a creative brief for my composers. It is a musical brief, but also we talk about the actual "ad-speak." There are issues with the story on film we are scoring that are important to my clients brand message, or a message a voice-over is delivering that tell the story. These things need to support or be accented by the music. Music, as we know, can tell you how to feel, and when to feel.

I also get to know my team or clients and their personal taste. I might tell the composer, "You know what, I'm working with creative director X and they just love a memorable melody or a branded theme, or I know this art director always pushes things to be darker and emotional than they really are, so let's put in a dark choir or go minor key." I also feel that the best way to work is to give them creative direction and then get out of their way and let them do their job.

In a project, more times than not there are revisions. There can be a lot of specific issues in thirty seconds. Music is *subjective*, so there are also a lot of opinions.

There may be a product shot that needs to be made a hero. There is fair balance copy of a pharmaceutical ad. The FDA actually needs to approve your final mix so the music needs to be simple and there. . . . [The "fair balance copy" is like, "*May cause bleeding from the ears, headaches, death, unwanted warts on your nose, bla-bla-bla-bla-bla.*"]

There are also always changes to the actual cut. If a client requests an additional three seconds to show how their products look, the music needs to be re-scored accordingly.

My job is to take in all this information and relay it to my composer in musical terms.

That's more how I might liaison and collaborate with a composer.

This sounds like something that has come with years of experience, and it takes a person that has a great depth of music knowledge, great ears, great feel . . .

Yeah, you need a lot of patience! As I said, music is subjective; everybody likes music and there are lots of opinions!

I've always embraced other people's creative ideas. My job requires handling a lot of big personalities. Not all composers handle changes as well as others. They take their music really personally and can push back in the wrong places. Likewise, there are a lot of talented creatives who are not musicians, but they have big musical ideas. There are times I need to work hard, and there are times it's just a question of me looking brilliant by making one phone call [*laughs*]. Why beat around the bush? I know this guy has seventeen vintage Dobros in his basement and burns his own custom 78s or something [*laughs*] who is the perfect man to call for project X.

And probably knows how to play those Dobros [*laughs*].

Yeah, so sometimes my "brilliance" is just knowing the right person to call!

You've done the Billboard music conferences and those types of things. Is that a requirement of your job or is it just something you do for the agency?

Not a requirement, I've just embraced it. Getting out and talking in front of groups of people is good for my own personal growth! I'm so excited about the potential of the music industry right now. We just did a project with one of our clients, Holiday Inn, and found a great song, an indie song, and released it as a single. We did some creative promotion for the song as well. My agency acted as the record label and shared in the profit. It's fantastic and I'm excited to participate in more opportunities like that in terms of the future of music and advertising.

Mike, What advice would you share with someone that wants to be in your shoes?

I think you just have to do what you love with music. If you are a player, learn how to play your instrument well, learn how to be a good musician. For me, my engineering background helped, and I don't know how I could function without that background. Without being able to load up Pro Tools, edit, bounce to picture, or even just kick up a loop to present an idea . . . it just helps me so much.

I remember a movie where one character owned this extremely successful restaurant. Someone asked him why his restaurant was so successful, and he said, "I don't know how I'm a success. . . . I just come from this little town where everybody makes a nice sauce! Your mama makes a nice sauce, your son makes a nice sauce, and even your dog knows how to make a nice sauce! That's what we do in Italy! I come here and I'm Superman because everybody likes my sauce!" [*laughs*] That's me, I found a place to make my sauce.

So find a niche where you are needed and are doing a functional job. Also, in this day and age, I think knowing Pro Tools and Logic and all the software programs composers use is absolutely vital. Be on the music blogs. If you're into music supervision, know where to find music and how to follow the trends in what people are listening too. Train your ears!

There are not too many music production jobs in advertising, and the best way to get in now is work somewhere for free. (Yes, it is the curse of an artistic career.) Find some way to do this if you can. If you're young, coming right out of school, you could live with your folks or with a friend, bartend, or play in a band part-time, and go intern somewhere during the day. Besides, there's nothing like learning in the real world.

If I was to come to you and say, "Look, Mike, I'll do whatever it takes, and I'd like to be an intern and just follow you around," would you take someone on?

I'm surprisingly not overwhelmed with those requests. Yes, I would use them.

What does the future look like for Mike Boris and the music world?

I think what's going to happen is that major brands are going to step in and do what record labels used to do. Everybody is talking about the record labels crumbling, but they're not going anywhere! They still do what they do. There are still developers and curators of talent, not to mention the gatekeepers for millions of copyrights.

I think there is also an opportunity for bands to be curators of talent or the modern-day House of Medici. I believe that's the future, and I plan to be involved.

Rudy Chung

Music Supervisor, Hit the Ground Running, and Co-Founder, Pusher

Rudy Chung's numerous credits include CSI, The Big Bang, Entourage, *and* Everybody Hates Chris. *At Pusher, he represents a boutique roster of artists, bands, and composers exclusively for use in film trailers, including trailers for* Prometheus, The Hunger Games, The Amazing Spider-Man, Transformers: Dark of the Moon, *and* Inception.

From what I understand, as a music supervisor you wear many different hats, but could you tell me what a typical day at the office is like for you?

What I like about this job is that there is no real typical day. In any given time, we might have four TV shows and one or two films we're working on. So my day starts with a team meeting, where Jason, our staff, and myself get together and talk about what that day's priorities look like.

We could have an episode of a television show that's dubbing that afternoon that we've got to finish and make sure that everything is cleared on time, or have meetings or spotting sessions for our projects.

Lots of meetings! [laughs] They could be with our productions if there's an upcoming on-camera performance, for example, or with records labels, artists, and managers who are presenting their music to us. Then in and amongst all of that, we have the actual work of finding music for our projects.

We also do quite a bit of paperwork and licensing in our offices, which we're quite proud of and quite fluent in. We wouldn't have it any other way. That takes up a large part of our days as well.

As far as actual music discovery goes, that happens nights, weekends, and in the car. It doesn't happen in the office. [laughs]

Fair enough! That's where most of us discover music. You must get a constant barrage of artists or A & R reps trying to get songs placed. How do you filter through the thousands of tracks submitted to you?

It's a struggle managing the amount of submissions you get, developing relationships with people that you already know, and introducing yourself to new labels and publishers, managers and artists. I've tried to make a concerted effort towards honing the number of submissions I get to a point that's manageable. That means getting more music from the labels and the people that I know and that I trust and that I love.

I'm constantly seeking out new music from labels from around the world and asking people to send us music. But that also requires sifting through the noise and the sheer amount of volume of submissions that we receive. Actually, if we give a label two or three shots at something and it's just not working out or the production level is just not there, we have to remove them from our list and the newsletters. It's not an enjoyable part of my job, but it's all part of trying to filter the number of submissions and music to make it manageable.

Rudy, what role do you think your formal education and playing cello has had on your career choice?

I actually studied law in university, and to an extent it certainly has helped with the business and legal affairs side of things, reading between the cracks in contracts of all sorts.

Being classically trained has really helped us out as well. Jason and I started a trailer music company a couple years ago in addition to what we're doing with our music supervisions, so I am also representing composers and artists for the first time in that arena. I represent artists, bands, songwriters, and composers exclusively for the world of film marketing and trailers.

I am very involved with the production of the music for our trailer clients, and being able to communicate and articulate briefs and direction to our composers is something that I have been able to do effectively. I find it easy and fun in part due to my classical training.

What would you say is the most challenging part of all of this?

I guess in a weird way, it's just a tremendous amount of juggling, but that's probably the most exciting part as well. Every day really is different, and it takes being meticulously organized and focused, which can be a challenge. I'm just fortunate to be doing this in a world I love, which is music, all things music. It's easily a job you can devote twenty-four hours a day to, but I'm also trying to carve out time to enjoy myself outside of my job. [*laughs*]

Do you get a fair amount of creative freedom in your job given all the different stakeholders?

That depends on the project. There are certain projects where your hope as a music supervisor is that you gain the trust and the ear of the head creative or the executive producer, but what goes into the show is *never* a music supervisor's final decision. It's always about us servicing the overall project, and I believe that's how it should be. There are projects where the head creative knows exactly what they want, and we act as facilitators to provide options that support that vision, and there are times when we are given the leeway to help set up the sound canvas and contribute. Both ways are okay.

I think the only time we have an issue is when there isn't a clear decision maker and we have a large committee making creative decisions. Our challenge is being able to navigate those situations politically and the ability to work with producers, egos, and the studios. It can be a delicate dance.

How do you deal with or think about the term "music supervisor" when every publishing house, indie label, and library has their own "music supervisors"?

That's been interesting. In the last couple of years, it seems like everybody is a "music supervisor." I think that the difference is that experienced supervisors are very fluent and knowledgeable with the business affairs side of things. Music supervisors understand the politics of how everything works—how a studio or a network interfaces with the producer or the writers or the directors, the entire creative process, how content gets made and music licensing.

There's a large amount of business affairs required as well, including negotiating fees, budgeting, managing of musical acts on camera, soundtracks. and so on. It's complicated, and a lot of people who call themselves supervisors don't really understand the scope of what we do. The creative component of our jobs is obviously hugely important but takes up such a small part of our days. It's our knowledge of how film and how television and how commercial production works that make us valuable.

The creation of media is exploding worldwide. Do you see a marketing opportunity for music supervisors to offer their services on a global scale?

I feel like the explosion of media only emphasizes the need for filtration and tastemakers because there's so much noise out there. Our job is to help filter through that noise and present the best music options to our clients creating the content. I think that the actual job title of Music Supervisor may not be here in a couple of years. I think there will be services, and there will be software with algorithms that will help people find music creatively.

The future is music supervisors leveraging their relationships, skill sets, and knowledge of music around the world and actually creating music content that they own and can license themselves.

With an emphasis on relationships, technology, and inter-connectedness, it would seem that social networking would have a big impact in your field. Has social networking affected you professionally?

Yes, I think it's made things a bit more complicated. I get pitched as much on LinkedIn or Facebook as I do on e-mail at my work, and it's getting out of control. But at the same time, I've met great artists and labels and have created relationships through the power of social networking.

It's been one of those things where I created a Facebook account for fun, and these days I literally know 20 percent of my friends; the other 80 percent are just trying to get their song heard on television. There are surely positive impacts of social networking making everybody more accessible, but for now it's just the Wild, Wild West out there.

What does the future of the music industry look like to you?

Two words, it's going to become *seamless* and *immediate*. With technology changing the way that music is being created and heard, it's going to be so much more than an artist just going to a studio, recording, and touring.

Information technology is going to allow the consumer to purchase and use music however they like. Methods of making business transactions and purchases through your mobile devices or your laptop or your cars are going to improve and be more prevalent.

Consumers will be able to go to a concert and buy the live show instantaneously on their cell phone, or purchase any music that you've heard anywhere, whether it is on your car radio or a shampoo commercial on television.

Also, I see artists being able to make a living composing for multimedia, touring, collaborating with visual artists and directors, the list is growing every day.

A COUPLE OF YEARS AGO, I was working on a new start-up called MyMusicSouce.com (one of the first fully web-based music licensing companies) and searched out several music supervisors in LA I thought might be able to help us get things rolling. If you've ever gone through the process of cold-calling, you know how frustrating it can be, but when Greg picked up the phone, he said in typical Greg style, "Hey, man, what can I do for ya?" "Well, I was hoping to meet with you—" Greg cut me off. "Of course I'll help, just tell me when and where."

It's easy to see why Greg Sill has been so successful in a business where you regularly need to give up an arm or your firstborn just to get a meeting. The people in this city of filmmaking are busy, busy, busy. Thanks, Greg, and I'm happy to call you friend!

Greg Sill

Independent Music Supervisor

Greg, life seems very good for you these days, working on the hit show Justified, winning all sorts of awards . . . how did you land this particular job?

Well, it's one of these situations, Michael, that you and I have talked about a lot. This business is based on relationships. The guy who created *Justified* is Graham Yost, who is one of my dearest friends, and I worked with him on *Boomtown* and *Rain*. He called me and said, "Listen, I'm doing this pilot and don't know if it's going to get ordered, but it's a show called *Justified*, based on an Elmore Leonard short story. He also wrote *3:10 to Yuma* and is a wonderful guy. Graham said, "Look, if it happens, I want you on it." So here we are!

Music supervision, as a career, encompasses many different roles. What kind of special skills do you need to be an effective music supervisor?

That's a great question and it actually takes a lot of skill and experience. I was an executive and ran a music department at Warner Bros. television for seven years under the guidance of a guy, Les Moonves, who is now the head of CBS. You have to be able to make administrative decisions, creative decisions, and you need to wear a lot of different hats. You also have to know and understand copyrights, records, managers, publishers, and all that stuff. It's not just about putting a song into a film.

Let me ask you this, Greg, where do you find music for your projects?

You have to be current and aware of what's out there because there's just so much music today. To be honest, I have seven or eight different people with whom I have full confidence, who know and understand my taste, and they usually get my first call. I go to the same folks *all* the time, and they never fail me, ever.

Do you create original music as well?

Absolutely. Steve Porcaro [Toto] is the composer on *Justified*, and I introduced him to Graham, who won't do a show now without Steve's involvement. We're like a team, you know? We're buddies.

How is the technology helping or hurting the process for you these days?

I'll tell you, I just did the pilot for *White Collar*, and I never met the executive producer, I never met the director, I never saw anybody. I did it all via computer and telephone. More and more, it's "Why do we have to come down to Sony to spot this thing? Why don't we just iChat and run the time code, and we can all see it at the same time.

I think that aspect of it has really helped the process. In my opinion, it makes my job a lot easier, but what I always do to find music, Michael, is call somebody rather than go fishing through websites. I'll say, "Hey, what do you have that will fit this scene?" Then send them a script page or a QuickTime movie file, and they will respond in kind with five or six songs.

Could you walk me through the process of supervising a TV project, starting from the phone call through closing out a job?

Okay. Here is basically how it works.

It starts with the script. I break it down; see if there is any music in it, how many songs, what my budget is. I work with the director, the producers, the studio, and the network. Then I go to work, and I find songs.

What happens next is pre-production, which is the script phase. Where there is existing music written into the script, I will clear it with different studios who do that in different ways. Some studios clear the music themselves, some studios don't.

The pilot for *Justified* was one of the hardest things I've ever worked on because FX had fallen in love with every piece of music, and I didn't do the pilot. The pilot had $400,000 worth of music, and I had $105,000 total to spend in my budget. I had to cut 75 percent of the cost and find new music, so I worked my magic. I found songs that were actually better in some cases, and the star of the show and FX were very complimentary. For me, finding the right music is a gift.

Once all the music is cleared and everybody knows that you're going to use the music, you go into the dubbing process and the dub stage. It's like a big recording studio, but more sophisticated with much bigger consoles. There are usually two guys, because it's more economically feasible. One guy does SFX and dialogue and one guy mixes the music.

What they do is they dub all that stuff in. Half the time, when you're shooting your show, you don't hear a doorbell, somebody screaming, a dog barking, because all that stuff is put in on the dub stage. Some of it is called Foley, then there is ADR [automatic dialog replacement], when lines are not discernable and you have to go back into the studio and re-record them.

Technology has really helped in the dubbing process because of the efficiencies of audio workstations like Pro Tools. You have a hard drive for literally everything you do. More importantly, once somebody makes a change, you have to re-conform the whole film because it's all timed out and PT is a lifesaver.

The last step is to put it in the finished show on what's called a digibeta, which is a digital tape format, and transfer that to what's called the DT3 [a three-inch digital tape] that goes to broadcast to a satellite, beamed to New York, and into your home!

Switching gears away from the busy work, Greg, what is your favorite thing about what you do for a living?

I think the best thing for me, putting a song up against picture and watching the magic happen, tears come to your eyes, and you know that you've created something special that wasn't there before. It makes me really, really happy. There's just no way to explain it.

Conversely, what is the toughest part about being a music supervisor—besides finding your next gig? [*laughs*]

Well, I think the toughest part can be the politics. There are so many different masters to television now, the network, a production company, or a couple of different production companies. Dealing with multiple stakeholders and waiting on decisions can be tough.

Also, if you need extra money on a show, you have to go to the network for "breakage." Breakage essentially means that you are getting extra money from either the production company or network and breaking your existing budget. In other words, if a song is going to cost me $30,000 and I don't have $30,000, but the network wants it, they might split it with the production company, saying, "You put in $15,000 and we'll put in $15,000."

Like I said before, the dance can be complicated.

How do music supervisors get paid? Is it per project?

It's based on an episodic contract, so you get paid for each episode, but you don't get locked in for a year. It's truly episode by episode. . . . I could get fired tomorrow! That would not be good. [*laughs*]

Are there residual dollars?

No, there aren't any residuals. Soundtrack albums have gone by the wayside, but what you can do is create an EP and put it in with the DVD when it's released. You can get a few points there, and the artist makes money as well from the EP sales. Our first week out, *Justified* sold over 130,000 copies, which is unheard of for a television show.

Isn't that something! I talked to one other guy and he started a company that supplies music, but not direct competition with what he is currently doing as a music sup. Is that something that music supervisors might find as a revenue source in the future?

Because we don't get rich doing this job, you have to diversify and do other activities. I'm doing a documentary right now, and it's the only authorized documentary on Bettie Page and it's amazing.

I got these amazing deals on Crosby, Stills, and Nash and Credence Clearwater. The director wanted to use a bunch of music, and Bettie Page is an icon, so I said, "I'm in!" A lot of people are searching for different revenue streams, but as for me, I don't want to create my own publishing company. It's a pain in the butt. But I do understand why other music sups would.

I may know your answer, but I'll ask you this anyway. . . . The role of music supervisors in the film and TV industry is very competitive, and shrinking, but there are many other media types that are exploding, like games and independent films. I would assume there is an opportunity and a market for a music supervisor to expand into the global market. Do you have any advice for somebody that wants to get into this business, besides "don't do it?

[*laughing*] Yeah, man, I mean, the advice is this: it's a relationship-based business. Create as many relationships as you can and make sure that you have the goods to back it up. I love to work with interns and I love to teach people. I love to give what's been given to me. That's why I'm talking to you, other than the fact that you're a good friend. It's part of the process, you know. Also, take classes!

I think my advice would be: "If you want to do it, be passionate about it, but get ready for rejection." Keep pushing, and push people just like me! Go to people like Gary Calamar or Alex Patsavas. Go to these people and say, "I really want to be a music supervisor. Can I shadow you for a couple of days? Can I hang out with you?" Become an intern, pay them or something, and don't be to shy to ask for some help!

Sometimes I need help, and I'll put an ad with UCLA or USC or an ad on Craigslist.

13

Orchestrator

Rapid Fire

Skill Set—A solid music education is a must because you can't do this job without one. The ability to concentrate for long periods of time with a single focus. Great ears as well as the ability to understand a composers sound and thought process is very helpful too.

Hours—This is a deadline-driven job, so the hours simply depend on the deadline. I could write some useful garbage here about hours, but it's pretty straightforward.

Upside—At the higher echelons, you will work with great composers, record in great studios, and collaborate with great teams of highly creative people like yourself. I can't imagine a more exciting time than standing in the control room of a fantastic recording studio listening to the fruits of my labor being played by some of the most talented musicians on the planet.

Downside—Depending on where you are in the food chain, the pressure can be enormous because of the deadlines mentioned previously. Developing the long-term relationships you will need to be successful will also take time. There are a limited number of orchestrators who make the big bucks.

Financial—$$ to $$$$ Union orchestrators who are busy and able to turn around projects quickly can make a fine six-figure income and create a long-term royalty stream for themselves. For those climbing the ladder, you will likely get by if you are good, but won't be buying a new home right out of the box.

Location—NYC and LA, primarily, and some European cities, like Prague, for example, where they do lots of film-score recording.

Future—As I've said before, like many jobs, orchestration is not going away; the number of productions that utilize orchestras will likely dictate the future. More and more composers are heading to Prague and other places to record for the cost savings, and that also adds to the competition as composers develop new foreign relationships and therefore more packaging of services.

HAVE YOU EVER WONDERED HOW IN THE WORLD A COMPOSER who's under a deadline to deliver a major film score gets it done, or how they write original music for a film with a 120-piece orchestra and choir and complete it in three months or less? It's an incredible feat, and to pull it off successfully takes a team of highly trained music professionals.

One of the most important members of that team is the orchestrator, who also sometimes takes on the role of composer and other times copyist and proofreader. The successful orchestrator is a chameleon, changing styles as needed to maintain the look, feel, and sound of the composer.

When I set out to write this book, I decided to include two or more people in each job category to get different perspectives on the same job, but after interviewing Conrad Pope, I thought there wasn't much else you would need to know. That's also the reason this is the longest interview in my book. I really struggled to edit Conrad's thoughts because they were all so relevant.

Conrad Pope

Conrad you are one of the busiest orchestrators in Hollywood and work on seven to nine A films every year. Could you explain a little bit about what an orchestrator does?

Basically we are people that help composers in whatever way they need in order to meet the deadlines that are imposed upon them to finish a film score.

I like to tell this story: Phil Ayling, who is a friend of mine and a session musician, said, "What's orchestration?" And I replied, "It's anything you say yes to!" What that means is that if you're going to help a composer, understand that every composer is different and needs a different type of assistance.

When I work for John Williams, he provides a very complete and accurate sketch that indicates who does what, so you're basically a secretary. [*laughs*] It goes from there to where I am essentially given four bars of music and told, "We need two minutes of music from this. It's gotta start this way, and it's gotta end that way, and we'll see you when you're done."

John Neufeld, for whom I worked for a number of years, once said, "An orchestrator doesn't have to be a composer, but he has to know *how* to compose because you need to know how a composer thinks." So you should have enough experience to be either a secretary or do the composer's job for him when he doesn't have time.

You touched on, and you are very humble about, your understanding of the orchestra. How do you go from John Williams to a James Newton Howard and

keep their style intact when you're orchestrating? Are you thinking about that?

Absolutely! Another of my mentors was a fellow named Arthur Morton, who was Jerry Goldsmith's longtime orchestrator. Arthur was a musician of remarkable ability and capabilities and was highly respected by his peers—of whom there were few. Arthur gave me very good advice when he said, "You know, Conrad, an orchestrator has to have a very good set of ears, and I'm not talking about musical ears because it's assumed you have those."

Artie Kane always said, "It's not the work you do, but how well you can work with others. You have to listen to what the client tells you he needs and wants. You have to hear the individuality in that composer." That's what I try to do, and I always endeavor to accomplish that goal for the composer.

You're obviously very good at it!

A composer once said, "You know, Conrad, I look at your orchestrations, and on paper they look like everyone else's, but whenever we get to the stage, they sound so much better!" Which was very flattering. I said, "I pay very close attention to what *you* do."

What made you decide to focus on orchestration and not composition?

My goal was not to be an orchestrator. When I moved here, I was told, "If you're not a rock star or an identifiable musician, and if all you are is a good musician, maybe you should orchestrate for people and they could advance you as a composer." I thought, "Wow, that sounds really right! It's just like the army; you start as a private, and if you have what it takes, you can end up a general."

Then I found out that it was more like the Ecuadorian army and that if you start out as a private, you're going to stay a private [*laughs*].

I came here in my thirties and had to make a living, so I took that advice. I attended some classes and luckily was offered a couple of jobs. Your first job will always come from someone that doesn't really want to hire you, but they've gone through everybody they know and finally ended up at your door. They're sweating bullets because they don't think you are going to come through for them.

Well, I came through, and that's when I started at the bottom of the bottom and tried to work my way from the bottom to the top of the bottom, and then to the bottom of the top. So I'm A-list orchestrator, but C-list composer.

Would you walk me through the abbreviated version of orchestrating a film and how you interact with the composer and the team?

Basically the composer will get the job and start by spotting the movie with the director. My suggestion to any aspiring composer is to find yourself a great music editor because they can help you and are also experienced about what to write for a film. You discuss things like "Should I take this approach to this scene, or that approach? What about the dialogue?" Blah, blah, blah.

I generally come in just before the movie is about to score, depending on the composer. If I am asked to orchestrate a film by John Williams, I will start when he starts, which is two or three months out. He'll spot the film, and as he starts to write [he will] pass the sketches on to me.

In the case of *Deathly Hallows*, I started about two months earlier because Alexandre Desplat meets with the director beforehand and has a very creative environment to work in. He starts giving me his sketches, which I send off to a copying office that creates a MIDI mock-up for me, and I start to translate those for the orchestra.

At this point are you working with the picture?

I generally do with Alexandre, as he insists upon it.

Another part of an orchestrator's task is that you have to understand the orchestra and how it first functions in the film world, and therefore the 5.1 Dolby world. You have to know where the trombones are going to conflict with somebody's dialogue; for example, you might say, "Yes, I can look at this and know the effects aren't in, and I know you'd like to have this be a single trumpet, but when they blast through the ceiling and everything starts caving in, we're going to need more body in the orchestra to actually cut through the effects."

Conrad, it seems as though this all comes with years of orchestrating experience?

Yes, I'm a very busy guy! A composer might write for forty or fifty films in his lifetime. If you look at IMDB, it looks like I've done 100 films, but I'm actually on the contract of over 400 films.

How are you involved in the actual recording process?

This is not true with all composers . . . but Alexandre is a very confident guy, has very good ears, is an excellent musician, and he conducts the orchestra. I can suggest things during the recordings, like, "I think the phrasing should go like this," or, "We should remove the slur here to make it more articulate," "The brass weren't together here; yes, they were out of tune," "The clarinet is sharp in the third of the chord," "We need to retake this, split this out, or do it in sections," and so on. It's quite a collaborative process in the recording studio, but that isn't the case for all composers, because some don't necessarily want your input, and others are actually intimidated by your ability to give it.

Conrad, what would you consider the key skills for an orchestrator to be successful long-term?

It's great if you have played in an orchestra; it's great if you can score, read, and have studied conducting or have been a conductor; but the major thing is to have a deep and abiding interest in current and present music. Stay up with everything that's going on, whether its pop or classical.

That's good advice! You mentioned arrangers. What is the difference between an orchestrator and an arranger?

Well, sometimes they are the same, but essentially arranging is more of a composing job. The task for an orchestrator can range from simply taking a piano piece and making it sound good with the orchestra to writing for one. An arranger is someone who takes a tune by someone else and re-imagines it as if *they* were the composer.

In almost every sense, an arranger is essentially a "re-composer," composing from his point of view. It's frankly a very unappreciated art.

That's interesting . . . the other night I saw Chick Corea and Gary Burton at the Lensic here in Santa Fe, and they performed the most beautiful arrangement of "Eleanor Rigby"; I was just blown away by it. I love the idea of "re-imagining" a song. That's a great description.

What would you consider the most challenging part of what you do for a living?

I would say there are two things—the professional and the personal. The most personal one is to always remember that it's *not* about you! [*laughs*] It's about what you can do and contribute.

Professionally, it's adapting to the changing environment of what music does, because music is a river, continually evolving. Don't expect the times to follow *your* lead; you're part of a larger parade.

As soon as those thoughts occur, take a vacation, because otherwise, you'll find yourself on a very *long* vacation that you didn't intend to take.

Is there a project or a time when it was really hard to push it across the finish line?

Sure, I can remember working for a composer on a very tough project because the studio didn't believe in the film. There was a big-time director, and they had spent hundreds of millions of dollars. The composer was not, at that point, as experienced as he now is.

I'd had my cues ready and we'd play it down, and he morphed into a record producer once he heard the cue. I just remember that his team were screamers. I was hired by the studio to work for him and [was] not his regular guy. We would sit in the control room and these people would start screaming at each other, blaming each other, and waste fifteen minutes of recording time trying to find someone to blame for what went wrong.

Then once they had exhausted all of the accusations, and realized that nothing had been solved, panic set in. It wasn't enough for there to be a mistake; someone had to be blamed, someone had to be punished.

I believe there are six stages to any project:

Stage 1—Great enthusiasm
Stage 2—Disillusionment
Stage 3—Panic
Stage 4—Search for the guilty
Stage 5—Punishment of the innocent
Stage 6—Awards for the uninvolved

[*laughs*] When something like this happens, and the composer has these great new ideas, do you find yourself sitting at the table doing rewrites?

Oh yes, it's not the most efficient way of working, because as Lionel Newman used to say, "Write your score *before* you get to the recording stage." And there's another one, "Who's the most expensive copyist in town? A violinist with a pencil!"

I would recommend to any young person that even if they've given you a ga-zillion dollars to record a score, don't waste the musicians' time. If you want to be loved by the musicians, respect them and they will do anything for you. If you are indecisive, unprofessional, not respecting their time, you must be prepared to suffer their wrath or indifference.

Also, I think that as a moral point, it's not good to take a million dollars when you have people starving in Darfur, or being killed there, and waste it gratuitously on 300 takes of "Skippy Goes to School."

Conrad, you have worked on such a large body of work—over 400 films. How long do you schedule for a project?

I never think about scheduling. I just think, "Can I say yes? Can I get it done?" Maybe not the best way to plan, but I've been fortunate so far that it's worked out just fine. Currently I'm doing *Harry Potter*, and when I return home, I'll do some of the orchestration for the next Harold and Kumar picture. One works on all kinds of films.

Would you talk a little bit about how orchestrators get paid and how that works?

It's a per-page rate, but as my father always said, "You do piece work." The union defines a page as four bars, which generally pays between $12 for a few instruments to $50 or $60 if you are getting double scale. As a rule, there will be between 200 and 600 pages in a film. Occasionally it will be as many as 1,400 pages.

Over-scale has been the same now for about ten years at about $80 per page. It doesn't matter if those four bars are filled with potatoes, or himi-simi-dimi-quicks, as one of my British friends would say, which means 32nd notes or 64th notes. It all pays the same.

You hope to have enough films with whole notes to balance out with films that are a bunch of black notes. [*laughs*]

You also have special payments, and every July 1st I get a royalty check that the union oversees for aftermarkets. So those 400 films generate a sizable sum in the long term. Sometimes it's only a nickel for being a proofreader, and my kids will make fun, "Dad, it's only a nickel!" To which I respond, "Any money that comes to me where I didn't have to lift a finger is a wonderful thing!"

Yes, it's a wonderful thing! I got a check a few weeks ago from ASCAP for $10,000 for twenty seconds of my music that was played on Japanese television, and I didn't even remember writing the music. It's amazing . . . I wish I could get those every day. It would be nice!

Well, some guys do! I should also point out that as an orchestrator, we get part of the whole union pie, and as a composer writing thematic stuff, your ASCAP check or BMI check will be far greater than any musician's royalty. Nonetheless, there is a kind of security that builds up over the time, and you can make a very nice living if you manage it properly.

What is the best time you ever had working on a project?

My favorite projects have been *Seabiscuit*, when I worked with Gary Ross, working with Randy Newman, and certainly any of the John Williams films. I feel like I should be paying him because I love his music and it's very note intensive. John writes so many notes!

I was once asked, "How do you do all those notes? How do you keep going?" Because one year John and I did five pictures together—*Star Wars, Harry Potter, Memoirs of a Geisha, Munich,* and *War of the Worlds*. Working for John is like reading a great book because you just want to keep turning the page.

If you are working with great musicians and hear music performed magnificently, those are the most rewarding moments, and believe it or not, they happen more often than not.

Do you have any advice for someone that's young and talented with regard to how they might get started?

I'd first say that you have to be serious about music and orchestration as a career, because if you come to somebody like me, guess what I do for a living? I don't sell shoes! I'm looking for somebody who knows music, who can tell me something I don't know when I talk to them, and somebody that when I ask, "What are you listening to?," they give me a very specific answer. "Beethoven" doesn't quite cut it; I know we all love Beethoven. I look for real passion.

I think you also should know Logic or Digital Performer and be familiar with Pro Tools, be able to help make mock-ups, and be comfortable with all changing technology.

It is very important to perform as well, because when I try to orchestrate something, I don't just try to orchestrate the notes or the colors; I sit there and let everybody, even the tuba, tell a story.

I try to put smiles on musicians' faces. I like to think of myself as a musicians' orchestrator, not just an orchestrator for film. A young person should be passionate about music, know music, and talk like a musician if they expect to get a chance to be hired by one.

Conrad, I believe that most people around you know you are at the top of your game. Some time ago, I met the head of broadcast production for Disney, looking for work, and he said, "Mike, are you good?" And I replied, "Well . . . I guess I'm okay." I was about twenty-eight years old, and he said, "Well, when you feel like you're worth a damn, come back and see me." Like I tell kids, "If you don't believe in yourself, why the hell should anyone else?"

You have to have the courage and self-awareness to say, "Well, I'm pretty good," which is a fair answer, but "pretty good" is just not what these people need. Almost everybody in the film business thinks they are on a sinking ship, and I've never met a director who thought his movie was any good, or at least as good as he'd hoped it would be. They're sitting there, and the support group has gone, the DP has gone, and all they've got is the editor, the composer, and themselves.

You really have to present yourself as somebody that can say with confidence, "We're going to make it through this!" And you have to always present yourself that way. Secretly that's what most people want to hear. It's okay for us to assess ourselves honestly, but remember we are in show business.

14

Part-Time Musician

Rapid Fire

Skill Set—The ability to at least play your instrument well enough that other musicians will want to play with you. You'll need free time to practice and rehearse with your band.

Hours—You make them up, except for the rehearsal schedule.

Upside—Low pressure, maximum fulfillment. You will be able to avoid lots of the typical band issues, and club owners who can, and do, become a pain over time when you perform professionally.

Downside—Not too much.

Financial—$ You don't play part-time to get rich and famous.

Location—Anywhere.

Future—The future is looking good, especially if you play for free.

I DECIDED TO INCLUDE A LITTLE BLURB IN THIS BOOK about part-time performance as a job option because lots of you reading this may already have a non-music industry job and are wondering, "What about me?." Being a part-time musician is not exactly considered a job, but I couldn't help addressing this option for all the musicians who may be juggling multiple jobs in today's economy just to make ends meet.

I'm sure that while reading this book you have noticed a recurring message from several of my contributors: "I really loved playing but knew I wasn't good enough to cut through the noise and make it as a performer." These folks understood early on where they were with their instruments and chose to pursue other careers that would keep them close to music. Being a part-time musician can fill that place in you that longs to play music even if you're not cut out for performing for a living.

Part-time performing can take on many forms, ranging from the once-a-month, one-night stint in a local restaurant playing acoustic guitar to the person who plays several nights a week as a supplement to his or her income stream.

Being a part-time musician also has its own set of benefits as well as challenges. The greatest benefit I see is the control over what music you play and how often you play out. The challenge is finding musicians who fit into the same life space as you at the same time. What I mean is that balance between playing for the joy of playing and playing because you need to make money gigging.

I recently tried to put a little band together that would play a combination of original music and covers of my favorite songs, and so far I'm not having too much luck. I don't need to make money playing, and all the good players I have found do! That creates a rub because I only want to play with accomplished musicians, and by and large, those people are performing for a living.

Working a day job, as it's called, is no excuse for not playing music. If you love music, you'll find a way to slip it into your schedule, like my friend Jeff Matz, who runs a very successful graphic design firm in Orlando, Florida.

Jeff Matz

Lure Design

Jeff, you made the conscious decision some time ago to get a regular job so that your bills would get paid, and pursue music as a sideline. Do you remember how or why you made that decision?

Honestly, I didn't think I had the ability or the level to take it to the professional level. I just never made the effort to pursue music because I didn't see it as a viable option for me.

I didn't really get into a good band until I started college and was working towards my design career. I also didn't play large shows until after I had started my design career. I don't know if it's because I liked design and art more than music; it's just that a music career seemed less realistic.

You run a very successful graphic design firm [Lure Design] and you play music part-time. Can you tell me a little bit about your band and the part you play in it?

I played in a band for seven or eight years after graduating from the Ringling College of Arts and Design. Stewart Grace was the singer-songwriter in the band. He and I worked really well together. When he left town a few years ago, we both just stopped playing. Almost ten years later, Stewart started writing again and sends me material to work on. Now we work on music projects long-distance. We do everything in Logic on our laptops, kind of home-studio style. We're not trying to get shows or try to get signed; we just do this for the fun and magic of making music. The process has even inspired me to write a lot of instrumental material of my own.

How do you juggle your music activities and running a busy design firm, or do you?

I work with some very talented people and I practice on my own in the evenings and weekends. It's just really free time—evenings and weekends. Somehow it all works out; I just make the time.

So how often do you play out these days, or do you play out at all?

I haven't played out in quite a while, and I haven't tried to get a band lined up here. I'm enjoying doing what I'm doing right now. Stewart was such an inspiration for me to work with, and after he moved, I felt like if something happens with another band, it'll happen. I'm not going to put an ad in the paper and try to make it happen, though.

I'm busy as hell with work and just don't have the spare time to put a band together, rehearse, and then find gigs. I have, however, been reaching out to more musicians and trying to find people to help put tracks on some of the songs that I'm recording. I can't say that it's an impossibility that eventually I'll have a band again.

Does what you're doing now, writing, using Logic, etc., fill that space in your heart that loves music?

Absolutely! I'm as much of a listener as I am a player. I actually feel more inspired now than ever. Even though I'm not playing live, I feel like I'm finally writing songs that are actually worth a shit. [*laughs*]

You don't regret not taking the path of being a musician then, right?

No. I really don't. Sure, everyone knows the dream of being in a band that actually makes it, and I'm sure it would be exciting. But I don't regret it at all. I actually enjoy my design career, running our studio and mentoring other designers. It's just another creative process, that's all. Designing, in a way, is very similar to music.

Don't you also design posters and CD covers and things like that?

Yep. More posters than music packaging, but we've been doing posters since '94. That business went wild back around 2004–2005, when we discovered that people really wanted to buy our posters. Now we're designing and screen-printing them ourselves and attending Flatstock in Austin every year, which is a rock poster show and part of South by Southwest [SXSW]. It's a pretty cool thing. Three days of selling your posters during the day and going to shows at night. It's awesome!

15

Music Producer

Rapid Fire

Skill Set—Communication skills are at the top of this list; music producers are simply great with people. Great producers also have the innate ability to understand what the public will like.

Hours—A producer's hours are varied and follow the production process. Producers work when the artist is ready. Most of the greatest recording sessions in history have taken place between 9 p.m. and 3 a.m. (the music hours) so you can work on your own schedule, but during the actual recording you may be drinking lots of Starbucks! (Stay away from the Mountain Dew, it will make you crazy!)

Upside—A record producer has some great highs. You are responsible (if not recognized) for the final recording and what the public will ultimately hear. You are the one that picks the best takes, sometimes the music, and works with the artist until the arrangement is perfect. You are the one that is also responsible for the overall sound. It's a very creative and gratifying place to be, even if nobody gives you credit. You are a direct contributor, just like the artist, and in some cases you're an equal partner.

Downside—Real opportunities to become a producer on the international stage are getting harder to come by. You might spend considerable time finding and producing the right acts to get you where you want to go. The pay will not be good at the outset of this job.

Financial—$$ to $$$$ There are still some producers who command six figures to produce an artist, plus points (a percentage of the sales). You may never be one of them. Like any other area where residual income is available, the more music you produce the more money you will probably make long-term.

Location—You need to be in a big music city! NY, LA, and maybe Nashville or Austin. You need to live where the artists live, where the recording studios are located, and where the music business is conducted.

Future—I am told that producing music is still a very viable career. Given technology and the huge amount of media being produced, I can see why.

FAMOUS PRODUCER/ENGINEER TOM DOWD, who produced one of the greatest songs of all time, "Layla" by Eric Clapton, once said that the producer's job "is to capture all the energy of an artist's performance and get it on the tape." (When there was tape!)

I have a friend, Tim, who is a very successful economist and art gallery owner, and he also yearns to share his ideas about life and love through his music. He decided to become a musician and record an album, but wasn't sure where to start, so he asked me one day to come to the studio and listen to what he was doing. The next day, I volunteered to produce his music. We've have been having a great time together; he is the artist and I am his sounding board.

I also have another friend, Fritz, who loves and lives music even though he makes a living as a headhunter. He plays guitar, sings, and writes great lyrics, but doesn't have the formal background in music to support the arranging and recording side of things. He's found it very frustrating at times figuring out how to put a great drum track together, and how to record his music. Fritz *needs* a producer.

There are literally millions of people like Tim and Fritz who have *no* delusions of grandeur or desire to become famous recording artists, but love music *and* can afford to record it. Opportunities exist to help these artists unleash their talents and get their music recorded.

I have produced many artists and recordings, and I've found producing to be every bit as fulfilling as recording myself. I once produced a record for a Spanish recording artist, Alfonso Sainz, and the project included writing songs for him, and even advising him on how to reach his target market: American females. He would write lyrics and then ask me, "Michael, will an American girl think these are sincere and sexy?" We had a great time as collaborators while I engineered and produced the recordings. I also made a great living that summer.

Besides capturing a performance, the producer's job can also include selecting songs, finding a recording studio, an engineer, and session players, as well as helping to negotiate a distribution deal, if there is one. I consider this to be one of the most interesting jobs in the music business because of the true collaboration between the artist and the producer. A producer is the artist's conduit to the public, motivating them, collaborating in some cases, and generally creating a safe haven for the artist to express themselves and their musical art.

A great producer has a skill set that is a bit different from the skill sets of others in the music industry. In many cases producers are well trained, like David Foster, who is as comfortable directing a rhythm section as conducting an orchestra. Then there are guys like George Martin, who worked quietly in the background and was responsible for the musical arrangements that contributed to the ultimate success of the Beatles' recordings, as well as those of Mariah Carey, Michael Jackson, and many other artists.

So what does it take to become a successful music producer? First, you need to have *ears*! Without great ears you won't have a chance. What I mean here is that you need to know what works musically and sonically and what doesn't work; you need conviction and a solid gut.

You must also have the ability to gently motivate and inch your artist towards his or her best performance without ruffling any feathers along the way. You need to gain the trust of everyone in the control room without alienating anyone, and instinctively know when to keep your mouth shut and just the let the music happen. A great producer has the inherent ability to understand and feel what the public will find infectious and want to hear over and over again. This is the producer's single greatest challenge, gift, and reward.

"Would you guys keep it down a little, please? I'm on the phone."

Russ Titelman is having work done on his spacious Manhattan apartment, and I can hear the piano being tuned in the background. I consider it an honor to talk with Russ, the man responsible for producing much of the music I love. I can only imagine spending a few days in the studio with him; man, what I could have learned. It was apparent to me, from his calm, reassuring demeanor, why he has been so successful. He is genuinely interested and engaged as we talk about the business he loves, and imparts a little wisdom. He is, by the way, the only contributor who spent two hours with me on the phone, dissecting this interview sentence by sentence to make sure it conveyed exactly what he wanted to say. A true producer, a great producer.

Russ Titelman

Russ Titelman is an independent record producer, who has won three Grammy Awards for producing Steve Winwood's "Higher Love" and Eric Clapton's Journeyman *and* Unplugged *albums. He has worked with numerous musicians, ranging from the Monkees and the Bee Gees to Paul Simon and Chaka Khan.*

Russ, you've been a huge influence on shaping today's music as a music producer; you've worked with everyone from Eric Clapton to David Sanborn.
Would you tell me a little bit about the actual job of a record producer?

When I get asked that question by laymen or a civilian, I usually say, "Do you know what a movie director does?" And if they answer positively, I say, "It's exactly the same role as a movie director, only in the music business they call it a producer." It's a different moniker, and different terminology for the same activity. So if you know what a movie director does, and some people don't, which is actually shocking to me really, I then explain.

The producer oversees the entire recording process, and you work with the artist, help choose songs if they're not writers themselves, or select the songs they write themselves if they are writers. Sometimes they've written more than ten or twelve songs, so you help them choose which ones that you feel should be on the record. Then if they don't have a band, you help put one together and suggest orchestrations if you're going to overdub things like horns and strings, or glockenspiel. [*laughs*]

Then you will look at the way to approach each song: full band, or, "This sounds like it would be better just guitar and bass," that kind of thing. I don't get involved with lyrics too much when working with people like James Taylor or Paul Simon or Randy Newman—they know best!

Along the lines of the sound, when you are working with James Taylor or another established artist that has a sound, so to speak, do you ever try to stretch them?

Well, sometimes it's good to stretch, but not too much. There might be some suggestions of direction, like on the new Jerry Douglas record where we threw around the idea of going to New Orleans and have Jerry record with New Orleans musicians because it fit him well as a soulful player. We did just that and it worked out quite well.

There's obviously a huge amount of trust that the artist has to have in you to allow that type of suggestion, right?

Exactly, trust is the main thing that you have to have with an artist. You must set up an atmosphere where there's trust and they can be comfortable with you when they are in their creative space.

What does it feel like when you're working with a well-known artist, like Paul Simon? What is your thought process when you start working on a project?

Well, each artist is different and requires a different skill set and a different approach by a producer. Because of that diversity, you have to adjust working styles, so you have to play give-and-take a bit here and there.

Basically, if you are hired to work with someone, it inherently means that the artist wants to work with you and chose you for a reason. For the most part, if there is agreement about what you're doing, then there's trust and an atmosphere of try anything. Any idea is respected, and sometimes even if it doesn't work, it may lead to another idea.

If you're lucky and you're on the same page, it can be quite easy and it should be great fun. If you listen to the old Louis Armstrong records, those cats were swinging. They were having fun, and they were all at the top of their game.

Speaking of luck, a good friend of mine once told me, "If you work hard enough, you'll get lucky." How does that play out in the studio?

Arif Mardin had a great quote that Barry Gibb [the Bee Gees] told me when I was working with him and they were at an impasse. Barry said, "Well now, what are we going to do?" And Arif replied, "Don't worry—something will happen."

[*laughs*] That's a great quote, but sometimes things don't just sort themselves out! Have you ever found yourself in the middle of a project, saying, "It's really difficult working with this artist," and if so, how did you work your way out of that situation?

Yes, there have been some difficult projects through the years, but you persevere by keeping your eye on the bouncing ball and remembering what you're there for, what the goal is.

Even when it's difficult, both the producer and the artist have the same goal, which is to make the best record you can. You may disagree at some point and get into arguments (which do, in fact, happen) but you know that at some point a certain amount of ego sublimation is required. You have to choose your battles and fight for things that are most important. Sometimes you just need to let other things go and trust the other person because it's collaboration, give-and-take type of thing.

Russ, you've been in the studio most of your adult life; are there any moments that stick out in your mind where you just sat back and thought, "Wow, I'm doing something that's really contributing to making a great song here"?

I can give you one example. I got a call to work with George Harrison [the Beatles] and went over to his house to listen to his demos. He had an instrumental, which at the time was just a guitar part. So we listened to all of the demos and then I went home and listened to them again. That night I called him and said, " I think you should finish 'Your Love Is Forever' because it is just so beautiful. You need to write a lyric for it. Please finish it."

He said, "Okay." So he did and it's on the record that I produced with him, which is called *George Harrison*. It's a beautiful song. So in that case, I felt really good about my contribution in pushing him to finish the song.

That's a great illustration. How important are those kind of relationships in the music community?

They are extremely important, because relationships are everything, and the music business, as most businesses, is all about people—even though they live online now on Facebook. [*laughs*]

It's a different way of doing things, so you have to adjust. I don't know if I've completely adjusted, but it's interesting. New artists really have to know how to use the new technology to get noticed. That isn't always easy because there are people who are better at it than others. There are great artists who won't get noticed, but the ones who are really sharp and know how to use the medium will do quite well.

Russ, who is somebody that you haven't worked with yet that you would like to produce?

Yeah, I'd love to work with Paul McCartney or Stevie Wonder, if I could stand the hours! There are a lot of people I admire and haven't worked with that would be kind of thrilling. Diane Reeves—the great jazz singer. I don't know . . . Sting, Aretha Franklin, Lady Gaga, Mumford and Sons; they are all so great! [*laughs*]

In your experience, how much do you need to know about music to be a successful producer?

Well, there are many producers that are extremely well trained and very knowledgeable arrangers and composers in their own right. Other producers came from engineering, and still others just have a good sense about music. It's kind of like Sam Goldwyn, who didn't really know anything about movies, but he did know what a good story was. He had a passion for it and loved it. There are music producers like Sam too that have a good idea about the big picture and have enough knowledge to reference things, make suggestions, and put them in a context that musicians can understand.

How do you, as a producer, make a living?

Well, typically you get an advance when you start the project, and then you get paid at the end when you finish.

When you say, "advance," is that based on an agreed-upon fee?

Yes, you make a deal and you say, "Producer gets $X" for making the record, and you also get royalties if it sells, so you can do quite well in many cases.

You make it sound simple enough. [*laughs*] In today's world and economy, do you think that there's still a place for a career as a music producer?

It's getting increasingly difficult to make money as a producer because music doesn't sell as much as it used to. CDs don't sell, and downloads are single songs, but there is an area where CDs are still strong, which is the adult market. I am currently the A & R guy at Decca Records. You know they have Andrea Bocelli, the Canadian Tenors, Renée Fleming (I'm producing her new album), the Leon Russell–Elton John record, and Sting. The adult market is Decca's focus. Alison Krauss is another artist that fits that picture and is doing very well.

The James Taylor–Carol King tour did phenomenally well. There are still people who can sell CDs. It's just different in that it seems like the younger audience no longer has the same kind of devotion and loyalty to an artist. In the '60s, '70s, and '80s, people would be dying to know,

"What's the next Dylan or Beatles or Sting record going to be like? When is it coming out?" You were dying to hear what they were doing.

It's also taking different shape. The Mumford and Sons guys, who I think are great, have an incredible online presence. Their live show is important, and lots of fans go to see them. You go to look online for a song and someone says, "Oh, go check out Katy Perry," and there will be like 74 million hits on one of her songs, or 34 million for the next one [*laughs*]. And then there's Spotify, a site for streaming music . . . that's where the money is probably going to come from in the future.

I know there are no shortcuts to becoming a music producer, but do you have any advice for somebody who wants to get started with the goal of becoming one?

Go out and listen to lots of bands! Find a brilliant act and start working with them, grow with them, promote them, and find success with them.

SEVERAL YEARS AGO, I SAT IN FRONT OF THE TV and accurately predicted that a young lady auditioning for *American Idol* would win. I'm sure I wasn't the only one, because Carrie Underwood is just an incredible singer. Now converting that talent to a recording that will not only be commercially successful but artistically relevant is no easy task. That's where a guy like Mark Bright comes into the picture. I would describe Mark Bright as a soft-spoken down-home guy with a slight edge. The edge comes from his internal drive to make the best music possible.

Mark Bright

Mark Bright formerly served as vice president of EMI Music Publishing. His current clients include Carrie Underwood, Rascal Flatts, Reba McEntire, Sara Evans, Danny Gokey, and Scotty McCreery, among many others.

What makes a great music producer?

A record producer needs to be a conduit for the artist. The most successful producer I have seen fill that role, starting from early in my life, and one of my idols, was George Martin.

As a kid, my sister would bring Beatles records home. When she went out with friends, I would sneak into her room and listen to "Hey Jude" and "Revolution" over and over. I would see George Martin's name and think, "I want to be that guy." What does he do? I found some articles, and when reading about him, I figured out that he was tuned into everything that the Beatles were about. He understood their music and what they wanted to convey artistically. He really got into their heads, and those records weren't about George Martin, they were about the Beatles. That's what I was able to ascertain early on. That's the most important thing.

You've produced some incredible music with, among others, Carrie Underwood and Rascal Flatts. What's your day like?

You mentioned those two acts, and while both of those artists are superstars, every day is different. If you're fortunate enough to work at a high level, you will be tracking or doing a track build on a daily basis while working on a project. If we're not tracking, we'll be writing songs or listening to songs people wrote that we might want to use. It's all about the song!

How involved do you get in the creative process? Are you involved in arrangements, lyric tweaking . . . that kind of stuff?

That's basically what I do—arrangements. When a songwriter writes the song, I'm going to listen very carefully to it, and sometimes I'll hear an arrangement as a stream of consciousness. I grew up listening to a lot more music than watching television, so my life has always been about listening to music. The arrangement is what I do, where instruments should play and where they shouldn't.

What challenges are there to working with superstar musicians?

There's not a whole lot of downside working with superstar artists [*laughs*]. They don't become superstars if they don't have a good sense of their artistry and musicality. The one big challenge is availability. Unfortunately, superstars are pulled in so many different directions, with photo shoots, magazine shoots, all these print opportunities, movies they have to make.

Superstars have to fit recording into an already tight schedule; not only are they working on an album but soundtrack recordings, and commercial recordings that are pulling the artist off the central task of making music. I always get enough time, but I always want more. With new artists, you get all the time in the world. With superstars, you will always want more time than you get. That's just how the business works!

Has living in a musical community like Nashville helped you grow personally? Professionally? Musically?

Nashville is a great place for music. For me, it's the elixir that pulses through my veins, the whole thing. You can find any style of music here. Clearly we do country music, but we also do alternative music, Christian music, and mainstream pop music . . . all day long! It goes on and on and on [*laughs*].

Would you tell me about the financial side of being a producer?

If you had asked me that question five years ago, I'd say album advances and royalty fees.

Now, except for superstar artists, producers are also being asked to help put the road show together because maybe the bandleader needs help. Some producers know how to put sets together at a high level, one-off shows, shows that require orchestras. For this type of extended service, you are paid like a production company. These opportunities are not available to everyone and will typically only exist, or be extended to you, if you are at a certain level as a producer.

If you were to pick one song, or one artist, that defines your experience as a producer, what would it be?

That's impossible! I have several artists where we lived a special moment in time, a musical moment. Everyone in the room heard it, felt it, it was a spiritual thing—and then you hear it back on the radio and it's a big hit! You hear it years later and the magic is still there. You never forget it. I've had four or five of those, dating way back to Black Hawk, several with Rascal Flatts, Carrie Underwood, a couple with Sara Evans, and a couple with Reba McEntire. I've been really, really lucky to be in the room with some exceptional artists throughout my career.

I'd say so! Do you think a career as a record producer is still attainable in today's market and music industry?

I think it's the new frontier for music industry and I love it. We're just weeding out all the wimps! [*laughs*] The people that remain in the industry are the ones that really love it.

You know, Michael, when I started out, I never thought that I'd make a nickel. [*laughs*] Hopefully people continue to want to make records because they "have" to, because it's in their DNA. Hopefully it has nothing to do with money. You hear an artist and you have the ability to come alongside that artist and improve on that artistic vision. If you feel like you're that person, that's what it's all about. If you're that girl or that guy that can come in and do that for an artist, then do it. If you want to become well known and just make lots of money—you need to stay home and stay away! [*laughs*]

Mark, you have an insight that few others possess when it comes to the state of the current music business and where we are headed. On a personal, professional, or industry level, what does the future look like to you?

Music has never been more relevant. When an artist makes a hit, people want to hear it and that's what I know! That motivates me!

How we monetize this new frontier is a big question, but that will get figured out someday, I'm sure. We are getting to the point where we just have to be smarter about how we get music to people—the way that they want to hear it. The same way we dish out cable programming the way people want to see it, or the way they want to run their smartphone.

Obviously, it's the way Steve Jobs gives people Apple products. That mentality works for millions of Americans. We tend to overthink things that we can't protect. When we overthink them, we wind up in the ugly quagmire that we're currently facing. If we can give a consumer the delivery that they want without overthinking it, we will all win. Maybe we should have a week where all music stops and nobody can play it on *any* device. Then we'll give it back to them for a nominal fee.

That way we can pay the composers and the artists what they need for their work. It'll come to something like that. People will always want to hear something great.

Is there anything that you haven't accomplished in your career that you've always wanted to do?

I've gotten to do what I love, from the day I moved to Nashville.

An incredible day would be to wake up and have the next breakout song. I want to have signed the next Rascal Flatts, the next Carrie Underwood. . . . I've never felt more competitive in my life! I feel like I'm that twenty-two-year-old kid again [*laughs*].

Lots of industry people say it's gloom and doom, but not to me! There is opportunity everywhere!

AT THIS STAGE IN MY LIFE, THE GIVING-BACK STAGE, I find myself often thinking about how lucky I've been and how I might share something of value with the rest of humankind. You know what I mean, right? We all pay lip service to getting out there in the world and helping others, but the fact is that 99.9 percent of us are just trying to keep our head above water, or are inexplicably engaged in some useless activity. Just this morning when I was taking a shower, I was thinking about joining a mission and getting involved with children so that I might in some small way contribute to the betterment of their lives.

Then I got out of the shower, came downstairs, had a cup of coffee, and off I go . . . to Lowe's, to the mall, not thinking about those children again until the next time I feel like I should be doing something of value.

You see, there are many people who think about doing something good, but are caught up in living, and then there are people like Eric Gast. Eric has found a way to expand his roots in the music industry as a notable producer to helping other musicians and children around the world. It was a privilege to speak with him, and I hope he'll let me join him on one of his trips so that I too can become fully engaged in our world.

Eric Gast

Eric Gast is a producer, mixer, and audio engineer. At Zomba Music Group,
his clients included, among others, Will Smith, Britney Spears,
Billy Ocean, and Kid Rock.

Eric, in your opinion, what are the most important skills of a great music producer?

There are several skills, and the one that's played a big role in my life is psychology. There is an intimacy that you are sharing with an artist, and it's very important that you set the right tone from the very beginning. As you know, the bigger the artists, the more you have to be careful with their ego.

Your goal as a music producer is to be the one that can bring the most out of the artist. You also understand that you aren't there to make your own record, but to make the artist's record, the best one they can make.

Then there are the obvious skills of production and knowing where arrangements will lie. If it's pop, what pop sensibilities work well but don't compromise the integrity of the artist that you are working with? You're there to enhance, not outright change.

Did you grow up a musician?

I've played several instruments growing up but didn't spend time with any of them. I literally wanted to produce music my entire life. I love shaping sound and arrangements . . . reggae, rock, and classical . . . everything. Playing and performing was never a road I wanted to go down, because I like control and being able to move styles around a bit.

You've worked with some exceptional artists, including Kid Rock, Will Smith, Billy Ocean, and a host of others. Could you talk a bit about working with celebrity artists? What's it like?

I have been lucky. I've had a good time and resonated with all of them. I think that I'm very good at feeling somebody out for what he or she needs from me at that moment. That's underplayed, but you can't just come in and throw your weight around, saying, "I've done this and that and it is going to go this way," because it just ruins the tone right off. Every project is a new horizon, and you are being invited into their world. It's their music, and they have to live with it for the rest of their life. It has to be the way they want it to be.

What are some of the challenges of working with well-known artists?

First of all, successful artists tend to lock into what has worked for them in the past, but obviously they should be growing. With that said, they are always conscious of their brand. I come in and need to establish a reason for being there without compromising my integrity and help define what "growing" might look like. That can be difficult at times.

Why do artists pick you to produce them?

You know, it's always different and sometimes it's just the strangest thing. You can get a rock artist who will tell you, "Part of why I want to work with you on this album is because of what you did on this other project," or, "I love what you did with the low end on that record."

For most artists, they just want something new; they want to stay current and they want things to change. What they don't want is to be making the same record every time. Even if their last record was a brilliant record, they still want growth.

Was any of this attributed to geography? The fact that you are in New York and there is a circle of people that you work with that all help each other?

I definitely think geography makes a big difference. You can't be a coal miner working in New York and vice versa.

Let's say you come up from the assistant level, because everybody starts as low man on the totem pole. Well, if that city happens to be New York, you are working with people of a higher caliber than some other places, so you are learning from the best engineers and the best producers.

Once you fall into the loop and prove yourself, someone will say, "This guy rocks, it's time for him to fly on his own. I'm going to give him a project." In a large recording town like NY or LA, there are places for you to grow and be successful.

Do you have a favorite project?

There were ones that weren't as successful that I thought were just brilliant. One that comes to mind is the band Enuff Z'nuff. I love the Beatles, and this band was so on point with that Beatle vibe, but unfortunately they fell victim to timing.

They released their record when Poison and all the glam bands came out and Atlantic wanted them to wear lipstick and spandex. Literally their writing was brilliant and their sensibilities for chord structure . . . everything was dead on. I was sitting there saying, "These guys are phenomenal," but it always comes down to marketing. You can make the best record in the world, but if nobody hears it, how successful can it be? It's like the tree in the forest thing—nobody hears it!

I was an engineer myself for maybe twenty years, and at one point I was working with Disney, and thought, "Disney needs great sound effects for all these animations they do . . . ,' so I created this CD called The Big Whoosh. It took another sound

designer, Dave Gross, and myself about a year to create, and it got rave reviews in Radio World as the "best sound effects disc ever"—I didn't have any idea how to market it, so I had 5,000 of those CDs sitting in my basement for five years.

How does the revenue stream work in your business?

Typically a producer gets a fee up front and included you in a point system as well. After a record recoups the money that's been spent on production, you'll get a percentage of the proceeds. If you have two points worth roughly eight cents per piece, that's sixteen cents every time a record sells, and it can add up pretty quick.

The way the industry has changed with the Internet, we really try to push to get that upfront fee as high as possible. A record that could have sold a million copies before will be a hit at 300,000 on the Internet. And stealing music is not helping anybody, even the consumer.

Is the idea of a mechanical royalty being attached to a CD disappearing because there's no way to attach it to a download?

Now that people are buying single songs, they don't care about CDs anymore. One thing that's fairly lucrative is soundtracks and movies because they are still locked into those mechanical payments. Now you have to be more vigilant and say, "Look, I need to get this much up front in order to cover my time." The funny thing is that I get checks from publishing companies that are sometimes less than the cost of the stamp. [*laughs*]

I've seen those checks too. It's almost like it's not even worth the walk to the mailbox. [*laughs*] You told me that you just came back from Thailand and Burma. Would you talk about FM World Charities, where the idea came from, and why it's relevant?

The Idea for FM Charities spawned from some film mixing I was doing in Prague. About six years ago, a lot of the film music was being outsourced to Eastern Europe because of the film permits and stuff like that, so they were flying people in from LA, New York, Nashville to mix.

I met some artists that were phenomenal and I thought that the only thing they are missing is upscale production. It's not that the rest of the world doesn't know how to make commercially competitive music; it's just that they are falling off in the area of pop music production.

So I opened a record company in Budapest and wanted to make sure I gave back. At that point, we were doing concerts and giving money to the homeless and the underprivileged, which was mostly the Gypsy population.

I also went into the Czech Republic and Romania, but when those countries joined the Union, they clamped down on Westerners doing charity work that wasn't medical, so I then decided to make my primary healthcare doctor the medical director for my charity, and it became a medical endeavor at that point.

Next, we began to implement ways to include medicine in what we were already doing. In North America and Europe, we went on huge music tours, but also did skin cancer screenings. That's what FM is; it's stands for "From Music." All the money that we generate for healthcare comes from our concerts and music media. We play to our skill set, but try to use it to make a difference in the world.

Do you think that a full-time music producer is still a career option today?

Yes, it's definitely a career option, although you need to be savvy and smart about it. Try to find new bands, and bring them from where they are to somewhere large, where they need to be. It can be very lucrative. It comes down to being smarter about the deals that you make. We didn't have to be quite as smart back in the day. [*laughs*]

Scott Mathews

Scott Mathews is a music producer who has had several Top 10 records and has sold millions for recording artists in all fields, from Barbra Streisand to Robert Cray to Santana.

Because this book is for people looking at a music industry job, is there an opportunity for someone to make a living as a producer today?

Of course, and in some ways more opportunity than ever before! But I think before you look at the money, you need to be honest with yourself. You *have* to love this particular part of business and ask yourself, "Is this my ultimate calling that I am will to sacrifice everything to achieve?" If the answer is unequivocally "yes," then you have a chance to make a go at it and perhaps earn a satisfying career as a music producer.

As a producer, do you work with artists on things like arrangements?

I do. Each and every project is different, so it depends on what a specific artist needs. In my case, I've pretty much worn every hat in the creative process that you're going to run into. Some artists clearly come in with very raw material that we work on together, and others come in with their music so together that they don't really need a hands-on producer; you can be more a fly on the wall. It's very important to make that distinction early on and to know that great production can sometimes be staying out of the artist's way.

I've been a major label artist myself, written songs, and my song catalog has gone to a lot of wonderful artists, so I understand their world. I've played and arranged and sung, and so from all points of view, I think I've been on the other side of the glass, if you will. It gives me an extra-added advantage to be able to convey and relate to an artist having been there myself. I really feel if I'm hired as a producer that arrangements and the song crafting are included in the job description, and the producer should pitch in anywhere if they can.

Some of what I've learned from the great producers that I've worked with coming up is, they're all willing to pitch in and make whatever is needed happen. And with no coming back later, saying, "Hey, I changed that lyric 'if' to a 'but'—I want 20 percent of the publishing or you can't use my 'but'."

How do you find new projects—or do artists and record companies come to you these days?

Yeah, well, it's a two-way street. While I am always on the lookout for incredible talent, the fact is 90 percent of the time, artists seek me out for the most part. I receive most of my submissions for production consideration via e-mail from the artists, management, labels, or entertainment business lawyers.

When I choose to work with an artist, it's based upon a variety of criteria. It's easy to say you're blown away by an artist's music, and based on that alone you'd be willing to do a project, but at this stage in my career that's not really true. I need to know the artist well enough to sense there is drive, ambition, smarts, humor . . . it all counts and is weighed out in the final analysis.

We have a small A & R department here, and we have weekly meetings when we review potential projects. The best always rises to the top, and I get a chance to reach out to an artist early on. I really try to pick my projects carefully because my reputation is riding on every release, and (on a more personal level) I develop long working relationships and friendships.

You also know the success of any artist-producer situation is based on trust and that often they're sharing their songs with you for the first time—nobody else has ever heard them—so your reaction means the world to them. The music is the easy part; I've already heard it and go, "Yeah, I really feel that." So I choose people that I believe I will have a great time working with, because I have learned those are the projects that always seem to turn out better than any of us thought they ever could. I really do love what I do, and I think that adds to the longevity factor.

You have a great recording studio, Scott, and I'm sure that aids in your continued zeal for producing records. Does having your own studio facility help you, either through productivity or the ability to advertise your gear and setup?

Yes, it's a huge factor. I confess, I'm spoiled and do own a dream studio, but it really helps my business because it inspires everyone that works here—myself included. What I've done is built a studio that I want to go to every day, because just by being here it lifts my spirits. This is my final stop after building four other studios. [*laughs*]

We wanted to bring that perfect vibe and feel to every production room, which if done wrong, can be like a cold hospital room [*laugh*]. So when we have our pre-production sessions, or writing sessions, or whatever phase of the project we are in, we feel like we're just hanging out in a very cool house on the edge of the San Francisco Bay—because that is exactly what we are doing!

What is the hardest part about being a music producer?

The most challenging part of being a producer is that you want to see your artists go out and make a great life for themselves based partly on the fruits of our labor in the recording studio, and that can be a challenge. I want to make sure that each project is provided the opportunity to be heard above the noise these days, and there is a whole lotta noise! I think it's fair to say that in the overall area of monetizing music today, it's very challenging as a music producer to be able to see how that's going to work out both for your artists and yourself in the short and long term.

When I am not in the studio working on a project, you will likely find me working on new business models and approaches that can help throw the music industry an economic lifeline. I spend a lot of my time in the Silicon Valley and have a separate building here at TikiTown strictly for work in the music/tech space. I am equally inspired to find solutions to artists' business needs as I am to make the music itself. Let's face it, I have enjoyed a wonderful career doing what I love, so it's only natural that I want to help pitch in to help get us out of this current hole we are all in. Either that or just join the bitter crowd that can only say how great it used to be . . . that would be tantamount to me bitching that there is no great new music today—it's my job to make sure that statement is untrue.

What about compensation? How is that working these days?

There's a fee to engage me as a producer, and then there's a royalty rate that goes along with that—the more an artist sells of my work, the more I enjoy the payday. These days, with the shrinking of sales, any and all other uses of the songs are being looked at as much (or more) as a major form of monetary compensation. These areas include film, TV, commercials . . . you name it. I have artists that make mighty incomes from simply licensing their masters for multiple usages. Many are recording artists who prefer not to perform live, so a large amount of potential income is left on the table—but they have made it work by working hard in other areas.

Unfortunately, some producers ask for the moon, but in my negotiations I always give artists deals that are very fair and all-in (that is to say you have me for whatever I can possibly do, which is a list of 1,001 things, so we have it in the contract) and our facility is included. I have a great staff, and everything on the creative end is provided. The way I work is great for those who say, "I have $X in my budget, and this is all I can spend." There is an art to budgeting, and I am thrilled to work on lesser budget projects if I know we can deliver productions that do not compromise on any part of the end result quality.

It's still the producers on the creative side and labels on the business side. I remember when I had a record deal and they were going to talk to the label to negotiate some tour or something. They said, "The meeting is tomorrow at 1 p.m.," and I said, "Okay, I'll be there," and they said, "Why would you be there? You're the artist!" It was very funny; I learned a lot from that single statement.

Exactly, and what a wonderful thing to be able to look back on as opposed to looking forward to! You're right, Michael, there are still a lot of artists that don't really see the big picture, so it's better to just keep them focused on what they do best and put the energy there. But I will tell you as a stone-cold fact, by and large, artists today *have* to be well rounded and understand the business they are in, as well as the music they make—otherwise, it's curtains. The competition is beyond fierce, and the smart artist that makes opportunities happen is going to trump the poor tortured genius who has no time for business.

Scott, what advice would you give somebody who reads this and thinks, "I've always wanted to be a producer. I think I could be really good at it. I am going to dedicate myself to this!" How do they get started?

I think one of the best ways for a producer is to go out and find talent in their local area that might want to go in and record. Go see shows, scour the local scene, and meet bands and develop a little back-and-forth. If you're able to convince them that it'd be worthwhile to go in the studio with you, all of the sudden you'll have an artist. The only way you're going to do that is to go out and ask people if they'll work with you for free with whatever primitive gear you've got or can make available to you.

It's also a great time to make deals with studios because they're not too booked up. So if you can, go out and do a spec deal with a studio, or with your own gear, or even if you have a friend who has a studio and can help you out. Do whatever you need to do to get yourself started!

If you have the opportunity to be around someone you really respect for any length of time, I believe you will pull a lot from his or her experience. There are many trade secrets to be had. It's like looking back on the days when Abbey Road Studios used to just spawn great producers. They all started as tea boys! Barely an intern, you're just a runner, a tea boy that jumps into action when water needs boiling. Not exactly glamorous, but you will be absorbing the real-life experience, not just dreaming about it, or even reading about it. You're finding your way *live*. Then one day the first engineer won't make it to work, and they'll say, "Hey, man, you're the guy today—go!"

Tell me, Scott, what's your take on where the music industry is headed?

Every artist should be giving away their music to gain the trust and develop relationships with what was once called a fan, which is now called a friend. It's much more about being able to relate to, and with, your fan base, and letting them in. I honestly feel strongly that this is a future we can all take part in. The old "first one's free" deal!

16

Music Publishing

Rapid Fire

Skill Set—Solid music-business relationships; a business education is helpful for contracts. You should be social and like people because you are always networking.

Hours—Most publishing companies I know work a regular 9 to 5. Depending on your position in publishing, you could be traveling or attending recording sessions, so your working hours may be all over the board.

Upside—Successful publishers do very well financially. Another benefit of this job is working directly with artists, and in many cases having a direct creative influence on the final music.

Downside—I'm not too sure about the downside at the present time, but I can tell you that the publishing business is in flux. There are a lot of publishers out there pitching for the same music placement business, which makes it difficult for the smaller publishers to get the meetings and get their music placed, especially the ones who are not located in the major markets.

Financial—$$ to $$$$ As mentioned previously, you can make great money in publishing, but it depends on where and how you work. If you work for a boutique publisher that is hot or has a notable artist, you could do very well. If you work for one of the corporate publishers like EMI, Universal, or Warner, you will be paid as an employee.

Location—NY, LA, and Nashville are the best places in the USA to locate, depending on the type of publisher you are. If you work for one of the majors, you can also work oversees.

Future—Publishing is still a growing market. I suspect it is due to all of the new electronic media being created that needs licensed music.

THERE ARE MANY JOBS IN MUSIC PUBLISHING and stories of both success and failure. If you have connections in the industry, love music, love people, and love the art of a deal, then publishing may be a good place to hang your hat. I'm going to go into some detail about publishing (not print publishing, which will be in vol. 2) because of its importance to the music industry and the future of the music business in general.

So check this out: Say you put a cool little band together called the Lame Ducks, and Jacob, the guitar player, writes some cool songs. You record them, and they start selling like crazy on iTunes and you make $1,000,000. The band splits up the money and you buy a little condo with your share. Jacob starts messing around with the drummer's girlfriend and the band breaks up. Five years later, you see Jacob driving a Ferrari while you're still struggling along and living in your little condo. What happened?

Well, Jacob, who wrote the songs, owns the copyright, and most likely the publishing, so if the songs are ever re-recorded by someone, played on the radio, licensed for a film or advertisement, Jacob gets the money—*not you*. It doesn't matter that you were in the same band and you created the best part of the song. Jacob owns it, end of story.

The moral of this story is: make sure you share as much of the ownership of the music you participate in creating as possible.

THIS IS A TRUE STORY. I have a friend, Larry, whom you would probably know; he sings and plays guitar. Several years ago, his band recorded a song that became a rock anthem of monstrous proportions that I am *sure* you have heard many times. Larry sang the song and played one of the most outstanding three-part harmony guitar solos in the history of pop music. My guitar-playing friends spent hours figuring out what he had done, in part because that song became a number-one hit and we played it in our cover bands.

Today, however, Larry is very bitter about his band, the song he sang, and one particular guy in the band. Larry now plays corporate business events for a living, mostly as a soloist, and struggles along. He plays that same hit song, lives in a very modest home, and is not a happy camper.

In contrast, the guy who wrote the song is a successful millionaire primarily because of that single song. Larry was the voice and guitar behind the song, but the other guy wrote it and owns the publishing. Larry hates this guy, and that's putting it lightly. Larry was not a savvy musician early in his career; his fellow band member was.

For some reason, I understood very early on that the guys in the band who made all the money were the ones who wrote the songs. When I recorded my record, I wrote the lion's share of the songs and another very talented songwriter, Lloyd Landesman (whom I interviewed for this book), wrote several songs. If our band had been successful and our songs hits, Lloyd and I would have made a bunch of money, while the rest of the band would only have received income from the physical record sales and touring, and as we all know, such income is declining.

It's a moot point because our band broke up and none of our songs were hits, but what's important to note and understand is that the real money in the music business is in the publishing. Publishing is the single reason that big record companies will be around for a long time. They own the publishing rights for most of the music from the '40s, '50s, '60s, '70s, '80s, etc. You get the point, right? Every time someone wants to use any of this music for a commercial enterprise, they pay the record companies for that privilege.

A few times a year, I walk out to my mailbox here in Santa Fe, New Mexico, to pull out the mail, and hidden among the bills, *Time* magazine, and *The Week* is a check. Sometimes it's from BMI, and other times from a publisher for whom I once wrote music. Mailbox money, there's nothing like it! What's funny is that I haven't written music for commercial use in a very long time, so when I get a check for $10,000-plus, it really makes my day.

Publishers make the deals with anyone who wants to use your music commercially. In other words, it is the publisher who negotiates on your behalf with the film companies, advertising agencies, doll manufacturers, and anybody else who would like to exploit your music for profit. Publishers are in the business of representing catalogs of works (songs) for commercial use. "Commercial use," for our purposes, is defined as any commercial venture that requires music.

There are also many jobs associated with music publishing that include the traditional business—jobs like accounting (a big one), technology (running a website, for example), sales, marketing, etc. What is unique to music publishing is the licensing side of the music business, which includes usage negotiation, placements, contracts, production, and other jobs. I know this may not sound interesting to you as a musician, but as you read on you may change your mind.

The music publishing industry is one of the few segments of the music industry that is growing and will continue to grow for the foreseeable future. The reason for this growth is the tremendous amount of media being created for every conceivable distribution channel, including TV, cable, Internet, museums, advertising, film. . . the list goes on and on. All electronic media uses music that has been published, and they need to pay for the license to use it.

To get an inside look at the publishing business, I talked with a few informed professionals who are experts in different aspects of the music publishing business, like David Simoné, who ran many large record labels and then moved into publishing. So why, after so many years of success in the music business, does he stay in it instead of sailing off into the sunset on his yacht?

David Simoné

PARTNER, PRIMARY WAVE MUSIC PUBLISHING

David Simoné was formerly president of Arista, Mercury, and MCA Records in the UK before moving to the US, where he was the president of UNI Records and PolyGram Music Publishing, and EVP of Geffen Records. Simoné has worked with numerous artists and songwriters, including Elton John, Jon Bon Jovi, Desmond Child, and Bono.

David, you've had a very successful career as the president of Mercury, Arista, and MCA in the UK and head of PolyGram and Geffen here in the states. What made you decide to make the move into publishing?

Publishing is a very interesting side of the record business. It's sort of the secret part of the music business, because it's not as glamorous as working in a record company. Basically, I was offered the job of president of a major publishing company in America, PolyGram, and didn't know too much about publishing. I soon learned it is a phenomenal business where all the music comes from. Without the songs there is no music business, and once you own a song nobody can use that song without your permission.

The real commercial potential of music publishing is in owning the rights to songs so that every time someone wants to use them in a movie, television commercial, or anywhere else, they have to come to you, the music publisher. For example, I was able to publish part of the Ellie Greenwich–Jeff Barry catalog. They wrote songs like "River Deep Mountain High," "Crying in the Chapel," "And Then He Kissed Me," "Be My Baby," "Da Doo Run Run," and a host of phenomenal pop songs in the '60s. Many of them were written with Phil Spector, and there I was in 1996, paying a lot of money to acquire the rights to those songs. They said to me, "When we wrote those songs, we thought they would hopefully become hits and then disappear again; instead they have become part of the fabric of our lives."

I love the art of the song, even though I'm not a musician.

Can you talk about the relationship you have with an artist?

With a songwriter it's more collaborative between the writer and publisher. He needs to get his song placed; they need to be pitched, and be put with artists and other songwriters. But if you are the publisher for U2, 90 percent of their songs are written for their record, so you don't need that day-to-day relationship.

A lot of songwriters are failed artists. They wanted to be rock stars, but instead became some of the most important songwriters of our time. For many years, I worked with Desmond Child, who had a couple of Top 40 hits but just never came through as an artist. He decided to concentrate on just writing songs, and the first one he wrote with Kiss became a huge hit. He has had seventy-four *Billboard* hits, most recently "Waking Up in Vegas" for Katy Perry, "Living la Vida Loca" (Ricky Martin), "Dude Looks Like a Lady" (Aerosmith), etc. He didn't make it as an artist, but he sure has made it as one of the world's greatest songwriters.

Could you explain what the role of a music publisher is?

It depends on what sort of music publisher you are—small, indie, or major. The major's role is often logistical. Getting songs registered, copyrighted, splits agreed, collecting the money if the song is successful, and retaining as much of that money as possible.

If you're a small publisher, you're much more involved in the day-to-day. If you're a medium publisher, you have a little of that, but you're starting to get overwhelmed by volume. As a major publisher, you're only fielding incoming calls. If you own over 2 million copyrights, it's all you can do. You can no longer focus on individual writers.

Then there's the creative side of working with the songwriter, marketing, or plugging the songs to get artists to record [cover] the songs.

What's been the biggest change in the publishing business of late?

I believe it relates to the collapse of record sales. Your upside is more limited today, especially with newer writers. For example, when Desmond Child wrote "Living la Vida Loca," which was a huge hit, you'd get paid a mechanical rate of maybe 9 cents a song, but you'd sell 22 million albums. They say publishing is a penny business, but with those sales that adds up to an awful lot of pennies. [*laughs*]

Your company is not a traditional publishing company, right? Tell me about it.

That is correct. In a traditional publishing company, there will be song pluggers who match the songwriter to the record maker. Primary Wave is essentially a company that has acquired the rights to iconic legendary artists, such as Steven Tyler, Maurice White, and Kurt Cobain. We have about thirty people who go out to develop opportunities for their music. We also have a branding company, an online digital company, film and TV supervisors, and people who pitch to advertisers, to video games. We use all of these resources to attract these iconic artists to join with us. We show them what we've done as a very young company that our competitors do not.

With the decrease in record sales, has technology opened up new revenue streams for publishers?

In 1996, I was not a technology guy. One day my son said to me, "I can get every song I want on the Internet for free," and I was shocked. At Geffen we would have weekly vice president lunches, and one day I brought up what my son had told me. I didn't really understand it, nor did many people in the room, some of which even refused to have computers on their desks!

When it came to controlling illegal downloading, it was already too late. Today music publishers are adopting new technologies and looking for new ideas, new concepts, and new things, from toys to sneakers. However, one of those will never replace a record that sells 22 million copies!

As with any job in the music industry, the better you are and the more connections you have, the more money you will make. What key skills separate a great publisher from the rest of the pack?

It is the love of music; it has to be in your heart, in your DNA. It can't be taught and you have to believe in the song. You also must be brave enough to talk to the writer if you think the song's not quite there. It can be scary directing a writer, particularly if you're not one yourself. You need to establish the writer's confidence in you and confidence in yourself to say what needs to be said.

I worked with someone when we had Paul McCartney signed, and the president of that label thought he'd become great friends with Paul. He had a new album that was about to come out, and the president was invited to present the artwork to Paul at his house in Scotland.

Before he left for Scotland, his A & R guy said, "I don't think there's a real hit on Paul's record and I'd like him to record two new songs that I think could be hits." The president said, "Sure." He had a fabulous day and that evening sat down with Paul and said, "I want to talk to you about the record. I think you need to add some songs to ensure we have a hit." Paul turned from his best friend to a man of ice. He said slowly and very clearly, "When you've been a Beatle, then I'll like your advice, but since that is not the case, I'd like you to gather up your things and leave my house." That was the end of a beautiful friendship.

To be a good publisher, you need to be able to talk with confidence to your writer and encourage them. Not an easy task.

One thing I think we can all agree on is that this business is always changing. If you were to start out today, knowing what you've learned, how would you approach things differently?

It's a tough business to break into. A great way to start is by beginning as an intern and working as an intern as much as possible. Instead of treating internships as boring, slave labor, etc., use your time there to make a great impression. It's still about your passion for music.

In America, going to music schools is a big plus. Both the people who work with me went to music schools. It's also a business of networks, and that's difficult when you're a young person without contacts. You have to do research, work at it, show initiative, and approach people the right way.

I recently received an e-mail from someone: "I'd like to intern at your office, John." I certainly won't waste my time answering an e-mail like that! Music lawyers are also a great funnel into the industry because they network with everyone. If there's a way to find a friendly music lawyer, that could be a great help to you.

When I tried to get in, my parents knew a lot of people, but not one of them did anything for me. It was a chance encounter, going to a wedding, talking to someone, that turned into my first job. Remember that even though publishing is an incredible business, more and more of the majors are owned by public companies, which leads to a lower head count. So at the end of the day, it's hard work and some luck.

Assuming that you have connections and a great catalog can you still make a good living?

Definitely! There is more and more media developed every day and it loves music. If you have great songs, then those will live on forever.

Mark Bright

CHATTERBOX MUSIC

So, Mark, you're a wonderful producer. Why did you decide to move into publishing?

Well, I've been in publishing ever since the get-go. When I moved to Nashville, I attended school and I took publishing courses to learn the song side of the business, because I was already an engineer and I knew the studio business pretty well.

My first jobs were not only at the studio but also working for a publishing company, so I've been a publisher all of my adult life. When I left EMI, I was the VP of the publishing company and started a joint venture company with Sony. That company was Teracel Music, and I'm still in that joint venture with Sony till this day.

Would you explain how the big money in the industry is made through publishing?

Yes, publishing is not sexy, but it's blue chip!

When a song is written and recorded and then plays on the radio, in a club, or performed anywhere, it generates money. When a song is downloaded, when a song is bought, it generates revenue. There are many different ways of generating revenue. Music publishing has all of these tentacles attached to it, and most people don't really realize that some of the richest people in the world have made their fortunes through music publishing.

A publishing company is set it up to put itself in the position of having hit songs in their catalog. You go out and find songwriting talent that are like-minded as you and sign those songwriters, and then get them to write the types of songs that you want to hear. We also set up those songwriters with other songwriters that hopefully are going to push them a bit to become even better songwriters. The idea behind this is so that I will have the first right to hear that hit song and record it.

How do you find music?

It really has changed a lot. In the past a publishing company would have a staff of songwriters and you would just cold-pitch songs around town. That has changed dramatically because there is not as much cold-pitching going on these days as more artists are writing their own songs. Culturally, you can't be a complete artist unless you are an artist-writer today. I don't know if I necessarily think that's the way it needs to be, but that's how it is. So you have to get your writers in with that artist writer. If you can't do that, then you're not going to be a successful publisher.

So does that mean one of your main goals is to try to put collaboration projects together?

Yes. It's all about the collaboration with that artist-writer.

What kinds of opportunities do you see for the music publishing industry, or your business specifically, in today's world where new media is created constantly?

Well, I think it all boils down to one simple concept: if you are the person that can spot a hit song, or you are a person who can spot the hit songwriter, the sky's the limit; but if you are not that person, then you're going to have to sit and watch from the sidelines.

Let's use *me* as an example. I have a very good ear and I find a band with some great songs, but I don't really have the connections that somebody like Mark Bright does. Would it make sense for me to approach a publisher like you?

I place a very high value on people that are actually talent scouts like myself and can bring me songs that are fabulous. When I do find them, I hire them because they're very rare indeed.

This happened just a few weeks ago, when this twenty-three-year-old girl approached me and said, "I have to play you this song from this artist who's incredible." She kept hammering me, saying, "I can play you two songs from this eighteen-song tape and both of them are hits." I kept putting her off, and she said, "No, no, Mark, you need to stop right now and listen to this." And so I finally I stopped.

I listened, and man, both of those songs, that artist, the whole bit was incredible! I said, "Come into my office; let's talk," and I hired her. Not only did she know the artist as an artist, she knew the two songs that the artist wrote [that] could be hits.

Speaking of demo tapes, do you typically record a lot of demos in your publishing business?

Yes; I do typical publishing deals. So unless it's terrible, they'll go and demo the song.

How many writers do you have on staff? And is there a requirement for creative output?

I currently have six full-time writers. Some of them are just there to write, and some have writer-artist deals. If it's a writer deal, they're there to write twelve complete written songs, meaning if you write a song by yourself, that's one wholly written song, and if you co-write the song, that's a half written song. That's how publishers with staff writers typically do it.

What is the perfect employee for a publishing company, besides having that ear to be able to spot a hit?

The perfect employee is one that *understands* media. They *understand* the Internet, social media, and what the music landscape is across the board. They see where music is going and know how to find great music, *period*.

I WAS ONCE IN NEW YORK promoting one of my new ideas for an online music library called MyMusicSource. At the time it was innovative; today you are expected to have your music online and available for immediate purchase and licensing. I contacted everybody I thought might have an interest and set up meeting after meeting. I did have some success, but new ideas require education, so it was slow going. I was told things like: "The Internet is just not going to take off"; "You can't play music on the web; it's too slow": and "It's not worth the investment." Oh well, I guess times have changed.

That week in New York I met a young woman, Jenna Rubenstein, full of energy and charged up about her job. Jenna worked for Jellybean Benitez and represented his formidable music catalog to film, TV, and advertising companies. She understood that the money comes from publishing, and also understood what we were doing right away; it was a breath of fresh air. Over the next couple of years, we kept in touch as she moved on from Jellybean and is now the main indie artist blogger for MTV.

Jenna Rubenstein

JELLYBEAN MUSIC

You once told me, Jenna, that you love music publishing and are very passionate about it. What is it that you love about publishing?

In simple terms, I love songs! And as you know, music publishing is a business of copyrights. I'm fascinated by song structure, hooks, melodies, lyrics, etc. On top of that, I love finding new songwriters because I firmly believe that at the core of any successful artist lies a catalog of strong songs. Lastly, I'm fascinated by the many ways one can, for lack of a better word, "exploit" a copyright. I love being creative and figuring out how to derive multiple revenue streams from a single song. It's a challenge.

Does the music publishing industry keep you tied into the musician community?

Absolutely. As a publisher, you're surrounded by writers, musicians, session players, engineers, producers, everyone!

Could someone just starting out make a decent living in the music publishing arena?

I think that it's hard to make a good living when you're starting out in almost any arena. But I'm an optimist! If you've got an ear for songs, align yourself with a great writer and either start your own company or bring that writer with you to a larger company. I also think there's always money to be made on the film and TV side of publishing. If you're consistent and can prove to music supervisors that you can quickly and efficiently deliver the songs they want, then pitching for film and TV might be a great way to get your foot in the door.

Do you ever go in the recording studio as a publisher?

Definitely! With writers, producers, artists, everyone. And hypothetically, if I'm in a session, it's my job to gently remind everyone to agree on splits before they leave the session. Whether or not that always happens is a completely different subject. [*laughs*]

Do you have advice for someone starting out?

Be out and meet as many people as you can. It's an obvious piece of advice, but a crucial one. Align yourself with producers, writers, and engineers and expand your network as much as you can.

Nowadays, if you want to do A & R at a major publishing company, for example, you've got tons more leverage if you come equipped with a hot writer in your camp. Lastly, make sure you know the nuts and bolts of music publishing! The best creative executives are the ones that know their way around deal structure, copyright rules and regulations, mechanical rates, royalties, etc. Make sure you learn the boring stuff before you get to the sexy stuff.

What are the must-have skills to work in music publishing?

Foresight and good ears. Though a record may not appeal to your personal tastes, you need to see through that and regard it as its own potentially moneymaking entity. Ask yourself how you can make this record even more commercially viable. What mainstream artist can sing this record? Who can throw a rap verse on to make it more interesting? If the song structure is good but you change the production value, who else can you pitch it to? Tenacity is also a must. Especially when pitching for film and TV, you've got to find a way to tactfully yet consistently stay on music supervisors' radars.

What does a music publisher do?

A *good* music publisher wears many hats. But in the traditional sense, music publishers manage songs. If you're a songwriter, a music publisher will collect all royalties on your behalf and make sure all monies are being collected in all territories. But that is just the tip of the iceberg. A good, creative music publisher will try to exploit your copyrights in unique ways and create multiple revenue streams for your songs. Whether it's getting a sync in a movie, a sync in a video game, or landing a lucrative cut with a well-known artist, good music publishers ultimately aim to make your songs work harder. They're also your creative advocate and in an ideal world, should try and set up strong co-writes with other writers.

17

Record Label

Rapid Fire

Skill Set—Working for a record label requires connections and a can-do attitude. Starting your own label is an entrepreneurial venture and requires that skill set.

Hours—Business hours primarily, but as you have probably guessed by now, they can vary based upon exactly what you are doing at the record label.

Upside—I think working at a label would be cool. Not as cool as twenty years ago, but the basics still apply. Working with artists on their music, recording, producing, and marketing, a record label has it all.

Downside—Well, first of all, the record industry is changing so fast that nobody, and I mean *nobody*, knows what is going to happen long term. Second, you might just end up at a label that doesn't survive the impending shakeout.

Financial—$$ to $$$$ If you're successful, you will be able to buy that big house and boat you always wanted. If not, you'll need to settle for a small condo. There really are many label executives doing very well, and you could be one of them!

Location—I would situate myself in the LA or NY markets because that's where they do the most music business and work the deals. These are the places you will meet other record company people and it will make networking easier as well.

Future—It is a bad time to make predictions about the record industry, especially since they don't make "records" anymore. Maybe by the time you read this book we might have an answer! My guess for now is they will be around for as long as there are networks and companies that need music with all the legal rights attached in a neat little package.

THERE WAS A TIME NOT LONG AGO when the life goal of every musician or band was to land a record deal. Just the act of making the deal was thought to ensure fame, riches, and a long career in the music business. Record companies of the past were hit-making machines; they found great talent and groomed them to be stars, earning hundreds of millions of dollars along the way. Those of us who have been down that road can tell you many stories of success and ruin. Mine was no different. Several years ago, I was working at a pizza place called Crusty's. Every day the owner of a recording studio across the street came in and ordered the same sandwich: "I'll have the meatball sub with onions and mayonnaise." Little did he know that I took the pizza job so I could be close to his studio.

One day, I brought the meatball sub to him at his office and asked if I could hang out. One thing led to another and his chief engineer, Peter Malleta, started letting me hook up microphone cables before realizing that I knew what I was doing. A month or so later, I started working there full-time as a second engineer during the day and was allowed to record my music at night. For about a year, I lived on less than four hours sleep a night and $150 a week, but I loved every minute of it.

Somewhere along the line, I met Ron Cangro, a wonderful drummer who introduced me to his friend, who liked my music and financed our band. We flew musicians in to audition, and ultimately we hired the best musicians I have ever had the pleasure of working with. They were all from NYC. Six months later, we inked a deal with Good Sounds Records, distributed by TK Records, owned by Atlantic.

My experience with the record company was not unlike many other artists, in that we had high expectations that didn't quite match up with the business side of the industry. We anticipated that the record company would take care of us and generally help us become the artists we hoped to be. We also thought they would promote us, market us, support our touring, and make us stars; yes, we were delusional, but oh well, we fit the mold perfectly.

Being on the artist side of things gave me ample opportunity to learn the business, which I did my best to soak up along the way. We worked with the best engineers in the best studio in the country at the time (Criteria Studios), met some of the top artists in the world, recorded a wonderful record, and for reasons I'll reveal later, we broke up after a series of tangled mismanagement, promises, and falsehoods, not to mention tension and dissent in our band. Looking back, I may have been the instigator of much of the internal band tension, given my artsy ego. I was a youngblood with lots to learn.

Today record labels look very different than they did even five years ago. The distribution model has changed dramatically and has been turned on its head, and most, if not all, major labels are struggling to survive. This new paradigm, like many in life, offers challenges as well as opportunities. A typical large label today has a smaller stable of artists, which they watch over very carefully, and may also have a catalog of copyrights (publishing) that is being leveraged to secure licensing deals. Just a few years ago, licensing a track to a film or for a commercial wasn't considered a big deal in the grand scheme of things, but now it's one of the most important sources of generating revenue for many labels.

There are many new business models emerging in the record label business, most notably the indie label that may be made up of one or more artists. There is one well-established record label model that is doing quite well. It's the label that only distributes and spends little to nothing on the production of the music. They are like a straight distributor in that they use their proven processes and connections to help artists sell their music, and then split the profits from the deals they make. The artist is typically responsible for all costs associated with recording, pressings, PR, marketing, etc. In some cases, especially for the more established artist, this is a great deal; for most new artists, it can be expensive and hit or miss.

As in publishing, there are many different jobs in the record industry and they aren't going away anytime soon. The bigger labels are well established with film companies and global distribution. The smaller labels are like piranha looking for every opportunity to eat something, especially a larger label if possible.

Tomas Cookman

NACIONAL RECORDS

Tomas Cookman, who heads the nation's biggest independent Latin label, said during a recent panel session that "labels can no longer just produce and promote records by their artists. They must be virtually full-service entertainment companies to survive."

Why did you choose to start an independent label?

I felt that there were not any labels at the time championing the kind of music I was successfully managing. It was frustrating to have my artists tour successfully and the record sales (when they were still robust) did not reflect that enough. Since the other labels were not going to do it, I felt that it was an open space. In addition, we already had a network of supporters, as we had often taken on the traditional roles of the label with our management artists (and they were all on majors).

Starting a record label is an entrepreneurial endeavor. What skills must someone have to be successful?

You have to be able to multitask. Even if you have the luxury of a staff, you still have to be aware of all the moving parts. Even if you are not the one doing it, you should have an idea of how everything is done.

It seems as though the indie label has finally come of age. How does one compete with so many players and cut through the noise?

I am a firm believer in that amazing music or an incredible performer will find its audience. Adele was a good example of that recently. Her ascent did not come with many of the trappings that you always see with the big singers of the moment. Think about how much you see or saw artists like Lady Gaga, Beyoncé and Katy Perry and then how much you actually saw Adele. She hit the world thanks to an indie label (even though it was Sony in the US). Some of the media playing fields have been leveled, and with that, it is easier to think that "anything is possible."

If I wanted to start an indie label, what are the most important steps I should take to head in the right direction?

You need to have the trust of artists. You should feel passion for music—and for running a business. Figure out how you are going to do royalty reports. Keep in mind that you are going to spend slightly more than you thought you were going to.

This is a big and interesting country we live in. It is one that allows for all types of tastes, trends , interests, and markets.

What has been the biggest challenge for you personally and business-wise since starting your label?

Keeping an eye on finances and making sure you budget well and spend wisely. As this is a passion business, it is easy to maybe spend a bit more than you should on a recording or release, but you really have to be frugal or things can get ugly quick. In my case, as I was (am) an artist manager, many of the time and attention demands that are needed were already part of my everyday workload. This is like having a restaurant, you have to be "on" all the time. If you are really going to give your label a shot at making it, you have to put your 10,000 hours into it.

Is it possible to make money in a market with so many players?

Yes, as long as you manage your expectations, spend wisely, and sign solid artists.

How much does placement in film, TV, and advertising affect your company?

It is very important. To make the process easier, we try to also control the publishing side of the tracks (through our sister publishing company, Canciones Nacionales) so that we can be a quick and easy one-stop shop for music supervisors. We have had tracks on *Breaking Bad, Dexter, CSI, 90210,* and many more. We have also worked with brands such as Target, Pizza Hut, McDonald's, Coke, Panasonic, been on countless video games and a lot of film placement too. We have some artists who may not set the sales charts on fire but are making good livings with their placements. We are firm believers in the code of "by any means possible."

What is the best part of owning and running an indie label?

Being able to hear an artist for the first time and be able to get excited about it, and then be part of their dream to get their music out to as many people as possible.

I understand this is a hard question, but can someone make a living operating a record label?

Yes, they can. You have to run it like any other business—on the pure business/financial side. As long as you have more coming in than is going out, you are making a living. The type of living is of course dependent on so many different factors.

Can you tell me what types of things you do on a daily basis?

Answer e-mails, listen to music, discover new favorite bands, talk on the phone with artists, partners, the creative community, our distributor, etc., interact with my staff, possible future partners, listen to demos, go over marketing and promo plans.

What does the future look like for the independent label?
What does your crystal ball say?

At some point, there could be some consolidation of some indie labels to join together in some 1 + 1 = 3 situations and some will be brought into the major label game via purchases and strategic partnerships. As we further explore the monetization process and how artists can be fairly compensated, there will always be room at the table for indie labels. That is not going to change anytime soon.

Thaddeus Rudd

Mom & Pop Records

What should someone think about before starting an indie label?

Starting a label is just like starting any business, in that it requires time, money, experience, relationships, and passion. Just as you wouldn't open a restaurant without having cooked professionally or ran a restaurant previously, it would be a good idea to have some experience in the music industry. It's essential to know the basics about how records are made, sold, and promoted.

However, perhaps the most important talent or experience is knowing and being able to attract great talent, and understanding what will connect and sell. We are only as good as the records we release and the artists we work with.

Finally, it's good to have a plan and to have clear budgets and expectations for your releases at the beginning. For example, if you are starting a label and putting out music by unknown artists, do you have the ability to get press, radio, and expose the artists? If you are taking on somewhat established artists, do you have reasonable sales goals and budgets? It's a good idea to expect that it will take a number of releases for the label to get established and in a good working rhythm, and that may include planning for losses on the early releases.

What kinds of jobs are there at a record label?

It can run the gamut, from owner-head-of-A-&-R-only marketing person to a larger label where there are often these departments/categories of jobs:

A & R
Marketing
Radio Promotion
Video Promotion
Online/New Media Marketing
Sales/Distribution
Licensing and Synchronization
International
Legal and Business Affairs

Can someone make a good living in today's economy in the label business?

Sure—we are! The business is smaller than it was at its height in the '90s and early 2000s, and we're selling fewer CDs, and understanding that not everyone pays for all the music they own. And that there are other ways of listening to music—YouTube, Spotify, etc.—that don't involve owning files. That said, there are great bands, and many of the costs of releasing albums have similarly been reduced. The key is having the right artists and the right records, and doing a great job, and keeping to a budget so everyone wins.

How does location play into the label business?

We're based in New York; it is great to be part of a community of others in the music business. The relationships you build and maintain with booking agents, managers, artists, producers, other label people, journalists, etc. are helpful in finding talent and putting out releases.

That said, some great record labels—Sub Pop in Seattle and Merge in North Carolina come to mind—have created their own cultures outside of New York and LA.

What's your biggest reward being at a label, besides financial?

Well, I have a leadership role here, and have owned my own imprint over the years (the

Rebel Group) and previously a label called Sugar Free in the late '90s/early 2000s. I can say that working for yourself and being able to create your own business culture and artistic identity are the reasons many of us got into this business.

Are there any specific challenges to running an indie Label?

There are many. Recorded music is more likely to be pirated and shared, and it's a business reality that we have to adapt to. We have lesser sales expectations than we would have a decade ago, and at the same time, the release of albums remains the key component in growing most artists' careers. In other words, a "big" rock album may only sell 400,000 copies, versus 1,000,000 a decade ago, but that breakthrough album is still the key to all the other aspects of a band's career—touring, publishing, TV and film synchs, etc.

Tell me about a typical (I know there aren't any) day at the office?

I'm a runner, and like to get a workout in, hit the gym, and get in early to the office. It gives me an hour before the day starts to think about our records, to listen to new things, deal with some of the big picture issues that don't get my attention during the more hectic part of the workday. I like listening to records that are getting press or radio in the UK, and also following up on bands getting played on college and some of the specialty radio shows around the country. I skim some music press to see what is getting great reviews, and check out blog aggregators like elbo.ws.

I also do all our budgeting work in the morning; it's easier to contemplate figures and think mathematically when I'm fresh and have just had a cup of coffee!

Around 10 a.m., the office fills up. My day includes new deals that are in progress, new releases which are being prepared—I deal with our distribution company, RED, and oversee the production and some of the big box and chain stores we deal with.

Additionally, I deal with the legal and business needs of our company, which includes making sure everyone is paid and inquiries get answered. We have a couple regular meetings as a company—a Wednesday marketing meeting and a Friday conference call with our radio promotion staff, as well as several breakout meetings on particular projects with the key staff.

Some days, I'll head directly home (I have a small child and occasionally have to be home to be parent!), and sometimes go to an after-work meeting or see a show.

How do you interact creatively with the artists you represent?

Some bands make their own creative decisions—who they record with, which songs they cut, etc. Others work closely with Goldie or Craig in a creative capacity—whether on producer choices, song selections, or more general artistic direction ideas and dialogue.

Is the future of indie labels bright or stormy?

There are great opportunities, in that the market has flattened over time, due to digital distribution and the importance of online media and organic, online word of mouth. Simply put, a smaller indie label with the right band can sell as many albums as a major label. There are some areas, like commercial radio promotion and video channels, where the bigger labels still have better reach and power because they have hit after hit record and aren't dealing with these media partners for the first time. But overall, it's gotten easier and less expensive to bring records to market. It just all comes back to having the right bands, the right records, and the right people to put it together.

18

Road Manager

Rapid Fire

Skill Set—You must be good with people and persuasive when needed. Very organized and have the ability to motivate others to work hard for you. It's nice if you understand the basics of mixing, lighting, accounting, etc.

Hours—Long, and you'll need to maintain a high level of brain function, sometimes on only a few hours of sleep a night for several nights in a row.

Upside—You get to travel quite a bit and hang with the band. Once a band hooks on to a road manager, it can be, and usually is, a long-term relationship that may transform into other more creative endeavors.

Downside—Like I've said, the hours and the travel can bite you in the butt and you're away from home and your family sometimes for months.

Financial—$$ to $$$$ Road managers might make an even split as a band member with smaller acts. Contracted salaries in the $150,000 per year/tour are not unheard of for established acts, but by and large payment is per tour and contract work, so it's job to job.

Location—Good question, because bands come from and live everywhere. Nashville and other cities with lots of touring acts are places you might look. I interviewed Mark Litten, who travels with Metallica, and he lives in a very small town outside Cleveland called Chagrin Falls, so go figure.

Future—As touring becomes more of the mainstay of every band's revenue stream, more road managers will be needed as more bands hit the road. The future for this job looks especially good for those with add-on talents like mixing, accounting, etc.

EVERY BAND NEEDS A ROAD MANAGER. The question is "Can they afford one?" In most cases, and from all appearances, you might think the right answer to this question is "no," but I'd dispute that thinking in a big way.

I was recently at a Basia concert in Cleveland at Night Town, a great little concert venue that hosts a wide variety of musical acts and serves a decent meal as well. We arrived early and I noticed one guy who seemed to be everywhere at once. He was at the console setting up the mix, changing strings on the bass guitar, socializing with people as they passed, and I think he even ran the lights.

After the show, I approached him and asked why he was working so hard. "What do you mean?" he replied. "I love this! I'm the road manager and it's my job." I shook his hand and told him what an incredible job he was doing as I left the show.

The road manager job can include many responsibilities, and as the title infers, you manage the affairs of a band while traveling on the road. You arrange hotels, collect money, wake the band up when they sleep in, work with the press, and with smaller acts, you do everything else too.

You see, every band *does* need a road manager, even if they don't know it!

Road managers come in all shapes, sizes, flavors, and colors. There are the people who work with small bands and do everything from mixing to settling the financial account for the shows, to the larger acts with five to ten people splitting these duties. One thing I've learned while speaking to these road managers is that experience translates into bigger jobs, bigger tours, and bigger paychecks.

My friend Mark fits this bill. He has been the road manager with Def Leppard for the past several years and recently surrendered that position. He told me he was considering other journey's he would like to explore aside from the touring path he has traveled for so many years. Within two weeks, he had offers from ZZ Top, who told him that if he went on the road with them, he could play golf everyday, to Metallica who are starting a European tour and would fly him home every ten days. He has agreed to take the Metallica job. Mark is one of the most sought-after road managers in the business because he knows what he's doing and can handle the responsibility that comes with large crews and very big dollar touring.

Mark Litten

Def Leppard and Metallica

Mark has been Def Leppard's road manager for the past nine years and has recently toured in Europe with Metallica.

Mark, you've been Def Leppard's road manager for a long time. Would you tell me about your responsibilities?

There are many hats that are worn, starting with paying attention to your clients and what their various needs are. From the travel part—the flights, trains, boats, automobiles, limousine services that you may use time to time. I also make sure the artist gets to where they need to be, whether it's an interview, a TV show, or a performance.

The other component of this job is the budgeting process and working within the means that are directed to you by the artist and the business manager while trying to make a profit.

How much are you involved in the actual show production?

Usually there's a production manager, a stage manager, and there's maybe a production designer that basically assembles what the show will look like and then works with the artist.

How is it traveling on the road with Def Leppard?

Basically, it was a brilliant experience. I got to travel around the world. They are a great bunch of guys to be around.

When you're actually on the road, what's your typical day like?

On workdays, I usually go to the venue, where I have a mobile office. Depending on what your needs are, you have special road cases built so that your desk basically collapses and folds up, so it can be rolled in and is sitting in a room waiting for you. The road crew is there at the venue to set everything up. The band may be busy during the day, doing interviews and that kind of thing, doing press for future dates.

If you're all staying at a hotel, then obviously you have to check out of the hotel, settle up the accounts, and that type of thing. A sound check would roughly be at 4 o'clock or so to test the equipment that's been set up. And then you've got doors at 5 or 5:30. Show time is usually 7 or 8 o'clock. The opening act . . . [then the performance at] say, 9:15–9:30.

Then we head to a hotel; some groups jump on their bus and head to the next city. If you're in that mode and you're heading to the next city, you stay up for a while and then you fall asleep. Busses are pretty comfortable today, and after you get used to the humming of the engine, it becomes a pretty easy environment to live in.

And then our day starts over again. You're in a different city, your office rolls out. Once you get in sync with the travel, your body digests pretty well and you become used to it.

So what would you say is the most important skill for someone to be successful doing what you do?

I really have to think that it's your people skills, because when you're on a tour, it's like going to Thanksgiving dinner with your family every day—for as long as the tour lasts. We've all been there, after Thanksgiving dinner is over, you're, "Wow, I'm glad that's over." I mean, you're living on top of each other for the most part. So you have to be considerate of space. Some clients are harder than others, and obviously you have to dial all of that in and sort it out.

Right. So you told me that you really like numbers. How does that play into your role as a road manager?

You have to be aware of what's going from the business perspective. You need to know when you can spend money, when you can't, and where you may be able to save a little bit of money so that you're able to spend more later.

If your show is packed to the ceiling in the trucks, sometimes just adding just one more truck and lessening the time that you're packing the truck is going to save money, even though you're spending a little bit more money upfront. That's because it takes a lot of time, and people get injured when you pack these things totally full. So you count on the production manager to figure that stuff.

Knowing numbers and understanding how it all works also opens up the opportunity for more work because you can do multiple jobs. You can be the road manager and be the tour accountant and settle the shows. I would tell people that if you're really interested in becoming a road manager, you can never go wrong understanding the financial side of our business.

Along those same lines, how do road managers get paid? Is it by contract?

Depending on who hires you, you negotiate what you feel is a fair rate or they may just tell you, "Hey, this is what the job pays." Every scenario is different. Every group is different. It's probably the only business I know of that's basically a handshake deal: "Okay, we'll hire you, the job is yours, you're going to work from June through September, and this is how much money you're going to make per week." Then you have to decide if you want to form an LLC or to become their employee and have taxes taken out. Some groups will allow you the option, and some won't.

Is there a career path for road managers?

It's really a networking occupation. Everyone starts with very little understanding about this job or they've worked themselves up through the ranks. Maybe they started out pushing road cases so they became familiar, then the stage manager, and then . . . they become the production manager. Somebody takes a liking to them and says, "Hey, can you be the tour manager?"

Other people start as a friend of a band they're there to help get rolling. They're the guy doing everything from selling T-shirts to putting gas in the van to loading equipment. As the band becomes successful, they just happen to be the guy who's been there since day one and they just kind of go with it.

It's a tough environment. It's not for the weakhearted. It's a lot of fun. You can have a great career. I've been really fortunate. I've had a lot good times, and I've met a lot of great people, and this job has allowed me to see the world. But sometimes I wonder how I got here. [*laughs*])

What's the future look like for this type of job?

Well, let's look at music itself. Even though some would say it's a lot more challenging now than it was in the '80s and '90s, there are still a lot of groups on the road at all the various levels and they all need help. So if you want to be a road manager, just go after it, the work is there.

If I wanted to get into this, and I had no idea where to start, would it be best to go to the band, or agent, or manager, or everybody?

If it's a kid in college who's looking at this as a career, colleges have programming boards where they schedule and do events. Maybe a local pub in town or the student union bar, maybe they have bands there.

Or you go get a job. "Well, I really don't want to clean the toilets. I want to figure out how to meet the entertainers." There's a whole process to that. If it's local bands, they're usually pretty approachable and you just tell them you want to help. Remember that when you're just starting out, you're going to work for virtually nothing. Somebody's gotta take a chance on you.

You could also go work on the tech side of it. If you have an interest in sound, you go find a sound company or a lighting company. Eventually you get around groups that hire out the equipment, and then you're off to the races in that respect.

There are also video opportunities in the touring market, so you can also look in that direction.

What has been the biggest challenge to you as a road manager?

Well, the biggest one is not being at home. You don't realize it, but life goes by very quickly. I've been doing this twenty-something years and it's like, "Wow, where did my life go?" But it's just plugging back in to home life. Getting out there, it's like being a sailor. You're on the road and there's a lot of freedom to it. Your sense of reality is distorted, because you're away and life is just way different.

So is there a story that really stands out? Something that's happened to you that was either really cool or really weird?

When we went to Russia. I stayed behind with the client and his wife in Moscow. Between the three of us we had eight bags, and when we left we had eight bags. We got to the airport and when our chaperone left us, we went through the gauntlet, which is where they check your credentials.

We walked up to the desk and the guy just starts checking us in. He looks at our bags and he says, "You have excess bags," and I say, "No, I don't, these are the bags I came with. We came with eight bags and we're leaving with eight bags." "No, you have excess baggage."

So the shakedown began. I asked the guy, "What are we doing?" and he goes, "Well, you have to go down there." I looked down the hall 150 yards away, and there's a little tiny mousehole type window with an eyeball looking directly at me. The guy says to me, "Go there," and as I'm walking the eye is continuing to evaluate me. When I get there two girls are smoking, and I say, "We don't have excess baggage."

"Yaa, excess baggage $900."

"Well, can I pay with a credit card?"

"Machine broken, $900 cash American."

"You're robbing me."

"No rob you, excess baggage, $900 please."

I had no choice but to dig in my pocket, pull out $900 just to get out of Moscow. It's one of those things that's unbelievable until you've gone through it. Very intimidating. The moral of the story is to make sure your chaperones don't leave you until you're getting on the plane!

What's the best thing about your job? if you had to look back and say, "You know what, this is why I love this so much"?

We used to go on these things called marches where we would march around the town with no map, sometimes getting lost. The world is a pretty big place. It's been a fascinating journey.

HAVE YOU EVER CALLED SOMEONE YOU DON'T KNOW, and when they answer the phone they talk to you like they've known you forever? This was the case when I tracked down Mary Lou Arnold. The phone rang, and this warm voice came over the line. "Hi, this is Mary Lou, can I help you? Oh, how are you, Michael? I don't know why in the world you would want to interview me. I'm not sure what I could tell would be useful."

Anyone who's been in this business for thirty years in one job knows everything there is to know about that job. So . . . yes, Mary Lou, we're listening!

Mary Lou Arnold

TODD RUNDGREN

*Mary Lou Arnold is tour director and personal assistant to Todd Rundgren.
She's a strong, straight forward thinker, in my humble opinion.*

Mary Lou, you've been working with Todd Rundgren for quite a long time. Would you tell me how you landed this job?

I have been working with Todd for over thirty years. One day I walked into Todd's Utopia Video studio, where they were shooting their first music video, and asked if I could help. I was just looking for a job and didn't know who he was.

They put me to work as a production assistant, cutting gels, wiring lights, painting sets, just whatever needed to be done. One day after I'd worked there awhile, Roger Powell walked up to me and said, "Todd wants you to be the tour manager for Utopia." I had never been a tour manager, but said I'd try it and went on the road. I think the first tour must have been the Suits Tour. I have funny names for them [*laughs*]. The band wore Beatles suits, and when I got to the airport carrying all of these suits, I said to Todd, "I don't know what to do," and he said, "You'll figure it out."

Would you tell me a little bit about your role as a road/tour manager?

It really depends on the size of the gig. Baby bands [new bands that aren't making a lot of money] will often just go out with just one guy who is wearing lots of hats. He'll often be the front-of-house engineer, production manager, and the road manager.

When you have bigger tours, in bigger venues with bigger paychecks, like Todd's gig with the Ringo All-Star Tour, they would have a tour manager, assistant tour manager, production manager, assistant production manager, as well as tour accountants traveling with them.

When I started touring with Todd, I would check them in and out of the hotels, deal with plane flights, hospitality, that sort of thing. In time I was given more responsibilities, which included managing the cash.

At this point in your career, are you working with the booking agents and arranging the tours?

Here's how that works. I suppose there are some artists and bands that book themselves, but Todd has always had a booking agency. Right now we're with Creative Artist Agency, and they have offices in NY and LA.

So you'll have an agent who reaches out to all of the promoters and says, "Okay, I've got Todd Rundgren and he wants to tour during this time period." Their job is to collect all of the offers from the buyers and cut the deals. They cut the deals in conjunction with Todd's manager, Eric Gardner. The negotiations are also dependent on the show's complexity. Some of Todd's shows have been extremely expensive, with a big band, lots of costumes, etc., while others are more plug-in and play. So once Todd agrees to the dates, they're sent to me, and I have the responsibility of putting the tour together.

And what does that require?

A lot! [*laughs*] I have to interface with the band members, of course, make sure everyone's up to speed, and get information to all of them. I book all of the plane tickets, hotels, create the itinerary, figure out how we're going to get from place to place, hire tour busses, and hire crew members, advance settlements, get passes printed, make laminates, etc.

Oh, and there's also coordinating and keeping track of when Todd has phone interviews and making all of that happen too. Just basically, "Okay, here are the dates, now make this into a tour."

What is the single most important skill of a road manager?

I think it would be organization. You have to be incredibly organized.

What are you up to these days? Are you still on the road as Todd's tour manager?

My last official tour was the Power Trio Tour. I stopped, though, because my immune system was becoming extremely depleted. One of the downsides of being a tour manager/ road manager is you don't get very much sleep because you're managing the show, and then you're taking Todd and the band out to eat afterwards. Somewhere in there you're supposed to do accounting, manage all of the money, advance your next hotel, and keep advancing gigs.

I was lucky if I got four hours of sleep and was always the first one up in the morning. Road managers are up early making calls; they're checking out of the hotel, paying the bills, and all of that.

Wow . . . given all of that, why would somebody want to be a road manager?

I love being part of the show and helping to make it happen! The other thing I really enjoy is the travel. Japan is one of my favorite places. I just *love* Japan. We've toured there eight or nine times. Not to mention that working for an amazing singer-songwriter-guitarist makes it all worthwhile. It's not like a vacation, though. Some people think, "Oh, you're so lucky, it's so glamorous, and you get to see this city and that city." Well, it quickly becomes checking into a hotel and working, and checking out of the hotel and traveling.

You also get to meet lots of people and other professional artists that come to the shows. It's an interesting social life, and you need to be socially inclined because most of my job is interacting with people. There are all the after-show parties, meet and greets, and being gracious to everybody even if you don't know them; you never know who you might be talking to!

It's certainly a fast-paced lifestyle. How do road managers get paid for juggling all of these intense responsibilities? Do you typically get compensated for an entire tour, a leg of a tour, or show by show? How does it work?

I can only speak for our organization, but I would imagine it's pretty much the same industry-wide.

Every organization has a pay scale, and typically uses a payroll service. The road manager gets paid just like the crew and band, usually by the week but some bands pay by the show. You set up a budget and that determines the salaries. Pay rates vary so much it would be hard to nail down the exact dollar amount, but it is fair and in some cases road managers on big tours do very well.

So what do you think the future looks like for road managers? Is there still a good career path for someone that loves music and is well organized?

Sure. As long as bands are performing and touring, you're going to need people who keep it organized and take care of them. I mean, it's really that simple.

A band can go out without somebody being in charge [playing the road manager role] but it's very difficult because then a band or crewmember has to be the person that settles the show, and be the person in charge who makes sure that everyone is where he or she are supposed to be. It's a complex job, even for smaller bands

Assuming I have the right skills and desire, how might I go about breaking into the road manager world?

I think a good way might be applying as a tour manager's assistant. It would teach a person a lot about the day-to-day job of overseeing everything, especially if you're dealing with money. I'm pretty sure if you networked with other musicians, other production managers, and crew guys, that you could hook up with the right people. But starting out is the tricky part, so you might want to connect with a small band just going out and do it on a small scale to gain some experience. That's why I said assistant tour managing is probably a great gig.

A FEW WEEKS AGO, I was given a couple of great box seats to an Alison Krauss concert at the State Theater. I was familiar with her name but not so much her music. In the past, I played pedal steel and banjo for a time but wasn't into bluegrass music; I just didn't connect with the seemingly repetitive nature and roots part, I guess. I am now a huge fan of Alison's, bluegrass, and her band; they just blew me away. I am converted!

The musicianship exhibited by Alison's band highlighted a dedication to near perfection in the way they played their instruments. This is not supposed to be a concert review, so the point is that along with the great seats we also were given backstage passes and met the band after the show. This is where I struck up a conversation with their road manager, Sean Murray, and was taken by his enthusiasm and even temperament. Two days later, I interviewed Sean, and this is what he had to say.

Sean Murray

Alison Krauss

Sean, can you tell me a little bit about what you're doing today, and who you're working with?

Well, right now I'm working for Alison Krauss, and I'm her tour and production manager.

What's the difference between tour and production manager?

Well, instead of just being a solo tour manager, I assist in advancement of all production requirements. That includes lining up the production budgets—from the local stagehands, catering, and timelines to the parking of the busses and the trucks and the sound and the lights.

Is that based largely upon the tour budget?

Yes, this is a smaller tour, and I split the duties with her front-of-house engineer. So he takes care of all of the intricate technical details like the techie talk, as far as getting things from A to B or 120 volts or 220 volts, where I keep things on budget and timelines that keep the tour moving from city to city on time and on budget.

Many times the tour manager just takes care of the artist and possibly the money, but the production manager takes care of the budgets for the show. I live in both worlds.

How long does your typical tour last?

Well, in a perfect world, they never stop because that's how I get paid, and tours used to go a lot longer, but now they tend to be shorter, with a weekend-warrior mentality.

Tell me about some of the challenges you face on a daily basis that people may not be familiar with.

Well, one of my mottos is, "You're only as good as your advance." So you spend a lot of time to make sure everything is just right. If you don't have a good promoter, you may arrive and it's not at all what you thought, or you didn't receive the best information.

You can often walk into a venue, and things aren't as they were laid out to be and you need an extra 100 feet of electrical cable to get power from one place to another, that type of thing.

You mentioned that in a perfect world, tours would never end because that's how you get paid. Could you talk a little bit about how road and production managers are compensated?

The pay is good and based upon the music genre, venue attendance capacity, radio and record label support.

Does location matter?

Eighty percent of the people who do the weekend and short tours come in and out of Nashville.

You can get to three-quarters of the jobs in our industry overnight from Nashville. If you look at it on Google Maps and start running miles out of Nashville, you'd be amazed at how many places you can be in ten to twelve hours. You can draw a circle from Nashville and you can be in Cleveland, New York, the top of Florida, all of Georgia, all of Alabama, Mississippi, Indiana, and Illinois, all the way to Pennsylvania overnight.

That's actually pretty nice if you're not the bus driver.

Yeah, well, it's a lot more economical to have two bus drivers than to fly everybody and pay for hotels.

It sounds like there's a lot of "best practice" on the accounting side and moving shows around, all of that stuff. How did you learn the ropes of this business?

I started in high school. I started doing local bands. And you can kind of map this to the Nashville idea, although I was in Cleveland, Ohio, going to Chicago and Ann Arbor and Toledo and Columbus and Cincinnati, going in and out of Cleveland. And I started at the bottom. I did drums, I did guitars, I still run sound every once in a while.

I used to run sound and just loved it! So what are the most important skills that you have to have to be a successful and healthy road manager?

Well, "healthy" is a word that doesn't get associated with what we do too much, but very important. Before I got my first bus, I was in a van tour with a guy named Charlie Hunter. He and I made a practice to seek out Whole Foods, which at the time were few and far between. He got me on the healthy path. That will keep you going.

For straight-ahead skills, you obviously have to be organized and have a good personality so that you can deal with difficult situations. Is there anything else that sticks out in your mind?

You have to be able to adapt, the word "no" shouldn't be in your vocabulary, and you must find solutions. If you can't give them exactly what they want, you have to come up with a good plan because there's no textbook for this. You're dealing with budgets, local crews, egos; there's a million factors to keep an eye on.

The other thing is, you're nothing until you've done a hundred shows. And when you've done a hundred shows, you've experienced everything you need to learn.

If somebody is looking at this as a career, can they make a good living being a road manager?

Yeah, you can. You just have to give 100 percent of yourself. And as you know from doing these interviews, our industry is littered with broken families due to the commitment.

So what's the best thing about your job? Aside from money, why do you do this? What do you love about it?

No matter what, no matter where, no matter a great venue, a big venue, 100 people, 1,000, 100,000, whatever. The best part is, no matter how many people are out there, they get to turn off their regular stresses and their usual problems for a couple of hours and get to release and surrender to the music.

Is there some story that you thought was kind of unusual or funny?

I couldn't tell my wife, but I was due to fly to Australia in February, and I was on a plane that attempted to land five times before we had to divert to another city. Sometimes there is information that just has to be filtered and left on the road. [*laughs*]

19

Session Musician

Rapid Fire

Skill Set—You should be able to read music as easily as you read the morning newspaper. Be able to deal with pressure-cooker situations from time to time. You are prolific in many styles of music, and being a bit of a perfectionist won't hurt you.

Hours—Vary, depending on the call and how you decide to conduct your business. If you work remotely via the Internet, you can make your own hours, but you'll need a reputation to get the calls in the first place, or be a whiz at social networking.

Upside—This is a very creative profession for very creative people. The money is good when you are working. It's fulfilling to meet and play with a variety of musicians in a variety of recording situations. Great fun!

Downside—Monetizing a changing industry is always a challenge. There are fewer sessions and more great players. There is also the Internet, which has opened up additional opportunities but also diluted the market.

Financial—$$ to $$$ There are still many musicians who make fine livings primarily as session players, and depending on the type of session musician you are and how/if the union comes into play, you can create some long-tail income. It wouldn't be too unusual to make $50,000-plus per year as a session player, but that's probably not enough to buy the home you want.

Location—You need to be where the work is (LA, NYC, Dallas, Chicago) for studio calls, or anywhere, if you are *very* good at social networking and understand technology.

Future—Partly sunny with moments of great enlightenment. Time will tell the future; there is no crystal ball on this one. What we do know is that the market is shrinking for session players, but at the same time, there is more media and work that arises from production.

ONE OF THE MOST FULFILLING JOBS I almost had was that of a session musician. These are the musicians who are called on to play and record for a variety of reasons. They serve in backup bands for artists that don't have one, replace a band member who isn't quite cutting it in the studio, play in an orchestra on a film score, or are added to a recording as instruments of color.

I say I was almost a session musician because I quite didn't make the grade, so to speak. It takes a very special musician to *make it* as a session player, as the requirements are unique and not necessarily part of the typical musician's tool set. For example, a session player needs to be extremely focused with flawless technique because even the smallest mistake sticks out like a sore thumb on a recording. A session musician needs to balance creativity with politics, as well as knowing when to add his signature chops to a recording and when to play exactly what is written on the chart. Understanding the pressure a producer must bear both financially and creatively, and fitting into their world can also be a challenge, especially when you may be doing four different sessions a day with four different producers, in four different studios, and playing four different styles of music.

Many people think that being a session musician is a dying art and career with very few opportunities and very little upside. My two cents is that it's thriving and full of opportunity, although the face of it and the process have changed dramatically over the past five to ten years. Musician artists, shrinking studios, record companies that don't record as many records, and of course the 315,000 home studios have all contributed to changing the landscape of session work.

Several years back, I remember doing a session as a guitarist at Bee Jay Studios in Orlando, Florida, and getting schooled. It was a typical session date with a rhythm section and two guitarists, Tony B., and myself. They gave us some charts and rolled tape (twenty-four-track at the time). I played very clean and right with the charted music.

When the producer stopped tape, Tony B. started in: "Hey, Eric, this second line doesn't work at all. I think we should change the chord from a straight C to Am7. It's more dramatic. Fantastic, Tony, why don't you do that, and, Mike, you come on into the control room for a while." That was code for, "Mike, we don't need you anymore." So what did I learn that day? There's much more to being a session musician than just playing well and reading a chart.

Great session musicians "bring it" to every session, giving their all and taking the music to places it could never go without them. Just ask Damon Tedesco, whose father was the famous session guitarist Tommy Tedesco. They even made a movie about him and the most notable session players in history. It's called *The Wrecking Crew* and they played on over 150 gold records!

Though I am high on playing sessions, you should note in my contributors' answers that playing sessions is probably not a full-time profession anymore; it is only one part of your combined income package.

Technology has and will continue to have a big influence on the role of a session musician. As you probably know, if you do a quick web search, you'll find great musicians whom you can send your tracks to; they'll add their parts and send them back to you. This may well be the future of sessions and the role of the session musician. The upside is that if you are talented, comfortable with technology, and play many styles, you could do very well.

I'VE TALKED A LOT ABOUT LEARNING FROM OTHERS IN THIS BOOK, but have not touched too much on the importance of working with people you admire, respect, and make you better at what it is you do. I owned a nice music house in Orlando, and many times had partners who were awesome talents in their own right. Tim Akers came to me on a recommendation from Ron Cangro when he was working at Disney. Ron, who is a longtime friend and incredible drummer said, "Mike, you need to have Tim come in and play on this track. He is one of the funkiest keyboard players I've heard in a long time, and has perfect time." Later that day Tim came by, played on the session, and I was blown away. We worked together for the next several years, composing some of the best music of my life, until he moved to Nashville.

I remember the day he told me he was moving, and I said, "Good luck finding a job, Tim. I've heard the studio guys only change out about every fifty years when one of them dies." As has happened so many times in my life, I was dead wrong. Tim went off to Nashville and within a week was hired by the famous Michael Omartian to play in his studio with Amy Grant. Since then he has continued to be one of the hardest-working and well-respected musicians in Nashville, and I'm proud to call him my bud. I don't think I've ever told Tim until this moment how in awe of him I am—Tim, you rock! Tim is a good friend, and working with people like him is what makes being in the music business worthwhile.

Tim Akers

KEYBOARDIST

Tim Akers, a studio session player, is the first-call B-3 guy in Nashville and has worked with many prominent artists and projects, including Rascal Flatts, Faith Hill, LeAnn Rimes, Stevie Wonder, and Michael McDonald.

Tim, you and I worked together for many years in the studio, and I have always been amazed at the incredibly positive attitude you bring to the studio and how you motivate people. How important do you think teamwork is in the studio setting?

Oh, I think it's extremely important. If somebody is a jerk on the session, it brings everybody down. And by the same token, if you get a couple of guys that seem to drive the session, you're just glad to be there.

There's one guitar player in town that I've worked with on a lot of sessions. He's one of those guys that do sessions at 10 o'clock, 2 o'clock, and 6 o'clock, and then he'll show up at 9:30 p.m. to somebody's session, and act like it's his first session of the day. You just can't get him because he's so busy. He's just a workaday, bread-and-butter session guy. This guy works all the time because people love his energy and attitude—he's always got a smile and an attitude to match.

Your hometown, Nashville, has changed a lot over the years, even more so in the last five; can you talk a little bit about how the session world has changed?

It used to be you would either be working on major country records or you'd do a Christian music record here and there. Once in a blue moon you'd see some pop music come through town. Everything else was songwriters' demos and what we call custom records. [Records self-funded by independent artists.]

Now fast-forward a few years. It's not just country or Christian music anymore. Nashville has become such a diversified melting pot of musical styles, because we have so many acts that come here. For instance, Jack White, of the White Stripes, moved to town and set up shop here, and so he has all kinds of indie rock acts and stuff that he's developing. I think, "Really? They came to Nashville?" or Rush just did their latest record here. Kid Rock is here all the time. India Arie came out of Nashville. The list goes on.

Another big thing that has changed is that almost every single studio musician I know has a home studio now. I've got a nice studio in my basement and it's fully finished out. I have my B-3, a seven-foot grand piano, all my synthesizer toys, my accordions, and my pump organ ready to go at a moment's notice. Last night is a perfect example. There's a songwriter-producer in town who produces a lot of major country acts, and he just sent me a text: "Can I send you a track to put piano, B-3, and strings on?" And I said, "Sure". He sent me an MP3, and I sat in my studio last night for about three hours and just overdubbed stuff right here in my studio. That's 50 percent of what I do now.

The third big change is that in the past, it was very unusual to see session guys going out on tour with live acts. Typically once the word got out that you were traveling, everyone would assume you were gone and the phone would stop ringing. This seems to be very unique to Nashville, because when I talked to LA musicians, it was never that way. If you went to a studio one day and went out on tour the next, you did yourself no political harm.

But now there has been a real change. A lot of the A-list session guys in Nashville are also out touring. The first example that comes to mind is Chris McHugh, one of the busiest drummers in town. Well, he's the music director for Keith Urban, and he does sessions as well. I also do both. I went out with LeAnn Rimes for a few years, and now I'm out with Rascal Flatts.

How important is reading music to a session musician in today's industry?

It's a matter of opinion. There are a lot of successful guys out there who don't read a note, and they're so good they don't need to. Most of what we do here in Nashville is using a number system, so it's not a huge deal anyway. But there are certain types of sessions and live shows that I contract musicians for, and if they can't sight-read, I can't call them because they just can't move fast enough.

My band, the Smoking Section, is a perfect example. We just did a charity event and were the house band for four different artists. There was no money on the gig, and I asked everybody to basically do it as a favor to me. I said, "Look, these guys are great readers. We're gonna come in and do this gig with no rehearsal, 'cause I can't ask them to take another day out of their schedules for a free rehearsal."

So I wrote these really meticulous traditional notation charts, and we went in and we played for Melinda Doolittle, Danny Gokey from *American Idol*, Russ Taff [legendary gospel singer]. Everybody just came in and sight-read 'em and it was just spectacular. We had the show recorded on Pro Tools, and when we listened to playback, our jaws collectively dropped. No fixes were even necessary. I think that is a testament to the skills of the musicians here.

Tim, how has playing sessions led to other gigs for you?

The best example I can think of was Faith Hill. I had worked on a couple of records with her [*Breathe* and *Cry*] and soon after was asked to fill in as music director for her live show. We did a series of shows at Caesars out in Vegas with a *killer* band . . . Vinnie Colaiuta, Paul Bushmill, Kenny Greenberg, Bekka Bramlett, etc. That was a lot of fun.

You may play a showcase for some new artist, and their career blows up, and they're like, "You know, that guitar player on that showcase gig just knocked my socks off; I love his energy, I love everything he played; I really want that guy on my record." Suddenly, you're the new kid on the block on the session scene. I was advised years ago to never allow myself to think that I'm too good to do demo sessions. They may not pay as much money as a master, but the next demo session you play might be the next new artist that blows up and can't live without you.

Knowing what you've learned, and if you were to start out today, what path might you take to break into this session musician world?

I guess under the current circumstances, I would say try to get on in on as many demo sessions as possible and network with all those new people. I also like the idea of having your own home studio and working remotely because that makes it easy and more affordable to work with you.

Also, show up on time, play whatever gigs you can get with a big smile on your face, and act like every gig you do is the hottest artist in the country right now. If you can get a showcase to help an artist and they say, "Oh, it only pays 50 bucks," you say, "Yeah, that's okay, I'll play it. I'll be glad to, man! I gotta learn twenty tunes? That's okay!" Show up and nail it, and have a smile on your face—you'll be remembered!

Conversely, the worst thing you could do is come to town thinking that you're this really hot musician, e-mail everybody, send hundreds and hundreds of demos out, and get in everybody's face, because you'll get shut down immediately and soon be working at McDonald's!

IF YOU'VE EVER BEEN TO A JAMES TAYLOR OR LYLE LOVETT CONCERT, you've probably seen Arnold McCuller up onstage. His voice is as smooth as they come. His devotion to his art and trade are deeply ingrained in his being as he opens up to talk about singing in the studio. Arnold is a funny guy and very pleasant to chat with. You can tell right away that his personal nature has been key to his longevity in a business that typically spits you out in about ten years.

Arnold McCuller

FEATURED VOCALIST AND SESSION SINGER

Arnold McCuller has worked with top recording artists such as Phil Collins and James Taylor, and is one of the music industry's most sought-after session singers.

Beyond having a great voice and personality, what are some of the other skills that someone needs to be successful as a session singer?

A successful session singer should know how to read music. I'm not a great reader, but I can usually find my way through a piece with a little rehearsal and help. The best singers can actually pick up a piece of music and sight-read it straight down. That's probably the number-one thing I would suggest, definitely be a good sight-reader. Sight-reading means having the ability to pick the music up and sing it correctly the minute you look at it, just like you're reading a book.

Can you talk a little bit about what a typical recording gig is like?

Every session can be completely different. For me, I did what they call head charts. Most of my sessions are generally "Arnold we have this song and we don't know what to do for background vocals; what would you do?" I listen and then we go section by section, "Let's try this in here, let's try some answers here, some 'oohs' here, some 'aahs' there; let's try a counter melody, and here are some ideas."

It sounds a lot like your creative side and your contributions are a big driver for your career.

Yes, I think so, sight-reading, being able to create head charts, and just having an amazing attitude in the studio. Don't get frustrated if the producer or artist wants more, not to get angry if they say, "We need more personality." Always remember it's got nothing to do with you. These are the same things you would go through as an actor.

Do you have any stories about sessions that where unique?

The first one that comes to mind was a Life Savers commercial. I was a huge fan of Valerie

Simpson and Nickolas Ashford. Valerie and Patty Austin were singing backup and I was singing the lead vocal. I couldn't believe that they had been brought in to sing backup for me! I'll never forget how awestruck I was.

Another one is Luther, David, and I did a disco album of all the Beach Boys tunes called *Good Vibrations*. Those were the most amazingly fun sessions.

What would you consider the biggest challenge while working in the studio?

I don't find it hard at all, ever. The only challenge is if a producer is unclear as to what they want. Sometimes they're so afraid of failing that they try too hard and they end up not getting the best performance out of you. Most producers come in knowing exactly what they want and have the parts ready in their heads, and they'll ask, "Now give me your input." It's so much easier then because at least we have a road map and my input is icing on the cake.

Another horrible thing that happens is when I've gone into the studio and they have us rehearse around the piano and they want to hear you sing it as loud as though you were recording. I always have to say, "No. I'm rehearsing." [*laughs*]

Actually, the only time I've left a session was during a gospel session. Andraé Crouch said, "I need you to sing louder," and I said, "Sorry, when the tape is rolling I'll give you all the volume you want, but I'm just learning my part right now." He left me alone, but the beating the part into everyone else continued. It was just a form of work that they weren't used to.

Assuming you are in the right market, you have a good voice, you sight-read, and all these other things, do you think there's a market for somebody who aspires to be a session singer today?

Sure, but there's no telephone number you can call and say, "I'd like to be in on your session." You can't walk in and fill out an application for this job. That's the problem. People think, "How do I get started?" Well, you get started by building a great reputation writing with people and demoing songs. When I first came to LA, I sang demo vocals for a publishing company. I did all the demo vocals for Almo Irving Publishing, and for writers like Will Jennings, David Lasley, Kevin Moore—or Keb' Mo'. Funny, I knew him as Kevin Moore for many years and all of a sudden he became Keb' Mo'.

There are lots of writers needing singers to sing their songs, because they might need a female version, a male version, a country version. They use different singers so they would be able to send them to different publishing companies to various artists. That's a great way to start.

But you'll need to let writers know that you're available and work for AFTRA demo scale, which currently runs about $80 to $100 for a two-hour session. The other reason I got into this studio scene in New York was because we undercut the established session-singer rates; not that proud of it, just a fact. [*laughs*]

Would you talk about how session singers are paid, and how the union fits into the equation?

When I started, I was working for less than union scale so that you could get more work, and we needed people to hire us. Later when we became more sought after, we became members of the union and worked for scale.

Then when we were working for people who were making more money, we would charge double scale. For instance, "Native New Yorker" is an old tune and we did all the padding vocals; we charged double scale because we knew we weren't going to get credit on the record.

So as you get more successful, you can raise your rates in line with how much you are in demand. A lot of the players don't work for less than double scale, and I always encourage singers to join their union so they get their benefits, and work through the union because they make sure that you get your residual payments. The union sees that you are taken care of and are not taken advantage of. People should get their first union gig, pay their dues, and work through the union, in my opinion.

Has singing on records, CDs, and doing sessions led to any other opportunities in the music business for you?

Well, my session work in New York landed me my first film. I did sessions with Kenny Vance, who had a group, Jay and the Americans. The music supervisor for *American Hot Wax* approached Kenny and Kenny said, "Arnold, it would be great if you could get your vocal group together and audition for this producer; he wants a doo-wop group for his movie." Well, they didn't like my group, but they did like two of us, so they paired us with two other guys and we flew to LA to shoot for the next four months. That was definitely a wonderful transition from session singing to another career.

Lee Sklar

BASSIST

Lee Sklar, a Hollywood session bassist since the '70s, has recorded more than 2,500 albums. His credits include work with Linda Ronstadt, James Taylor, Hall & Oates, Jackson Browne, Phil Collins, Reba McEntire, George Strait, Willie Nelson, and hundreds of other artists. His signature long gray beard can be spotted from a distance . . . enough said!

Lee, you've played on over 2,500 albums, which I find to be a staggering number. Would you tell me how you got started as a session musician?

I was in college in the late '60s and was always in bands. One of the bands was called

Wolfgang and the drummer, Bugs Pemberton, was friends with a guy named John Fischback. John was friends with James Taylor and brought him by a rehearsal, and that was how I met J.T. When James started his first gigs, he had Peter Asher contact me, and the next thing you know 2,500-plus albums have gone by and forty years of touring. Where did the time go? I always ask the drummer that, but it is another story.

I would have to guess that you are one of the most-recorded musicians of all time! Your home base of LA has changed quite a bit for session players over the past few years. Can you talk about that a bit?

The whole business has changed, and not just in LA but NY and Nashville and all the musical centers. The labels are becoming a thing of the past and people are doing so much on the Internet now. There is still label activity but not like it once was. Also, in the heyday of sessions, we worked in studios all the time. Now at least half of my work is in guys' homes. Generally it is just me overdubbing bass on existing tracks, and I miss the magic that happens when a group of players gets together and creates. Occasionally I do dates where there are a group of players in the same room at the same time and then it still is *magic*!

How important is the ability to read music to a professional session musician?

If you want to be a studio musician in the classical sense, you *must* read music. There are so many times when you show up and the arranger or composer will have your parts all done, and it is up to you to interpret them. You have to be able to read the parts to even get the session started. I cannot say it enough: learn as much as you can about the entire recording process, as it will only make you a better player and in more demand.

How has technology influenced the recording studio business? Have you ever worked any Internet-based sessions? If so, can you tell me how they work?

Technology has had a huge influence on the business. Very rarely do I do sessions that are not on Pro Tools or some other form of digital recording. I love tape and that sound, but it is what it is now. I still do some projects to tape, and usually it is tape and Pro Tools in combination. There are aspects of both that I dig. The main thing with the technology is that almost anyone can have a decent studio in his or her home now. I have people contacting me all the time about sending me files and recording parts at home and just have not done it yet. I am still busy enough with regular work that I value my time away from music and like being home not working.

Since there are more independently owned studios today, would you say that new talented players or singers can still break into the higher-profile session gigs these days?

Absolutely! The only thing that has really changed is the amount of work that is available compared to when I started. But if you are good and can find yourself in a situation where someone in the right position hears you, everything can change for you overnight. The main thing is to love what you are doing and keep yourself focused on what really counts—the music. Don't get caught up in the bullshit of the business side if possible. Always maintain a strong work ethic.

As most people know, the music industry is primarily centered in New York, Los Angeles, and Nashville. Would you say there is a best place to be?

As I said, the technology is so good now that you can make great recordings anywhere. As for studio work, it is still Los Angeles, Nashville, Chicago, and New York as the main centers. It is not easy to break in and you really do have to pay your dues doing demo work, playing clubs and funky gigs. You just never know where or when a break will come your way.

While we're on the subject of location, does your work as a session player take you to other countries?

Yes, I have done sessions everywhere. Most of the time, foreign artists love to come to LA to record, so that limits the amount of overseas recording that I do. I will probably be doing a few projects in both Asia and Europe this year.

What was the hardest session you've ever played?

When I first started doing Motown sessions and was working with the great Gene Page, who was one of the great Motown arrangers. He wrote fly shit and I had to double the left hand of the clavinet player. I hadn't read in a long time and suddenly I was reading like crazy. I got my shit together real fast and then it was easy, but my heart stopped when I saw the charts of one of his dates! [*laughs*]

That's great! How about the coolest session you've ever played on?

So many of those . . . to name a few: Billy Cobham (when we did Spectrum) to working with Phil Collins and Genesis at their farm in England. There is also something inherently cool about just going to work every day as a musician. That never gets old.

Can a competent musician make a good living just playing sessions in today's industry?

It is hard. If you get into the inner circle you can, but it's a tough road. I feel very blessed to have made my entire career in the studio and on the road. A new musician might make a living, sure, but the notion of "good living" is subjective; it depends on each individual's lifestyle.

Why do producers pick Lee Sklar to play bass on their session?

I think they have a confidence in hiring me because I have done this for over four decades and have a track record of having played on many successful recordings. Now, just my being there won't make a recording successful! [*laughs*] You still need a great song, a great artist, and all the things that make for great music. It is good for me that most of the producers I work with know that I am very instinctive,

"Look! It's the ISS." My eyes darted to the night sky and scanned from side to side. I didn't see the familiar glow of the International Space Station reflected from the sun that had recently set over the Atlantic.

"I don't see anything," I said, turning my attention back to the bar, where my once-full beer stood at half-mast. "Ha, ha, ha, Mike, thanks a bunch." Another lesson: Don't ever look away from your beer when you're with a bandmate and both of you are broke.

Like some of you reading this, I once lived at the beach, but unlike most of you, I lived in a warehouse. I moved to Florida with my good friend Michael McAdam with the intent of "living the life" and starting a band that would become wildly popular. Hmmm . . . didn't work out exactly like we expected, but looking back we had a lot of fun.

Mike and I found our way to Cocoa Beach, Florida. We made the rounds looking for musicians for our band and met two incredible players, Paul Ill and Mike Wright. You are correct if you're noticed three Mikes in the same band. Mike M. (as I'll call him) and I had only a couple hundred dollars between us, which wouldn't get us through the front door of an apartment complex, and we didn't have jobs. But one day we did find this little warehouse on a side street next to a surfboard carving shop and spent our money making little dividers for bedrooms.

We would stretch the remaining few dollars at happy hour at local bars so we wouldn't starve. At happy hour, if you bought a beer, you could help yourself to the hors d'oeuvres, so we would each buy one beer and eat what sometimes was our only meal for the day.

We practiced day and night and wrote obscure songs, what were mostly instrumental because we loved to play intricate, complex music and none of us could sing. Needless to say, that band lasted about six months, and we disbanded never having made a dollar.

We lost touch with each other for a time, but years later all of us are still in the music business and have been successful applying the survival skills we learned during those early years. One guy in particular, and the only guy *not* named Mike, moved to LA. Paul Ill has made his mark on the town and has his fingers in all types of music-related activities that he's pulled together to make a nice life for himself. He shared a little about the session playing he does with artists like Christina Aguilera.

Paul Ill

BASSIST, SONGWRITER

Paul is a bassist and songwriter whose recording credits include Linda Perry, Christina Aguilera, Pink, James Blunt, Alicia Keys, Courtney Love, and Daniel Powter.

Tell me about the coolest sessions you've played. Why you love doing this for a living?

My best session ever was being flown to England to record songs for a Tina Turner record with producer Guy Chambers. He had asked Tina Turner, "Who's your favorite songwriter, and she said, "The singer in Train." Guy called him and asked, "Do you want to write for Tina Turner?" So they wrote a bunch of tunes. Guy flew me and the brilliant drummer Brian Macleod first class from LA to London and put us up in a four-star hotel in Primrose Hill, just walking distance from the studio.

We cut the tracks, and Tina loved it so much she said, "Are those guys still in town? Can you get them in the studio? I want to cut this live with them." So Brian and I got the call while I was sitting in a cafe with an ex-girlfriend living in London. I walked into the studio, and we're introduced to Tina, who is the kindest, sweetest, most humble person you would ever meet. So Guy played guitar, Brian played drums, and I played bass. We re-cut the three songs with Tina singing live in the room behind glass gobos.

There I am, this kid that grew up playing in soul bands on army bases, and I can't believe I'm here; this is so much fun. That was absolutely a high point in my career and my life. I work hard, fast, and come prepared; I am not magical. I am just a working musician and have spent a long time perfecting my craft.

Paul, you have multiple income streams as a musician and do quite well for yourself. Would you give us a summary of the different revenue streams and how you've been able to diversify?

I have five income streams, and it's one of the reasons why I've been able to stay successful in the music industry. My first income stream is through recording sessions as an electric bass player. My second is as a songwriter, having copyrights that create income with prominent pop stars like Christina Aguilera, Pink, Linda Perry, Courtney Love, and others. My third channel of income is as a composer of instrumental music for film and television. My fourth is as a writer of prose—I wrote *the Studio Musician's Handbook* for Hal Leonard Music Publishing and technical articles. Finally, my fifth income stream is performing live music. I juggle them all without a manager or a wife. [*laughs*]

You are one incredibly busy person! I'd like to talk about some of those different disciplines. For starters, could you tell me exactly what a day is like in the recording studio?

My days are scheduled anywhere from "day of" to two days in advance to a month out.

I may get an MP3 that I'm supposed to transcribe, or they might say, "Learn this song, but we want your vibe on it." Sometimes they'll just say, "Show up, we're going to hit it cold," which means you need to be prepared for anything.

Most of the time, guys in my line of work get paid to come up with a part on the fly. Usually they want me in the room because I'm going to create something that serves the song, a really cool part for their track. Very rarely do they want me to duplicate something they wrote note for note. What they're paying for is that kind of bass part that they go, "Oh, that's f-ing great!" [*laughs*]

So the day of a session, I pack a bag with my chart and have the song on an iPod so I can listen to it on the way to the session and keeping it fresh in my mind. Prior to leaving, I will also have a discussion with the producer, the artist, or the contractor about what to bring because I have a lot of instruments and bass-oriented toys.

What I typically bring is two Fender Precision basses, one with flat wounds and one with round wounds and a third really cool bass with that "ooh-aahh" factor, like an old Hofner or Kaye. By "ooh-ahh" factor I mean something like this: if the producer is a keyboard player, then the I may bring a Stylophone—it's a little synth that Bowie used on "Heroes"—you actually play it using a stylus that looks like a little pencil. It's called "value added creativity."

I might even bring a one-octave keyboard controller and my laptop and say, "If you want, we can make some bass sounds on this," and usually they'll go, "Holy shit, you have software synths?!" [*laughs*] I always participate in the creativity if it's allowed. In some sessions, that will be a determining factor for a callback.

Alternatively, some producers will tell you, "No story telling today, no extra stuff; I want you to play exactly what I showed you on the MP3. It's easy, but don't distract the artist with any creativity at all." In those cases, you are invisible and you say, "No problem." Remember that a lot of being a successful studio musician is having the presence of mind to know when not to do anything except exactly what someone else wants you to do, not to say a word, to just be a fly on the wall and let them have their moment.

You certainly have a large toolbox to work with when you go to a gig! Is carting all that equipment around covered in your compensation? How do session players get paid?

You get paid either directly by the artist, the contractor, or the producer or the record company through the union.

There is this very successful Latin producer, Gustavo Farias, and when I work for him, he takes control of the budget, and he doesn't pay through the union. He will tell you what your rate is for the session and always pay you more. He looks at it in a pretty unique way. Let's say you're cutting a track and you nail it in less than ten minutes; he'll pay your rate and sometimes put in an additional 20 percent like a tip. I look at the check and go, "Thank you very much," and he says, "You're welcome, because you saved me some time."

Another way of getting paid is the "backend deal," where someone will tell you, "We will pay you when this track generates some revenue." In those cases, the rate should be considerably higher, but it may never be paid. I also do sessions for a trailer company, and when they place the track I get paid. It's mailbox money.

On that note, do you see technology working its way into your life as a session musician and changing the way you work? Do you have experience playing Internet-based sessions?

On most of the sessions I do, you have to perceive yourself as more than an instrumentalist. You have to be like Todd Rundgren or Paul McCartney that blew our minds in the '70s.

Case in point: I did a TV show called *Fast Track Advantage* last year. We did thirty-six cover songs and it was aired on the Speed channel. It was like NASCAR meets *American Idol.* So it was singers and instrumentalist and dancers competing on pre-race day on a live stage over pre-recorded tracks that we created.

On Monday, my boss would meet with the producers of the show and they'd decide what songs were going to be performed and would then edit cover versions of four to six songs. They would do two-minute edits of everything from "Ramblin' Man" to the latest Taylor Swift hits. Then they would clear those with the publishers immediately, digitally. As soon as the songs were cleared, they would send us MP3s so that we could write our own charts. On Wednesday, the drummer would track the drums in his studio and post them on an FTP site Wednesday night.

Thursday, I would be working on the bass part in my studio, while guitar parts would be played in other studios. Bob Burnstien would be doing the pedal steel and Chris Joyner would be doing the keyboards. Then we would all post wav. files on guitarist/mixer Chris Henry's website and he would mix it.

Boom—music meets tech meets creative!

20

Songwriter

Rapid Fire

Skill Set—Something to write about helps. Having been in love and then broken up is a plus. Heartache, love lost are all good. Relationships are helpful, and a good education is important to understanding publishing contracts and writing lyrics that are worthy of publishing. Being social and a good networker is required.

Hours—Depending on what songwriting path you follow, hours vary. If you are working as a staff writer, you will work business hours but have to deliver songs weekly. If you write as a songster and pitch your songs to artists, you may be able to write anytime you are feeling it. However, you better be feeling it often or you will starve.

Upside—Creatively, songwriting is very fulfilling and, I believe, tremendous brain food.

Downside—Again, depending on the songwriting path, it can be quite challenging to find work and make a living.

Financial—$$ to $$$$ Let's say you *are* a working songwriter. Money can enter the picture from several directions, including up-front fees, simple work-for-hire fees, as well as long-tail income from residuals, performance payment, and publisher royalties. If you are successful as a songwriter, you can make real money for a real long time, so invest it wisely.

Location—Nashville, LA, NY, and other cities where publishers tend to congregate and artists live; otherwise, anyplace in the USA will do just fine, but you may be limited as far as collaborative writing and pitching opportunities go. You'll also need an agent or song plugger to get your music in front of the right clients.

Future— Songwriting is an art form unto itself and will not be going away anytime soon. There will always be a need for a good song. So the future is bright for the lucky ones, as always. You might want to have something to fall back on if you pick songwriting as a job.

No doubt that writing songs is one of the coolest things you may get to do in your musical life. It allows for an open and free musical expression of your thoughts and emotions, and for a lucky few, songwriting can be a lucrative endeavor and a career with a very long tail financially. As I see it, one of the keys to a successful career as a songwriter is to approach it much like you would approach any business: research every aspect of songwriting to fully understand the inner workings of the industry before you jump in.

You might start by looking at all of the places where songs are used, both in the record industry and commercially, for such things as TV ads, advertising jingles, corporate meetings, etc. You may be surprised by the sheer variety of songwriting opportunities available to you even in today's uncertain musical economy.

I have written songs for Fox, jingles for Coke, theme songs for Apple, songs for Universal, and a host of others. I was pretty thoughtful in developing my client base, though I didn't live in the right city for much of my work. With careful research, you too can discover where you *should* live depending on the type of songwriter you aspire to be. Most of my songwriting was also classified as work for hire, which means in essence that you are giving up your rights to the music you write.

I wrote a lot of music for Disney, and I mean a bunch—over 1,000 jobs—and they were all work for hire. Some weeks I would get three twenty-five-page contracts from Disney legal that went on and on about how they would maintain all rights into and beyond eternity, and I couldn't even use my Disney music for demo reels. It was kind of humorous, so one day I picked up the phone and called Disney's legal affairs department, the one that issues all of these contracts. You see, the problem was not the number of contracts; it was the requirement that I have each one notarized at my bank that was eating up a few hours of my week. So when I got the person on the phone who was creating all these contracts, I said to him, "I am doing so much work for you and the contracts are driving me crazy. Can we just make it a one-pager that says, *"You wrote it, we own it,"* and call it a day?* I'm sure you can guess the answer.

Songwriters who have their music recorded by others stand to make the most money because the more people that record your song, the better chance you have of selling more downloads, and the back-end publishing and performing rights revenue will increase exponentially.

I may make songwriting out to be an easy career, but it's not without a multitude of challenges—including the simple fact that there are boatloads of songwriters, meaning there's a lot of competition for the same work. So . . . find a niche, meet the right people, be creative and accommodating, work hard, and use the money you make to further your personal creative songwriting goals. I have always thought that if I could use my talent to make some money, then I could do whatever I wanted creatively and not worry too much about the outcome of my creativity. It has worked so far.

Harold Payne

Harold, you've had a very successful career as a songwriter. Can you tell me why you made the decision to become a songwriter?

It wasn't like I was going to make songwriting a career. It was more like being driven to do this because of my love for music. I started playing wherever I got the chance, and when I realized that I had a gift for writing, I began knocking on doors to expose the songs. It all evolved from there. I've been very fortunate to do something that I love, and then to make a living from it—that is truly a blessing.

Could you share with me your personal process of writing a song?

Well, I think a lot of songwriters, especially when they're writing for projects, usually start with a central concept or theme. I like to start with what I call an "organic seed," which is usually a word, phrase, idea, or concept that arises out of a conversation, a situation, an article, or a story. I write those down or record that initial idea, and then nurture those organic seeds by adding craft to them. It's the old saying, 10 percent inspiration and 90 percent perspiration. If you've captured the emotion that originally moved you, it usually rings truer.

Next, I write the chorus to the song, including both the music and lyrics. I go, "How does this naturally flow, the feel of that phrase?" I try to sing that phrase and see if a musical expression comes out of it, and if not, then I'll pick up an instrument and just get a groove going and strum it out playing chords.

Then when I get a chorus melody, I'll write the lyrics for that chorus, and then I tend to work backwards from the chorus—in other words, everything leads back to the chorus, or central theme. I usually like to keep a flow going for a while without too much editing, before going back to revise it.

It sounds as if your process is very fluid. You've written songs that have been recorded by everybody, from Rod Stewart to Snoop Dogg. Do you ever work directly with an artist collaboratively when you receive an assignment?

I do. My principle collaborator has been Bobby Womack, and most of the songs I write with him are recorded by him, and often by others later. At the end of 2011, I worked with him on a project in London with Damon Albarn (of Gorillaz and Blur) and Richard Russell, the owner of XL records. We were all in the studio together writing and recording a solo project for Bobby, to be released in 2012.

My very first collaboration with Bobby was a song called "Daylight," and Vicky Sue Robinson, one of the first disco acts, recorded the song, then Leon Russell did it, and then I had a connection with those artists. In the past few years, that same song was a hit single in the UK by Kelly Rowland (of Destiny's Child).

The Snoop Dogg recording came because Bobby Womack is kind of the godfather-like figure to a lot of rappers. Other acts like 50 Cent just found tracks I had written that were on old R & B or dance records and then sampled them.

Is songwriting a learned art? Did your education in the language arts play a role in the process?

I really do think so. Everything I've learned and every experience I've had helps me to be a better songwriter. I also think that travel, experiencing other cultures, and meeting people from other countries helps you to view your own world from more than one angle. I think a good songwriter not only observes life but has to have empathy to be able to effectively shine a light on what others might be going through. I find that many of my songs come from everyday life experiences and the little idiosyncrasies that make us all a little different from one another.

And sometimes what seems really personal ends up also being universal.

I also believe in the Nike theory. Just do it—every chance you get to write for a real or imagined project or play your songs in front of an audience makes you get better at it.

Where does the money come from for a songwriter? How do you get paid?

First of all. I'd like to say that if you start off writing music just to make money, you're probably in the wrong business. Not only will you probably starve financially, you'll probably dry up creatively as well. That being said, there is definitely money to be made in songwriting, even if it's by a small percentage of those who undertake it. And when one of your songs really takes off, it can keep the royalties coming for a long time.

As a songwriter, you primarily get paid from mechanical royalties, which is a fixed amount (currently 9.1 cents in the US) for each unit of that recording that is sold. And, in addition, you get paid for performances (by the performing rights societies like ASCAP, BMI, and SEASAC) primarily on radio, TV, and some live shows. When your song is synced to a film or a commercial, the fee is usually negotiated

Then there are the other ways of generating revenue, like performing your original music and selling CDs and downloads. In my case, I also do custom songs for individuals and corporate events.

Do you have any advice for somebody that's like-minded and has a real passion for songwriting? How might they start looking at songwriting as a job?

If you're a singer songwriter and you feel like you're not performing enough, find a coffeehouse or a neighbor's house or a church or anywhere to keep improving. If you're a writer who's not a performer, then find like-minded people, go to meetup.com, writing groups, and inspire one another every chance you get.

Write, perform, collaborate, connect, whatever it takes to get yourself out there.

John Vester

John Vester delivered his first album, My Heart Is in Your Hands, *in 1998, followed by* Half a World Away *(2002),* Things I Wish I Would Have Said *(2004), and* All the Way Out West *(2007).*

Would you tell me about your approach to songwriting?

I started way back playing in bands in Cincinnati, without any real knowledge of music at all. Then moved to LA and attended a great music school . . . in Studio City, California, called the Grove School (then called the Dick Grove Music Workshops). That's where I bridged the gap between my uneducated, playing-by-ear approach and a more literate understanding of what songs are made of (words and music) and learned the tools of the trade of songwriting.

These days I also teach songwriting, and students often ask: "What comes first, words or music?"

My answer: Be prepared to start from either, words first (title or lyric idea) or music first. When I'm writing alone, it starts from either, or sometimes words and music arrive at the same time.

When I'm called to consult and work with other writers on a record project, like my work with the band Venice, I make it my business to write from any point that is required in the process. Working with Venice, sometimes we start with a piece of music that suggests a feeling that they (the artists) want to convey and I help them find the words, or starting with a good title can be a good way to begin collaborating.

What would you call the must-have skills for a great songwriter?

I'm sure everybody who's been in this business for a while would say the same thing. Develop your creative skills as a song craftsman, and cultivate your marketing side, which is a completely different skill set. Being able to do the work is important, but so is finding work!

How do you go about finding work?

Well, it helps to live in a city like Los Angeles where the record companies, the film studios, the opportunities are. When I first arrived here, I was represented by a number of different agents looking for [songwriting] opportunities for me in films, TV, and commercials. I had a streak of TV-show themes in the '90s via representation. Since then I've focused on my original intent, to write good songs to be recorded by other artists but I made ~~most connections with recording artists myself,~~ as opposed to through agents.

When you moved from Cincinnati to LA, did you have a backup plan just in case the whole songwriting thing didn't work out?

You know, if I had a backup plan, I probably would have gotten out of this business a long time ago [*laughs*]. Working without a net can be scary, but after all these years I still don't see an alternative for me.

Do you have some career high points that you would like to share?

When I first heard my band on the radio, heard the first record that I wrote, first song in a film in a theater, first TV theme showing on TV, first solo concert tour in Europe, first [European] gold record [with Venice], first time I worked with people that I've always admired, like David Crosby; for me, it's been graduating levels of firsts through the years.

John, do you have any special skills that have helped you be successful? Are you a player, a producer, do you record, engineer, any of that type of stuff?

A skill I developed twenty years ago was reading a [pilot] script for a TV show and writing a sixty-second song based on that script. I would read the script and write down words, just stream of consciousness [salient] words from the script, then feed them back to the producers who were doing that show, using their own words but in song form. Tricks like that worked very well.

I've been teaching music for twenty-plus years. When you're teaching young people, it really keeps you in touch with what's current these days on their iPods. . . . Sometimes I'll teach a Santa Monica College guitar class with as many as sixty students at once and it's awesome!

What advice would you have for someone who has that same feeling you had in Cincinnati many years ago and just wants to write songs?

In my early years, I wanted to learn from people doing what I wanted to do, who were more experienced than I was. I still do. I've found that the advice and critique of artists whose work you admire can be very helpful. Early on, when I was studying songwriting at the Grove School, I went to a local gathering of musicians and met a famous songwriter, Jim Webb. I boldly went up to him and naively said, "I really admire your work, and I'm studying songwriting. If you wouldn't mind, I would really benefit from you critiquing my work." He welcomed me to his home a number of times, and in the course of those sessions, Mr. Webb basically trashed the hell out of my early efforts, but in a very specific way that really helped me.

So while you're developing your craft, I would suggest being open to advice and critique from experienced pros and don't take it personally, just learn from it. It can make you better than ever.

John, what's the future of the music business look like to you? What do you think about when you're not worrying about paying bills?

Mixed feelings. The positive side is that we songwriters can all put it out there with the unprecedented accessibility provided by the Internet, but the downside is that we're all putting it out there, the yin and yang. I'm optimistic about my ability to get it out there, but I'm also concerned about all the competition . . . being heard through all the noise.

Kevin Quinn

Kevin Quinn is an Emmy-nominated songwriter/producer, who has composed hundreds of songs for television, records, and motion pictures, including featured songs in Disney's High School Musical *and a long string of national TV commercials.*

Is it different writing music commercially for a client as opposed to writing for an artist?

Certainly there's a difference between writing for television and writing songs for people to record on their records. Television has many specific parameters with regards to time and what you can say. For instance, you may be asked to write a sixty-second theme song that has the title of the show in the lyric or maybe a thirty-second commercial that needs to say "super-low prices."

The difference when you write for an artist is that there's much more freedom because there are less restrictions. Again, when you're writing commercially you're always trying to please the client . . . but writing for an artist allows for a much broader canvas.

Let's pretend I am a would-be client, and I called you because I need a song written for a TV show. What are the steps in your process?

Usually I'll have a meeting with the producers, and many times they're not very musically inclined at all [*laughs*]. They might say, "Well, can I have something kind of like this," but you don't know exactly what "this" means—it's just a vibe. Most of the time, I just read the script and try to understand the vibe.

As far as the process of writing for the show, I usually work with a collaborator, a number of them really. What we'll do is to try and come up with a title to write to, which might be the name of the show or something that expresses the emotion of whatever scene it is that needs a song.

How do you get hired? Who hires you? Do you have long-time clients that come to you for any project they have in the works?

I don't know, and if you find out let me know! [*laughs*]

When I started out, the studios would have agencies or music supervisors and we would get brought in on cattle calls. My first break came when a friend who was doing a bunch of kids' videos asked if I wanted to contribute. So I wrote a couple of songs and they were picked up. Next, I was asked to work on a television special for that producer, and during the project, his secretary moved on to another show. I remember she called me on a Tuesday and said, "Hey, I'm doing this new series with Eric Idol and they don't have a theme song. They need one by Thursday. Do you want to throw something at them?" And I did and we got it.

One day you might just get a call and go up against anywhere from four to fifty writers to compete for a job. When you get that call, make sure you answer it!

Do you belong to the union?

Well, I'm a SAG member and a BMI guy, but I'm not a union player, I guess. I'm a union singer, though. I don't know if there is a union for songwriters.

It doesn't sound easy . . . what would you say is the most challenging part of being a songwriter?

For me, it's just the being self-employed thing; every time I finish a project, I don't know if I'm ever going to work again. That's what you have to deal with.

What instruments do you play, Kevin?

I play guitar and a little piano. I'm a professional hack, and honestly I doubt I would hire myself to play on my own recordings. [*laughs*] Actually, I can play fine; there are just so many musicians that are so much better than me, and I know that to be true.

For an aspiring songwriter, what advice or guidance might you give?

I would say, of course, write all the time! The biggest tip I might give someone is to re-write. Re-writing doesn't hurt, because you never lose what you've started with. I approach it as *serving the song.* You may have a brilliant line in a song, but it might feel like it's out of left field, so don't be afraid to look for a better line to serve that specific song. You can always go back to the line you loved . . . or use it in another song.

I would also suggest that people collaborate, because it's a good way to expand your craft and network at the same time. It's something that has become invaluable to me; it helps you get your ego out of the way and be honest with yourself.

I've also known a lot of musicians who are afraid somebody's going to screw them over, or that everybody is trying to rip them off. Get over it! I always say that 50 percent of something is much better than 100 percent of nothing. Let it go! Keep working! Work is better than no work; it's just better. Don't live your life in fear!

One last piece of advice and understanding is that it ain't sold until you get the check, or at least it's on the air.

If you had a crystal ball, where do you see the music industry heading?

[*sigh*] Well, that's a big question. . . . Do you know about that book *The Long Tail*? I kind of follow that thesis. I think that we're going to have *more* opportunities to sell songs for less money.

I think that a lot of people are scared because the paradigm has changed . . . but music isn't going away anytime soon. So it's just figuring out how to deal with the new music world that we live in now, and forget about the past. The people that are going to be the most successful are the ones that are innovative and find new ways, new places, and new niches to place their music. It's the new do-it-yourself music business—which I find very exciting!

21

Software Developer

Rapid Fire

Skill Set—Education and more education. I recently read an article that said that 86 percent of all software engineers were recruited in their second year of college. I also heard an interview with a Harvard professor, who said, "If you aren't studying computer engineering, communication, or medicine, you needn't bother going to a university because that is our future." You decide, but I think he may be right. Twenty years ago, you could learn software design on your own—not anymore.

Hours—Every developer I know likes to work all night, but I'm sure there are day jobs as well.

Upside—Software development is a very creative field and extremely rewarding on a personal level. Software folks tend to do well financially, and it is nice when you make something new—*and* it works! Did I mention that many of the companies that develop new software are very cool places to work?

Downside—Not too much. Being a software engineer in a company is much like working for yourself, in that you develop parts and pieces and then someone else hooks them together.

Financial—$$$ to $$$$ Some software developers clean up, especially if they create software that others often use. Even typical corporate jobs in this segment pay very well.

Location—You can work in a variety of places as a software developer, including Seattle, Boston, LA, Minneapolis, Charlotte, and so on. Music software is being developed everywhere.

Future—It is a great time to have the this job and it will only get better.

"WE COULD MAKE THAT."

"What?" Greg said.

"A system where people can upload music. We could license it. The music could then be downloaded right into Avid and Final Cut Pro."

"What's an Avid?" Greg said.

"Another software system for editing video, and we could have the first system of its kind that could integrate music right into it."

"Okay, let's make it," he said.

And there I went again off to the races, setting up meetings and getting excited about building something new.

For me, software development is about building stuff, but stuff for the music industry, processes that can make it more efficient and accessible to all. For others in the software development side, it is creating systems that manipulate audio.

I've always been interested in technology and at one time pursued a degree in software programming. Moving through the years as a gearhead, I was an early adopter of every new gadget. This probably was not the best use of my time or money, but I sure learned a lot.

As an industry, music software is expanding in all directions. There are music apps for iPads, Pro Tools, third-party development of every kind, web-based social music systems, and the list continues to grow and change every day. This is one area you might enjoy researching because the options seem endless, and software will no doubt drive the future of the music business. It also ties in nicely with the entrepreneurial world as well.

Bjorn Roche

INDEPENDENT SOFTWARE DESIGNER

Bjorn wrote one of the first, and still most powerful, audio editors that runs entirely in a web browser. Recently he has been working hard on his own project, called Xonami.

Bjorn, you're a programmer that specializes in web-based audio software. Would you tell me about the challenges that presents?

I think that one of the biggest challenges is communicating my understanding of how audio works with the users, customers, and clients that may not have the same technical grounding that I have. I think the hardest part of my job is the language that I speak is not necessarily the same one my clients speak, but it's a fun challenge. Often I start with the language of music to help them understand a technical concept.

Can someone make a good living as an independent music software designer?

It's definitely possible, but staying independent is a challenge: while there is a growing acceptance of hiring contract workers, some employers are only interested in full-time workers, even if the work in question is highly specialized, like programming for audio. That said, I could probably be making a lot more money now if I weren't working on my own software, and certainty when I'm consulting I do very well.

Are you a musician?

I'm an amateur musician. I play upright bass and a little guitar. In my band I do most of the arranging and always write really simple bass parts for myself [*laughs*]. I've been playing on and off for years, though, and having a grounding in music, music theory, music recording, and editing not only helped develop my love of what I do now but also gave me the skills I needed to accomplish the tasks.

When and why did Indaba Music contact you?

I met Jesse, one of the founders of Indaba, at a club one night and we started chatting music software. I don't know if he was testing me or actually interested, but he sent me a few e-mails with questions, which I answered. Then a month later, he called and said, "We have this project. Do you know how to do it?" It turned out the project was the online digital-audio workstation, called Mantis.

At the time, Mantis was the only web-based audio editor that could record, mix, and add real-time effects. We took a very careful approach, tested a few things, did a little research first, and set aside a little money to research things we weren't as sure about. And then we jumped into development.

What formal training have you had that prepared you for the job of a software engineer?

My school had something called a concentration, which is a little less than a minor, so I got a concentration in computer science. I think if you're interested in computer programming and software design, it's really helpful to have a complimentary skill. A lot of people say, "Oh, there's money in programming and I'm interested in that, so I'm just going to go program." And then ten years later, they're a code monkey doing something that's not interesting or profitable.

I majored in math, which I don't know if I'd recommend to somebody in my shoes at that age. If I were going to do it again, I would probably go with engineering because that's really where the audio skill sets are. I also took some music and engineering classes, which were very valuable.

So tell me, Bjorn: what's the best thing about what you do?

I just love it. I have a list of what needs to be done each day and what little bugs need to be fixed and things like that. But as long as I can connect my software development back to making music, I hardly need to make the list. Of course, in every other area of my life I have a terrible memory and I need to write everything down. [*laughs*]

Do you have any advice for somebody that loves music and programming?

Well, this is a really interdisciplinary business; so the advice is not to not focus all of your energy on the computer science. If you are in a specific program for music technology, such as one of the ones offered at CCRMA, IRCAM, Queen Mary University, Universitat Pompeu Fabra, or Carnegie Mellon, you are probably in good shape to learn the various skills you need.

If not, there is still a lot you can do. For example, by working on an open-source project, helping friends record their album, and learning how everything in the music business works, you can start to understand how the computers fit in with the music.

WHEN I FIRST MET ED GRAY AT THE NAMM SHOW IN LA, it was to pitch a partnership with our company, MyMusicSource, to provide an integrated music licensing engine that would be available to users from within Avid systems and Pro Tools. Ed welcomed me and my partner, Greg Sims, and arranged a powwow with his counterparts, even though he didn't know if what we were presenting had any value whatsoever. That's the kind of guy Ed is: welcoming, straightforward, smart, quick on the uptake, and open. He is also in touch, meaning that he has his fingers in the pie and is in the know. There's not much happening in today's digital marketplace, especially as it relates to audio and video software, that Ed isn't aware of.

Ed is a perfect example of someone who doesn't perform professionally, but has successfully entered a closely related music field that fills him with rewarding challenges and keeps him close to the music he loves.

Ed Gray

VP, AVID TECHNOLOGY, INC., PRO TOOLS

Ed, you played music when you were younger. Does your job at Avid developing audio software keep you close to the music industry?

I'm as much an Avid customer as I am employee, and I'm fortunate to work in a building with professional recording studios. Most of us subscribe to multiple music publications and we're quick to share web-based news of interest. We cover music-related trade shows all over the world and design our own events to connect with the industry and with customers constantly. All this said, I wish I had more time to play—not only in the electronic medium but also on the other instruments I play (badly), including piano, percussion, banjo, and tuba.

Your formal title is Director of Partnering Programs. What exactly do you do?

Avid offers technology to help people create the most listened-to, watched, and loved media in the world. I work with an organization that gives third parties the information and resources they need to develop products for our platforms and help them when they have questions and issues. My team is also charged with feeding that information back to Avid.

I'm also in charge of screening inquiries from companies who want to develop software for our platforms—they are sometimes simple requests for access to our software developer kits (SDKs) and tools, but just as often, they are requests for unique kinds of technical and marketing help.

I've been doing this job for fifteen years and it's always full of new people, companies, and challenges.

So what is a typical day or week like for you?

My California location means that I start out pretty early with any calls to Europe, and then work my way west to Avid's HQ on the East Coast. The developers and issues have me on e-mail fairly constantly during the day, so it's sometimes a challenge to get out of crisis mode. I also am on several video conferences a day, interacting with my colleagues and developers as much as possible. I use Skype and WebEx many times per day and try to make it my business to learn about tools to keep in touch.

Would you talk a little about formal education (your MBA and Russian degrees) and how they have played a role in your success in the audio software industry?

I'm extremely proud of my education, but I also see tremendously successful people in the music industry without the parchment paper on the wall. I not only work on partnering programs, but also in corporate development, and merger and acquisition. My business training has been indispensable in those roles. A great education is forever—and it has provided me with degrees of creativity, experience, and gratitude for which there are no substitutes.

What's the toughest part of your job?

It would probably be getting to all of the requests for information and support that require personal interaction. There is just not enough time in the day. Each time one of these things is handled late or dropped, I've risked or squandered an opportunity to help an important person or company succeed.

Conversely, what is the most rewarding part?

Two things, really. First, seeing a company grow from an idea to a prosperous business using the tools and programs we've shared with them; and second, seeing one of our products gain recognition, not only because of its own features but also because of the offerings delivered by our partners, many that are also personal friends.

Do you come in contact with high-profile musicians in your business?

Too many to list, and I'm one of the guys for whom this never gets old. I have asked Béla Fleck for his security badge, performed onstage with George Clinton, been credited on a Yes album, had a synthesizer shown to Devo and—in an incident I'd like to forget, I waved to Stevie Wonder. So the answer is yes. At on-site events, at trade shows, and at parties, I've enjoyed meeting not only legendary artists but also the engineers that help them sound the way they do.

Does the Internet play a role in the audio software business? Will we be seeing audio editing platforms moving to the web anytime soon?

There are already audio-editing platforms on the web playing a large and growing role. Musicians are discovering each other, sharing, buying and selling content, collaborating live (with limitations of bandwidth), and editing multi-track compositions with video. However, the heavy lifting required to manipulate hundreds of multi-channel tracks and high sample and bit rates with tons of audio effects is prodigious data-processing work. The Internet is not yet the medium for creative people who need these guaranteed levels of performance, but we are a creative, innovative, and tenacious community who will find a way to get it there in time.

How about Facebook, Twitter, and iPad? How do you see social networks and new platforms fitting into the puzzle?

The growth of mobile computing and social networking are certain to make these technologies central to the ways we consume and distribute our music—hardly a new observation. I'm also convinced that they'll play an increasingly key role in the way tools for music creation is made. Social media is being used to evaluate developer programs, to locate talent, and to support others in the same developer communities, from reporting bugs and answering developer questions to previewing apps and sharing code.

What does the future of the music business look like to you?

I remember the Ensoniq ESQ-1 I purchased with my summer earnings in 1987. It came with an EPROM and eighty sounds on it. Some of them sucked, some were okay, and there was a piano and a trumpet, which for the day, sounded exquisite. Over that year, I spent $40 for an E2PROM with 160 patches, some of which were pretty good. A year after that, I dropped $50 on a floppy disk with about 1,000 patches, some of which sounded great and the rest unusable.

Fast-forward to 2011. Fire up Pro Tools and a virtual instrument created by one of our developers, and play the first ten randomly selected patches. If you're like me, you will ask, "Who did that and how the hell did they do it?" The sounds and content available today is limitless and in many cases, sonically fantastic. It's a great time to be in this business!

22

Studio Owner

Rapid Fire

Skill Set—Owning a studio is an entrepreneurial venture. It is also foremost a business, so you need all of the typical business skills to make it fly. You'll need an understanding of people, accounting, expenses, marketing, you name it. I would suggest an internship at a good studio before jumping in.

Hours—Ha-ha, if you are a studio owner, you can forget about sleep for the first couple of years as you sweat it out establishing your studio. Or conversely, if you already have a bunch of money or angel investors, you can hire someone else to do the sweating.

Upside—I have owned many studios and loved almost every second. It is such diverse work, and there are just so many different things you might get into, from recording bands to audio post for film.

Downside—You might find yourself becoming a workaholic. Capital investments in equipment can drain your bank account (fortunately not as much as in the past) and to make real money you need a couple of studios humming along, which means hiring people! The human relations part of the job can be tough.

Financial—$$$ to $$$$ If you do everything right, you can make a very, very comfortable living. I would start a studio with the endgame of selling it to someone else when you're ready to move on. But if you do everything wrong . . . you get the drift?

Location—Place yourself in a major market for film, TV, advertising, or mid-size markets with lots of corporate headquarters where they create training films, promotions, and marketing media.

Future—Owning a commercial studio is a pretty solid opportunity both as an investment and a job. Some have told me it's dying, but I don't buy into that thinking. I bet I could go out, open a studio today, and start making money in thirty days. However, I do think you should consider getting some help and finding a mentor to get you up to speed and trained in the ways of business before venturing out.

AT SOME POINT, IF YOU ARE A COMPOSER, like I was, you are faced with a few important business decisions. I'd like to introduce you to my thought process and why I decided to start a business as opposed to being a hired-gun composer. In my case, I was the composer who sat in the back room writing music while my partner was in the front office lining up our next job—or so I thought. He was, in fact, lining up *his* next job, which didn't include me. Looking back, I guess I couldn't blame him, because we weren't making the kind of money either of us wanted.

One day he came into the room and announced, "Michael, I have taken a new job and will be running a large music library and won't be coming into the office anymore." I smiled but was devastated because I didn't know what I was going to do. I had been the good partner, writing music and engineering along the way, but now it was decision time. I could go back to work as an engineer for a guy I really didn't like, or face the world as a composer and open my own little studio to commercial use.

I chose the latter, and after a bit of a rough start, was able to break into the market as a one-man shop both composing and engineering. One of the most challenging parts of my decision was that I needed to understand the economics of running a business, which included accounting, marketing, utilities, rent, taxes, etc. Having dealt with the business issues, I was rewarded with the benefit of being my own boss and keeping the fruits of my labors (after taxes). I was single at the time and sometimes worked eighteen-hour days, but it sure felt good to see my own personal wealth growing and enjoying the freedom that it brought.

While I scoured the local market for work, I finally realized that almost every business needed my skills as an engineer. Marketing departments created videos, did in-house promotion, and made training films; the local TV stations did radio sweeps every eight weeks or so. There was money to be made. A couple of days ago, I met with a nice young fellow at a friend's request to offer career advice at my local Starbucks office. He was a guitarist and recording engineer who was struggling to decide which path he should take. I could tell right away that he was pretty knowledgeable about the tech side of things and loved music. I also sensed the trepidation about his future in the music business. We talked for a long time about the business, and he seemed happy when mentioning a track he had written for a TV commercial. He thoroughly enjoyed the process. I immediately honed in on how he might turn his skills into dollars by starting a small commercial recording studio that specialized in advertising and marketing. In a small market like Cleveland, Ohio, there are several advertising agencies, but the larger competitors don't bother to spend time marketing to the corporations and ad agencies.

I made most of my money in the advertising industry and have a broad understanding of that market, so I proceeded to give Jake advice and recommended strategies he might employ to make it all happen. As a studio owner, Jake could make money in a variety of ways, including studio fees, licensing, music fees, and composition, and as a sole proprietor, the business side of things is simple. No human resources, payroll, etc., and the only overhead is rent and equipment (which is inexpensive today).

I was very lucky in the studio business because I worked with professionals who actually knew what they were doing. This led to a certain measure of freedom for me. Owning a studio can be the best part of many worlds if set up in a way that allows you to generate money in the studio while you're driving revenue as a composer, as an example.

New business owners, here's a story of warning.

I once hired the chief operating officer of Disney to work in my small film-production company in Orlando, Florida. We were so excited to have a guy of his stature working with us, a guy who could assure our success. His name was Dave, and Dave would sit at the computer day after day, working on Excel spreadsheets and running numbers for our little organization. I didn't really know what he was doing, but it seemed very important!

Everything was going well for the first few months, until one day when I spotted something strange on our bank statement. I went to Dave's office and asked him to have breakfast with me the following morning.

At 7:30 a.m. we met at a business club next to our office, and halfway through a cup of coffee I asked, "So, Dave, how's it going? What does our future look like?" He opened his briefcase and pulled out a binder with at least 200 pages of Excel spreadsheets. "Michael, we're going to have unbelievable growth next year. I have us doubling our staff, and at least another million in equipment acquisition."

I did my best to give a calm response. "Dave, yesterday I looked at our bank statement; did you see it?" Dave replied in the negative, so I continued, "Well, we have a problem, and if I am doing the math right, we will be out of money in twenty-one days, and out of business in thirty. I have to let you go; you don't need to come back to the office."

There is a moral to this story. Surround yourself with great people, but never take your eye off the ball. When you own a business, you have people and their families depending on you.

Andrew Sherman

Butter Studio

Would you talk about the difference between owning and running a commercial music house as opposed to being a composer that works in one?

More than anything, I tend to blur the line so much that I can't really tell the difference anymore. It does make it easier to accept the moments when somebody doesn't leave the legal on the screen long enough and I have to go back and redo music that I've already done *[laughs]* . . . knowing that that's going to keep the lights on makes it easier to swallow the pill. The other stuff is just business as business, paying the bills, insurance, etc.

What would be the criteria for signing a new composer to work for your company, Butter?

It's rare that we hire full-time these days, and I say this with a tear in my eye, to hire staff composers here at Butter because we have so many out-of-house composers that are available to us with the technology that currently exists.

Having said that, anyone will tell you that if you come with a client list, they will hire you. If you come as a high-caliber person, amazing programmer, and composer, you're on my list. It's a short list but great one, not necessarily a list of employees. It is a list of our composer resources.

Running this kind of studio is more about whom you know, keeping track of people, letting clients know you're still around and doing great work. Hopefully your client had a great time the last time they worked with you and will bring you their next job. That's the owner part.

It sounds like you can make a good living, and Butter is thriving even though budgets are lower than they were five years ago. That's great! How are you handling this era of smaller budgeted projects?

I remind myself every day that budgets were completely and grossly inflated to begin with, and I don't look at it like the world's going to hell. . . . it's more like, "They're finally waking up," you know what I mean? We watched it with the music business twelve years ago when the big studios in New York went out of business. It's just the nature of a shrinking economy, and I'm not discouraged by it. I think that it's actually a sign that people are starting to pay attention, which I don't think is such a bad thing.

And you just have to get more jobs. Twenty years ago, if I wrote the Dr Pepper jingle, that would be all I would have to do for a couple of years because it would net me six figures a year. Today, the only thing that can net you that kind of cash is singing on high-profile spots, and that's not long for this world either. It's sort of the last bastion of the unionized thing.

I feel we're approaching it pretty quickly, but people still argue:

Me: Well, for *that* kind of money, you could just go license a piece of stock music.

Client: Yeah, but I want to own it!

Me: Yeah, but you can't buy stock music—that's why they call it stock.

Client: I want it tailor-made for my track.

Me: Well, you can't do that with stock.

There is a pretty funny version of this conversation on YouTube somewhere. . . .

So there is a line for custom music price-wise that won't get crossed, and I think we kind of know where that is.

That's very insightful, Andrew. Advertising music itself can be very lucrative, but it's also extremely competitive; along the line of the "value add," how do you position Butter to stay in the game and top of the mind?

First, we maintain a strong position in the community. If you're going to do music for advertising, the places to locate are New York, LA, or Chicago—however, there are always emerging markets like Austin with GSD&M down there. . . .

There are events we sponsor or attend that can keep the social aspect fresh, and then we just try to constantly over-deliver.

Simply put, this business is the sum of its parts. You can go to some music company's website and see the super-sexy Nike spot that's music driven (with no dialogue and really cool footage) and the spot is amazing; but those big brands make very few of those a year . . . and the competition gets pretty fierce.

If you want a company that's going to thrive in this business, you also have to be able to do a Pampers spot with tons of copy in it also—I feel like we have creative composers who understand the role music plays in the overall presentation . . . they know when to step up and when to back off.

We started out as a company that primarily created music for comedy spots, and we were A list in that department. The trend has shifted these days, and music simply isn't in the comedy spots the way it once was. When it first became evident, my reaction was, "Shit!" [*laughs*] but it caused us to evolve. . . . these days I think it has actually come back a bit.

If you had a crystal ball, what would the future of the music business look like? What do you see coming?

This is not going to be a short answer [*laughs*]. For the last ten years, I've been watching record production shrink because of the fat they couldn't get rid of. If you were ever in the Hit Factory building in Manhattan, you know what I'm talking about—tons of overhead in a market that is bleeding. To me, what's happening in the music business is actually a very, very positive thing, for two reasons.

We're putting the power back in the hands of the musician in a way that gives them many options. There's no easy way to make it in the music business if you're not great at what you do. Assuming that you're good, I think that the music creation tools are readily available to allow musicians to create their own career.

Places like Kickstarter are fantastic for artists. I know for a fact that you don't need $100,000 to make a great record; you can do it for $20,000. You can get $40,000 on Kickstarter if you pre-sell it properly, promise a certain amount of people your record, and create the appropriate pitch. You can pre-sell 1,000 copies of your record, at which point you have the money to make it, and after that everything's gravy. . . . I've just finished such a record.

Yes, the days of me sending a limo to pick you up at the airport when you get into town to come and sign your contract before I ever hear a peep of music out of you are over, and I'm personally glad they are. It was nothing but bullshit anyway . . . enough with the waterfalls in the lobby already.

Musicians don't need to sell a million copies of their record to make money today. They can sell 10,000 copies and forget the label-oriented overhead-generating machine.

If you have 500 friends on Facebook that are actually your friends and not just people that you friended, then 500 people at 10 bucks a record is 5,000 dollars. Five hundred people at twenty bucks with a free T-shirt: $10,000. Or 500 people at $50 get a free concert. . . . There are all kinds of ways for the artist to create their own income now.

Of course, labels are now trying to take percentages of ticket sales to live concerts, etc., calling it a 360 deal, so the Kickstarter thing looks better and better.

What better way to make money as a musician than to be an entrepreneur and not necessarily have to be a businessman!

Right . . . keep more of it! The old model was getting $250,000 for a record deal. It happened to me; I got $250,000 to make a record; $200,000 of it went to making the record, $50,000 of it went in our pockets to live on for what was probably going to be a year at the time. Our agent got 20 percent, boosters got 60 percent . . . that money got carved up immediately into things that had very little to do with our music.

So yeah . . . to get to the same number, it doesn't take a record deal anymore . . . just a little self-reliance and creativity . . . and a good video pitch.

Michael Redman

REDHOUSE

Yes—it's my turn again!

What is the best part of being a studio owner?

Well, I would say for the larger studios I have owned, it is being a part of a talented team of individuals and working towards a single goal, which is to bring creative ideas to life, be it an attraction for Disney, or the perfect music for one of our client's projects. It would be the team.

Is the studio business still viable?

Starting a small studio is not only doable today it's inexpensive. That translates to less overhead and a smaller financial commitment to meet each month. There is lots of work if you are creative and don't limit yourself to a defined piece of business, like perhaps radio spots. You need to aggregate many different clients and put yourself out into the community to build a variety of relationships.

Can you make money running a recording studio?

Yes, I made a very good living even when I was a one-man shop, like many studio owners are today. Again, I would say that you should to be versatile, creative, and a great problem solver.

How would someone get started?

Start by developing a business plan. It doesn't need to be a plan, like what would be developed for raising capital, but one that helps you think through the important stuff. You need to know who your clients might be, where they are, your costs, including rent, equipment, etc., and how all of that relates to you financial investment and profits.

You might also consider renting a small office space in a central location that's convenient to your potential clients. I say this because the home studio, for the most part, does not have the professional environment that many of your clients will expect. Next, only buy the equipment that you need to get the job done and avoid the equipment junky syndrome.

What was the most fun you have ever had in your studio?

I think as an owner, fun might be defined as landing a job and the relief that goes along with knowing that payroll will be taken care of for a while, so it may have been the day we won a contract with Universal Studios for $750,000 to create the music and sound design for a great animated film in Barcelona. It had to be dubbed in three languages, and the attraction had multiple little films that supported the main motion-based ride.

How much can I make with my own studio?

This is a very hard question to answer, but let's just take one scenario. You have a little studio and record radio spots for ad agencies, maybe a couple of spots five days a week. You would make money for the studio, and a mark-up on the music, talent, materials, and possibly remote recording, etc. So you might gross a profit of $1,000 a day. That translates into $250,000-plus a year. Not bad, but you need to pay your expenses and such.

Is there a downside to owning a commercial studio?

As a one-man shop, it wasn't bad, because you are the master of your own little universe.

When work slowed, you just looked for more. I really can't say there was much I worried about.

With my bigger studios the stress was on the human resources side of our business. We had about thirty employees, and when there was a slowdown, we still had a sizable payroll to meet each week. My partner, Tom, and I would sit for hours worrying and trying to figure out how we could make it all work. Through the years, we had to let many great people go and downsize our business. It was tough. This is the reason you don't see very many big studios these days; technology has changed everything in the studio business.

23

Touring Musician

Rapid Fire

Skill Set—You must be personable, a terrific player, maybe like to play golf, like to travel, get along with others, and did I mention be a terrific player? Being able to read charts helps too.

Hours—Your hours as a touring musician follow the tour schedule. You sometimes rehearse and sometimes don't. There are typically sound checks in the afternoon. In the evening you play the shows, and then potentially do a meet and greet. Or it could be onto the bus or plane and off to the next gig.

Upside—You get to play and are paid for it! Like I said—if you like golf, you might get to play a lot. You are usually working with other great musicians and sometimes become a family. Travel is a plus if you're into it and don't have small children at home missing you.

Downside—Although there is probably more touring than a decade ago, the big gigs are few and far between, which makes it harder to build a fulltime career as a touring musician.

Financial—$$ to $$$$ Pay for this job runs the gamut. There are musicians who stay on an annual contract, like Tim Akers, and then there are contracted numbers of performance, etc. You can, however, make nice money as a sideman touring musician. Just ask around.

Location—I would say that if you want to do this and supplement with other music jobs, I would live in NY, LA, or Nashville because that's where a large majority of the concert tours originate.

Future—I talked earlier about bands needing to tour to make a living. If you want to specialize in this field, do a great job and get your name out there. I believe the future to be bright for touring. Bands and solo artists need great musicians to make them sound great!

I WAS TALKING WITH A LONGTIME FRIEND, Michael McAdam, who is an extraordinary guitarist and spent much of the past twenty-five years touring the USA and Europe as a side musician. As we were driving by a parking lot in Nashville, where he lives, he said, "Every Thursday, this parking lot used to be filled with musicians loading up their gear to head out on tour with everybody from Clint Black to Alabama. It was surreal because touring was just a way of life and nobody gave it a second thought. Today this lot is empty most of the time. Things have changed and the big acts don't tour the way they used to."

Michael now travels from Nashville to Key West, Florida, every four weeks or so, as he has for the past nine years, to play with multiple bands, including Bill Blue, the Hog's Breath Allstars, Pinmonkey, and his band, the Holt/McAdam Band. For Mike, touring is his life and he loves it.

If you talk to most experts, they will tell you that monetizing music today is a moving target, but at some point it will get figured out. The experts will also add that there are a couple of traditional avenues for bands and artists that are growing, one being touring. Artists can still make a good living by touring and selling CDs, downloads, and merchandise; this revenue stream won't be disappearing anytime soon.

Many acts that tour, including solo artist', don't have a full band and fill the ranks with touring musicians on the road. There are musicians that specialize in touring, and others that just go out on occasion to tour with specific acts. The touring musicians who are in the highest demand are those who play multiple instruments and sing as well. These folks are called utility musicians because they might play keyboards, percussion, violin, and sing equally well. These utility players do very well financially and can charge more, since they are saving the artist the need to hire multiple musicians to play instruments that only play a small part in the overall concert presentation.

Tours today can be local, national, worldwide, small venue, large arena, three days or 9 months in length, and there are a lot of them. Some of the musicians I interviewed for this section make a living by including touring as one of the many revenue streams they leverage as part of their career. As you will read, touring is not for everyone but it can be exciting, and it's alive and well as a job option.

I MENTIONED EARLIER IN THIS BOOK about the need to be versatile and connect several income streams to reach your financials goals. Many people who are great players in the music business, but not necessarily artists in their own right, look to jobs that make good use of their skill set. For example, if you are an incredible pianist or keyboard player, you may be able to make a very comfortable living as a session player, touring musician, arranger, etc.

This is exactly what my longtime friend Tim Akers has done. He is cool, positive, a joy to hang with, and yes, an incredible player. So much so that he doesn't need to look for work. People are looking for Tim. Well, I found Tim and we talked about being on the road with Rascal Flatts and what it's like to be a touring musician.

Tim Akers

KEYBOARDIST

Currently touring with Rascal Flatts.

Tim, you're under contract with one of the hottest bands in the country, Rascal Flatts. Would you tell me a little bit about being a touring musician?

The Flatts gig is great! I consider it a pretty easy touring gig, from the standpoint that we're not gone for five weeks without a break. We pretty much just play weekends, then once a year or so we'll go out and do a couple of weeks on the West Coast. I feel like the Flatts have really figured out the balance of being able to tour and support your record and do what's necessary to keep the act alive.

You have to get out there and let people see you, but at the same time, all those guys have families. I have a family. Nobody wants to be gone for long, long periods of time. That's a game for the young and single.

Are there guys that make a living solely doing the touring sideman thing?

Oh yeah, there are hundreds of them! There's a lot of touring acts that travel to such an extent that it's difficult to do anything else. LeAnn Rimes is a good example because when I traveled with her, we would go out for three weeks at a stretch, come home for four days, and go back out for a few more weeks. When you do that, it's hard to keep your session accounts alive. Everybody gets the impression you're out of town even when you're in town for four months straight!

What are the different ways that tour musicians get paid? Is there a union, that kind of thing?

There is a union, but there are some problems on the touring side. On the recording side, the union has a very strong presence, and we have a pretty decent pension fund that the labels and publishers contribute to every time we do a recording session. However, in the touring world, it seems that the presence of the union is not as strong. My suspicion as to why that is, is that the official union scales for live performances are so low, most touring acts pay well above that scale; therefore, there has not been a lot of motivation to get all the live acts on the card. I know the AF of M would like to change that, if for no other reason than to get pension contributions for us from our employers. However, the sheer number of live acts out there on the road today seems to make that almost insurmountable.

Is there a typical scale for touring players?

It really runs the gamut. I know that there are guys out there making $150 a show, and then there are guys making $1,000-plus a show. A lot of the busier studio guys will charge a per-day rate, as opposed to a per-show rate, because every day that they're out of town, they are most likely losing money.

There are some acts that use a salary system. They figure up a rough annual per-show number, like, "We know we're going to do eighty shows this year," for instance. They will figure that into an annual salary and give you a bi-weekly paycheck. You don't get a really fat paycheck from a two-week run, but the trade-off is that you'll end up with several weeks every year where you're off work with pay. That's a nice thing.

What is the biggest challenge on tour?

Um . . . probably personal space. You're on a tour bus, which is basically an aluminum tube, with anywhere from eight to twelve other people, and it's very difficult to find any privacy. That's really the only challenge, to tell you the truth, that and being away from family.

Yes, that's definitely a trade-off. Is there one touring gig that stands out in your mind? A time when you were sitting up there, playing, and thinking, "This is where I've always wanted to be, this is where I belong"?

I think it would be the first time that I played live with Michael McDonald. I had just been such an enormous fan of Michael's my entire life, and never dreamed in a million years that I would ever get to work with him. I played several charity events with him as music director, and I ended up writing some arrangements for his next record, *Blue Obsession*, which led to more shows, and ultimately I even did some touring with him. I think the other one was playing with Stevie Wonder. Playing with those guys was really the pinnacle for me—like, "Okay, I'm done, shoot me."

Arnold McCuller

VOCALIST

Arnold McCuller has worked with top recording artists such as Phil Collins and James Taylor.

Can you describe the role of a feature vocalist in a touring band?

I've only toured with a few bands: Lyle Lovett, Phil Collins, and James Taylor. I'm brought in to help create the vocal sound and monitor it throughout the tour. If parts are getting sloppy or if someone's not carrying or changed the part inadvertently, I'm there to bring it back into line.

As a featured vocalist, I sing [step out] to James Taylor. Step-outs meaning shout chorus on "Shower the People" or duet with James on "Knock on Wood." A solo bit as well. With Lyle Lovett I do a couple duets with him and a lot of shout chorus stuff where I'm singing ad libs. I'm the only singer he trusts to do ad libs. I just got home from a tour with Lyle last Thursday, and I told him, "I've never, ever worked live where someone gave me the latitude you give me."

That's just great! Did touring with Lyle and James come from your recording with them?

I toured first with James in 1977 and then recorded *Flag* in '79. With Lyle, I recorded a song for a movie with Don Was. It was a Robert Altman movie and he was doing the title song. After we recorded the track, he said, "Would you be interested in touring with me?" And I said, "I'd love to." With Bonnie Raitt, I mostly record with her, but I've also done a little bit of touring with her, and sometimes I'll be in the audience and she'll bring me up to sing.

I would love to sit in the studio with Bonnie and just observe.

She really knows what she wants. She's very persnickety and it takes her a long time to figure out what's right, but when she's clear, when she finds it, she knows exactly what it is. She's great.

Tell me a little about touring. How do you travel? What's the typical tour length?

The last Lyle tour was three weeks and we traveled in a tour bus. There's usually a bus for the band and the bus for the lead artist. I almost always travel on the lead artist bus and the band bus is usually for the guys.

The lead artist bus is where we take care of ourselves: we eat healthy, we sleep more, and all that. The band bus is a little looser, and the guys will be drinking a little more, or stay up watching movies, or playing more tunes late at night.

Is there one tour that just stands out in your mind as one of the best tours you've ever been on in all these years?

I think the first time I did Rock in Rio was great. I went to Brazil and it was overwhelming. We did this rock festival, and there were 600,000 Brazilians singing in English in the middle of the soccer field. We got stuck in a horrible bus traffic jam trying to get into the parking lot and sat all night until daybreak. We had finished our gig at 2 a.m. but didn't get back to the hotel till 6 or 7 a.m.

There were also some Phil Collins tours that were really wonderful. I toured with Phil for years and then recorded with him. He is a very generous man, and we had an amazing band. He also paid more and gave us bonuses at the end of the tour. It was because of Leland Sklar that I got that gig. He told Phil to "get Arnold and let him put together the singing group for you."

Would you talk a little bit about preparation, rehearsals, and that kind of thing?

I've only rehearsed once with Lyle and we never rehearsed again. We've recorded tunes and practiced live versions of them, but he doesn't rehearse. He just doesn't. Sometimes he doesn't even show up for sound check.

James, on the other hand, rehearses a lot. We rehearse a full day even for a private date. Everything he does is two, three, or four days of rehearsal.

Tour schedules are all over the place. James Taylor's are two days on and one day off, while on the last Lyle tour we did ten shows in a three-week period with only two days off!

How has social media affected your career?

Digitally, everyone is involved in the social medias and interactive stuff. I think James is trying to stay on top of it and is inspired by the younger artists. They set the bar for the new path and distribution models. Not being in the younger crowd, the video thing is not so important to me, though. You see fewer and fewer older artists making videos to coincide with their music releases, unless it's just a live show.

Please sum up a path for someone wanting to follow in your footsteps.

The best thing to do is live in New York, LA, Nashville, or a city where there are lots of recording sessions. Meet producers that are hiring singers and send them demo reels. At the end of the day, it's whom you know and who's willing to bring you into a session to help you get started. Good luck!

Lee Sklar

BASSIST

Lee, you are a long-standing member of James Taylor's and Lyle Lovett's road band. Do you spend a lot of time on the road?

It's different every year. I've spent seven months on the road this year, but maybe less next year. I never know.

What advice would you give someone who wants to be a touring musician?

Have the full support of your family; it is a hard life. The shows are a gift each night, but the travel and lifestyle are tough and not for everyone. Try to stay focused and not waste your time getting high and drunk because you'll probably lose your gig; it is a *job* and you are a professional. Treat your gig and fellow players with respect. *Enjoy* every minute of it—it is *magical*.

What kind of travel accommodations do you have and does it vary from band to band?

This varies a lot from band to band. We have used private planes in the past, but most of the time we are on busses nowadays.

What's the coolest touring gig you've had?

All the years with James Taylor were amazing, as was this year with the J.T. and Carole King reunion tour. Phil Collins was always a great joy to tour with, as was Jackson Browne when we did the Running on Empty tour. The main thing I enjoy about touring is simple: I love working *and* playing.

What are the challenges of touring? Your family? The hours? Band politics?

There are always things that will make you crazy, but that is life, and when you throw a group of creative individuals together, anything can happen and usually does. It is an interesting dynamic.

What would be a good start for someone who wants to be a touring musician?

You just have to meet people and make connections. Try to let people know you are there and want to do it. There are no shortcuts.

What does the future look like for Lee Sklar— beyond sessions, tours, and fast cars?

I think that is about it! [*laughs*] I never thought at this age that I would be an in-demand recording and touring musician. I pinch myself every day and am happy when that phone rings and I get to play and hang with the greatest musicians and artists in the world. Holy crap! It does not get any better!

IF YOU'VE MADE IT THROUGH THIS ENTIRE BOOK, CONGRATULATIONS! You now know that there are many paths to success in the music business besides the elusive stardom as a performer.

Now I'd like to ask you one last question. For those of us who love music, what makes us pursue it for a lifetime? Contemplate this question and try to appreciate what it could mean to you personally. It will be your guiding light in troubled times as you brave art as a career.

I've come full circle from those early days playing drums and running with abandon towards a record contract, to finally understanding the economics of life and then turning to business . . . it's been an interesting journey.

There has always been one constant for me, and that's the beat. I love that 105-to-120-bpm groove. It makes my body move in sometimes a most uncoordinated way (I have never been a good dancer). The other thing that gets to me is a good blues scale, not necessarily blues music but the raw nature of the notes themselves. Adele, the young woman who swept the Grammys, has that magic combination, as does Bonnie Raitt, Robert Cray, Johnny Lang, and a host of other artists.

Hey—did you know that music is the only phenomena in the human experience that electrifies all four quadrants of our brain at the same time? Maybe that's why we live to play music, and those who don't play long to hear music, to experience something very special inspired by the almighty, or spirit, or universe. Whatever you believe is the reason why we are here.

I'd like to leave you with a few thoughts, and then it's up to you to discover who you are as an artist, or where you might fit in and be the most comfortable and effective in the music business.

next steps

MY FINAL ADVICE TO YOU would be to spend a little time away from your instrument and work on both your career and life plan. The time you spend thinking about what you might like to do, what will make you happy, and what you are good at may well be the most important time you ever take for yourself.

You see, most people, including musicians, don't plan much of anything and just react to current situations and possible outcomes. I am a big believer that we all can make our own future, but it requires due diligence and careful planning. Your plan may fail, but you will feel better knowing you had one, and I guarantee you will do better in life with a plan than without.

A good next step might be to create a simple "like" list. Remember in the beginning when I told you make a budget? Well, let's make a more detailed list of the things you would like in a job. For example, say you like to stay up late at night, and you don't want to live in LA but NY would be okay. You are good with numbers but bad performing the same task for an extended period of time. Your list might look something like this:

LIKE:	DON'T LIKE:	SKILLS:
New music	Doing the same thing everyday	Good with people
Late nights	NY	Technical stuff
Movies	Pressure	Great player
Travel	Stressful situations	Play multiple instruments

Next, match up some of the jobs in this book that fit your skill set and aspirations. Then if I were you, I might take just a little more time and track down a few people like the ones I have interviewed and ask them the questions that you are no doubt deliberating. You might be surprised that most successful people in the music business are more than willing to share their experience and advice with you (if approached in a friendly, non-threatening way.)

In the process of writing this book I have also become enlightened. You see, when I started researching the different jobs in the music industry, I must admit that I was not bullish on the future of the business. It's easy to think that the music business is a mess, like much of our economy, but somewhere along the line while talking to some of my contributors, I changed my mind. I realized that this is the most exciting time in recent history to be in our business because the gatekeeper record companies are disappearing. It's like the wicked witch is dead. Now, that's not to say that the large record companies are the devil or anything of the sort. It's more like, "Come on, everybody can be a record company." Technology is allowing everyone who loves music to have a chance to create it and make it on a level playing field that has risen from of the ashes of the music industry. I focused on some of the higher-profile jobs in the music business, but in future editions I'll expand on at least fifty other jobs that can be found in the music business, like a friend of mine who blogs about indie bands for MTV, or the personal manager who guides the careers of artists, or the editor at a music book publisher like Hal Leonard, or the music-prep person who helps a film composer get ready for a recording session. There are many, many great jobs in this industry, and I know in my heart and gut that there is one that will keep you close to the music you love and provide a secure living as well.

So it's time now, time for you to plan for your future in music!

Thank you for reading, and I hope in some small way I have shined a light on a possible future in music for you. You can follow this and future publications on my website: www.thebestmusicjobs.com

contributors

I BRIEFLY MENTIONED in the beginning that one of the greatest joys of writing this book was getting to know the people that I interviewed. I cannot stress enough how important their views have been, and I will be forever grateful for the chance to meet them and the time they have shared with me.

Tim Akers

timakersmusic.com

Tim Akers is a keyboard player, session musician, songwriter, arranger, and producer living in Nashville, Tennessee. He has been a studio session player for many artists and projects, including Kid Rock, Kenny Loggins, Michael McDonald (including the platinum-selling *Motown* record), Faith Hill, Keith Urban, Megadeth, Michael Bolton, Rascal Flatts, SHeDAISY, Jewel, LeAnn Rimes, Trace Adkins, Glen Campbell, Barry Manilow, actor Jeff Bridges, Pam Tillis, Patti LaBelle, Joss Stone, Wynonna, and Josh Gracin (of *American Idol* fame). He has also performed on the movie soundtracks for *Chicken Little*, *Evan Almighty*, *Herbie Fully Loaded*, *The Prince of Egypt*, *We Were Soldiers*, *Kissing Jessica Stein*, and *Anastasia*.

From 1997 through 1999, Akers was the music director for TNN's flagship music/talk show, *Prime Time Country*, starring Gary Chapman. He has performed with hundreds of artists from all genres, including Dolly Parton, SHeDAISY, Bruce Hornsby, Paul Williams, Jimmy Webb, Lou Rawls, and actor/performer Kevin Bacon. His songs have been played on television shows such as *Lois and Clark*, *Late Night with Conan O'Brien*, and *Lifestyles of the Rich and Famous*. Akers's most recent projects include the new Kid Rock record, *Rock n Roll Jesus*. He also recently conducted the orchestra for Kenny Loggins, Travis Tritt, and Patti LaBelle at an all-star bash in Los Angeles.

Chuck Archard

Chuck Archard is an accomplished bassist, composer, and educator. He is a member of ASCAP and a primary composer for the Power House Music Library (mymusicsource.com), and his original works have aired on the major TV networks as well as Fox, HBO, Showtime, and in thirty international markets. Archard's music has been used in numerous motion pictures, including *Career Girls*, *Substance of Fire*, and *Santa, Jr.* Archard has performed and recorded with artists, including Isaac Hayes, Larry Coryell, Peter Erskine, Danny Gottlieb, and Gene Bertoncini. He is in demand as a studio musician, and has played for national television commercials and more than one hundred CDs. He is the bassist for Warner Bros. and Shawnee Press educational publications. He is the co-owner of World Time Music, where he is also the composer.

Archard holds BME and MM degrees from Morehead State University, and is currently an artist in residence at Rollins College in Winter Park, Florida, where he teaches numerous classes, directs the jazz ensemble, and gives private lessons. Currently, he is working with legendary bassist/composer Stanley Clarke, transcribing all of Clarke's compositions for future publications.

Mary Lou Arnold

Mary Lou Arnold is tour director and personal assistant to Todd Rundgren and his band, Utopia. She began work at Rundgren's Utopia video studio in 1980, and within a few years became road manager for the band. Arnold managed tours and worked as a production coordinator for Utopia for many years. She was also one of the singers in Rundgren's "eleven voice orchestra" on his a cappella tour in the mid–'80s.

Arnold graduated from the State University of New York at Buffalo with a degree in art education, and sang throughout her college years. Arnold currently sings with the State University of New York at New Paltz College/Community Chorale, performing classical works as a chorale member and soloist.

Brian Black

zoophoriamusic.com

Brian Black is founder and president of Zoophoria Music, a music supervision and soundtrack production company based in West Hollywood, California. His feature film credits include *Meet Me in Miami*, *Sam's Lake*, *A Dance for Bethany*, *Cupid's Arrow*, and *American Flyer*. Brian has worked in the film/TV music department at PolyGram and Universal Music Group and in various capacities at Geffen/DGC Records and MCA Records.

Mike Boris

mikeboris.com

Mike Boris is an independent music consultant who brings musicians and the advertising world together. Over the course of his career, he has placed, scored, coordinated, and recorded the music for over 6,000 commercials. Boris's awards include the McCann-Erickson Producer of the Year for 2006, a CLIO, and several Effies. Prior to becoming an independent consultant, Boris was SVP Executive Music Producer at McCann Erickson in New York, where he produced music for a wide range of clients, including MasterCard, Verizon, L'Oreal, Kohl's, Nikon, Intel, the US Army, Applebee's, Holiday Inn, Weight Watchers, Staples, Avis, Unilever Brands, Xbox, MLB, Sony Erickson, Nestle, and NASDAQ.

Boris began his career as a recording engineer and transitioned to the role of music producer. He honed his craft at several New York ad agencies before joining McCann. Boris was also the drummer of the band More F*ing Cowbells, which won *Adweek*'s Battle of the Ad Bands for two consecutive years in 2008 and 2009.

Ron Boustead

resolutionmastering.com

Ron Boustead is a mastering engineer and owner of Resolution Mastering in Los Angeles, California. Before Resolution Mastering, Ron spent fifteen years at legendary Precision Mastering in Hollywood, and served for three years as chief mastering engineer at CMS in Pasadena, California. Ron has had the privilege of cutting CD and vinyl masters for artists like Prince, the Rolling Stones, Seal, Kiss, R.E.M., Johnny Cash, Aerosmith, Beck, and a host of other hugely successful artists.

Mark Bright

Mark Bright owns Chatterbox Music (formerly known as My Good Girl Music), a co-venture of Sony ATV Music. The company has celebrated multi-week #1 songs, "Do You Believe Me Now" by Jimmy Wayne, "American Ride" by Toby Keith, and "Without You" by Keith Urban. Bright is best known as a hit record producer of various artists and as a Nashville publishing company executive. His production projects include Carrie Underwood, Rascal Flatts, Reba McEntire, Sara Evans, Danny Gokey, and Scotty McCreery, among many others. Bright's success with Carrie Underwood has resulted in many multi-week #1s, including "Jesus Take the Wheel," "Before He Cheats," and "Cowboy Casanova," and has sold over 9 million units.

Bright formerly served as vice president of EMI Music Publishing and co-founded one of the most successful co-ventures, Teracel Music, which had staff writers including Brett James, Rascal Flatts, and Danny Wells, and was recently acquired by Dimensional Music Publishing.

Gary Calamar

gomusicsupervision.com

Gary Calamar, president of Go Music, is a four-time Grammy-nominated producer and music supervisor for his work on HBO's *True Blood* and *Six Feet Under.* He currently oversees the music for *True Blood* (HBO), *House* (Fox), *Dexter* (Showtime), and *Men of a Certain Age* (TNT).

Calamar also hosts a Sunday-night show on public radio powerhouse KCRW in Santa Monica. It has been a listeners' favorite for over a decade.

Daniel Carlin

Chair of film scoring at Berklee College of Music since 2007, Carlin has worked as an Emmy-winning music editor (*Under Siege*), Emmy-nominated music director (the Temptations), and conductor, music supervisor, soundtrack producer, or consultant on over one hundred projects, including such multiple-award-winning films as *An Officer and a Gentleman, Days of Heaven, The Black Stallion, Sister Act, The Body Guard, Steel Magnolias, The Last of the Mohicans, What's Love Got to Do with It,* and *Bruce Almighty.*

Carlin served two terms as chair of the Recording Academy's board of trustees (the Grammys) and over twenty years as a member of the Motion Picture Academy's Music Branch Executive Committee (the Oscars). Carlin co-founded Segue Music, the industry's largest independent provider of on-set and post-production music services, and was for twenty-five years its CEO. He also co-founded the Sundance Institute's Composer Lab and was a charter member of the UCLA film-scoring advisory board. In addition, Carlin served as executive director of the Henry Mancini Institute. He has taught at UCLA, UConn, and Belmont, and has lectured or served on panels at USC, NYU, MIT, CSU Northridge, and Loyola University New Orleans, as well as at institutions in Ireland and India.

Chuck Carr

chuckcarr.com

Chuck Carr is a producer and songwriter for high-profile video games. He uses SONAR X1 to compose, produce, mix, and deliver his projects, all within an end-to-end 64-bit environment. A short list of games he has worked on include Twisted Metal, Gran Tourisimo, God of War, NBA, MLB, Everquest, Supercross, and over fifty other titles.

Gary Chester

praguerecording.com

Gary Chester is a New York–based engineer who recorded and mixed albums for Nancy Wilson, Funkadelic, Jay and the Americans, and the Belmonts. He is the founder of Counterpoint Studios and the Edison Recording Studio, which specialized in advertising recording.

Gary moved into film-score recording, and his credits include films composed by Howard Shore, Carter Burwell, Rachael Portman, Angelo Badalamenti, Tan Dun, Mark Isham, Mychael Danna, Dave Robbins and Stephen Endelman. He's also worked on the films *Dead Man Walking*, *Silence of the Lambs*, *A Bronx Tale*, *Naked Lunch*, *Delovely*, and *Sweet Charity*, among others.

Rudy Chung

pushermusic.com

Rudy Chung is a founder and partner of Pusher, a Los Angeles music licensing agency created in 2009 that represents artists, bands, and composers exclusively for use in film trailers. Pusher was created as an alternative to traditional production music libraries. Chung has been a film/TV music supervisor at Hit the Ground Running, Inc., since 2003.

Chung's numerous credits include music supervision for over thirty episodes of *CSI* (2010–2011), *The Big Bang* (2011), *The Paul Reiser Show* (2011), six episodes of *Nikita* (2010), nineteen episodes of *Dark Blue* (2009–2010), eleven episodes of *Kath & Kim* (2008–2009), ten episodes of *Eleventh Hour* (2008–2009), and twenty-two episodes of *Everybody Hates Chris* (2005–2006). Chung was also music coordinator for *Goal! The Dream Begins* (2005), four episodes of *Entourage* (2004), twenty-four episodes for *CSI: Miami* (2003–2004), and twenty-three episodes of *Cold Case* (2003–2004). He was the assistant music supervisor for sixteen episodes of *Jake 2.0* (2003–2004).

Philip Cohen

Philip Cohen has been the senior vice president of music business affairs at Universal Pictures since 1995. He is the head of the business and legal music staff, and coordinates with creative affairs, production executives, finance, marketing, producers, and directors to ascertain music needs on projects. He negotiates composer, publishing, recording, artist, and soundtrack agreements for all Universal movies.

Cohen began his career at Sony Pictures Entertainment in 1984, where he started as legal assistant in the legal rights department. He became administrator of the labor relations department, and went on to become the assistant general counsel in the music legal department. From 1976 to 1983, Cohen was a freelance musician and songwriter, who wrote, recorded, and performed in NY, LA, and on tour in the US. He earned his JD at Loyola Law School in 1989, his California paralegal certificate in 1983, and his BA from NYU in 1981.

Tomas Cookman

nacionalrecords.com

Tomas Cookman is the president/owner of Cookman International, a multi-platform company that includes artist management, record label, publishing, and marketing. The Nuyorican, Los Angeles-based entrepreneur first established himself as an artist manager, working with many notable artists such as Los Fabulosos Cadillacs, Manu Chao, Tom Tom Club, and Nortec Collective, among others.

Cookman founded the Latin Alternative Music Conference (LAMC), the only major conference geared toward the marketing of cutting-edge Spanish-language and bilingual music. He also heads Nacional Records, a successful independent label.

On the content side, he produces *La Hora Nacional*, a weekly show on MTV Tr3s, and curates and hosts a three-hour radio show every Saturday and Sunday on Sirius/XM called the LAMC Mixtape.

Joel Dean

joeldean.net

Joel Dean is in-house composer at the Lodge. Dean has written and licensed music for a variety of TV shows and commercials, including AT&T, Cotton, Converse, Discover Card, Ford, Toshiba, McDonald's, FreeCreditScore.com, Lexus, Toshiba, Verizon, ABC, CBS, MTV, NBC, and USA Network. His work was nominated for an AICP award in 2010; he won first place in the International Songwriting Competition (2008) and second place in the John Lennon Songwriting Contest (2004).

Dean grew up in Niagara Falls, Canada, studying classical guitar. He graduated from Berklee College of Music in 2004, where he honed his skills as a writer and arranger and began producing demos for himself and his collaborators. He then worked as staff producer/engineer at Sanctum Sound in Boston, before relocating to New York to launch Deasel Music, a production company and recording studio.

Paul Degooyer

relativecomfort.com

Paul DeGooyer was the senior vice president for electronic games, music, and programming at MTV Networks. He is the award-winning producer, music supervisor, and marketing executive responsible for shepherding the bestselling Rock Band music video-game platform. He is the key architect of Rock Band's industry-leading music download business, which has sold more than 75 million songs to date. DeGooyer also served as executive producer of The Beatles: Rock Band, and led the global marketing effort that resulted in that game being named one of the Top Brands of the Year by *Ad Age*. Rock Band and Rock Band 2 have garnered more than 50 industry awards, including *Entertainment Weekly*'s Entertainers of the Year.

Prior to joining MTV Games, DeGooyer served in a broad range of senior creative, marketing, and management roles for MTV Networks, Warner Music Group, Palm Pictures, and Sony Music Entertainment. His experience covers music, film, television, and electronic games, with particular expertise in digital distribution strategy and complex licensing scenarios. In addition to the groundbreaking Rock Band interactive music platform, his credits include the Grammy-winning Concert for George, and the acclaimed Directors Label series of video anthologies, for which he was an executive producer with Spike Jonze, Michel Gondry and Chris Cunningham, among many others.

Jimmy Douglass

jimmydouglass.com

Jimmy Douglass, also known as the Senator, is a four-time Grammy-winning recording engineer and record producer whose career has spanned more than four decades. He started his studio career at Atlantic Records in the early 1970s as an after-school job: as a part-time tape duplicator, Douglass learned how to operate the studio's custom-made sixteen-channel console. He also observed, was trained by, and worked with some of the greatest engineers, producers, and record moguls, including Tom Dowd, Arif Mardin, Jerry Wexler, and Ahmet Ertegun. Douglass went on to work with artists such as Aretha Franklin, Hall & Oates, Roberta Flack, Donny Hathaway, Foreigner, Led Zeppelin, and AC/DC. During the 1980s, Douglass continued to hone his engineering skills while also producing. He engineered and produced established artists, including the Rolling Stones, Slave, Odyssey, Roxy Music, and Gang of Four. He began the 1990s working mainly on jingles and post-production.

In 1994, Douglass began work with contemporary R & B/hip-hop producer Timbaland and served as his main engineer for more than a decade. They collaborated on projects, including Grammy-winning albums for Justin Timberlake, as well as for artists such as Aaliyah, Missy Elliot, Ginuwine, Jay-Z, Snoop Dogg, Bjork, Rob Thomas, Sean Paul, Kanye West, Ludacris, Al Green, John Legend, and Duran Duran. Douglass is best known for bringing unconventional techniques into the studio and encouraging artists to transcend genre restrictions.

Larry Epstein

paradiseshow.com

Larry Epstein is founder and president at Paradise Show and Design, a full-service staging and production company headquartered in Orlando, Florida. Paradise works with show producers, designers, directors, meeting planners, and talent managers in entertainment, corporate theater, business meetings, music festivals, live broadcast, sporting events, and special event industries.

Epstein is an entrepreneur from Ohio, where he attended the University of Ohio and majored in economics. During college, he worked with local bands and accepted a job with a tour management company. This led to a career as a sound engineer, touring with well-known artists. After touring for several years and honing his skills as an audio and monitor engineer, he settled in South Florida and began working as a freelance engineer. Epstein was accepted into the IATSE Theatrical Stage and Film Union. He started Paradise Sound in 1988, and it became Paradise Show and Design. In 2009, Epstein began Launch, a creative event-planning company that supports corporate meetings and other events.

Brian Felsen

cdbaby.com

Brian Felsen is the president of BookBaby/CD Baby/HostBaby. BookBaby digitally distributes the works of independent authors, poets, memoirists, and publishers, making their e-books available to digital retailers worldwide, including through the Apple iBookstore, Barnes &

Noble.com, Sony's Reader Store, and Amazon.com. At CD Baby, the world's largest online distributor of independent music, Felsen is responsible for all business development, operations, customer service, marketing, and technology.

Before heading business development for CD Baby, Felsen joined Disc Makers in 2003, launching and growing major new initiatives, including the merchandise and film/DVD replication programs. His prior credits include founding and running one of the largest independent music conferences in the world, composing several classical music works, creating art photography, poetry, and plays, and producing an award-winning documentary film about Turkish military coups d'état.

Eric Gast

fmworldcharities.org

Eric Gast is a producer, mixer, and audio engineer, who has worked in genres as diverse as rock, hip-hop, jazz, gospel, and world music. At Zomba Music Group, his clients included Will Smith, Britney Spears, Billy Ocean, Kid Rock, and A Tribe Called Quest. Eric left Zomba in 2000 to freelance, and explored jazz, gospel, and various international recordings. He worked with artists such as James Moody, Jonathan Butler, John P. Kee, and Cissy Houston.

Gast is also the founder/CEO and managing director of FM World Charities. In 2003, he started FM for Music LLC, a production and management company. After extensive film and record projects in Eastern Europe, Eric opened label/media companies in the Czech Republic, Hungary, and Romania. From the outset, he built charity into his business plan. Over time, Gast enlisted the medical community in his charity efforts and started FM World Charities.

Lance Grode

Lance Grode teaches Legal Issues in the Music Business at USC Law. Grode received his JD in 1966 from Michigan Law School, where he was the note and comment editor of the *Michigan Law Review*. Upon graduation, Grode was the senior law clerk to the chief judge of the Federal District Court (EDNY). After several years as a criminal trial lawyer, he moved to Los Angeles to specialize in the music business. His clients included Bob Dylan, Michael Jackson, the Eagles, Neil Diamond, Jimmy Buffet, and Donna Summer.

In 1983, Grode began working in the MCA records business and legal affairs department; he eventually became the head of worldwide business affairs for the MCA Records Group (currently the Universal Record Group). In this capacity Grode oversaw the negotiation of thousands of contracts for artists, publishers, merchandisers, concerts, distribution, manufacture, and home video. In 1992, he became the executive vice president of MCA Music Publishing. From 1997 to 2007, Grode was the executive vice president of 20th Century Fox's music division, where he oversaw all aspects of music for motion pictures and television, including soundtracks and music licensing. Grode is currently writing a novel about the music business.

Lloyd Hanson

peytonentertainment.com

Lloyd Hanson is an entertainment agent for Peyton Entertainment Productions, where he books musicians and entertainers for different clients and events. In addition, Hanson has made a living as a musician for most of his adult life, playing in the bands Fire Creek, the Mischief Makers, Myth, Sarabande, the Gatton Gang, Teaser, Sophisticates, and Paradise. He continues to perform as the drummer in Paradise, for which he is also the administrator, managing partner, and music director. Paradise has provided entertainment for many events during twenty-plus years together, including a corporate dinner-dance program with Ray Charles in San Juan, Puerto Rico, for American Express; opening for Bruce Hornsby and the Range at Light-Up Orlando; New Year's Eve parties with the Commodores, Chubby Checker, Richard Elliot, and Ramsey Lewis; sharing the stage with Wilson Pickett for Publix Corporation; backing up Donny Osmond and Marilyn McCoo for Children's Miracle Network at Epcot Center and MGM Studios; being the exclusive band for the PGA Merchandise Show for four years in a row; and corporate shows for Legal & General Insurance Group in San Antonio, Aruba, and Sun City, South Africa.

Hanson studied music performance and composition at the University of Central Florida. He is a Florida native whose first instrument was the accordion.

Paul Ill

paulill.net

Longtime bassist/songwriter/multi-instrumentalist Paul Ill lists playing bass at Willie Dixon's Los Angeles wake, tracking live with Tina Turner in a London studio, and playing the Sunday gospel music services while in junior high at the US Army Base Chapel in Munich, Germany, as three definitive career highlights.

Paul has toured internationally with Linda Perry (whom he sites as a crucial influence and mentor,) Courtney Love, Daniel Powter, Wayne Kramer (MC5), Juliette Lewis, and Bill Ward (Black Sabbath) to name a few. His multi-platinum recording credits include Linda Perry, Christina Aguilera, Pink, James Blunt, Alicia Keys, Courtney Love, and Daniel Powter. He has written songs with nearly all of the aforementioned, and his instrumental compositions grace numerous films and television shows.

"For all this I am so truly blessed," says Paul. "That's why we named our psychedelic blues-rock duo Truly Blessed. We may be the only piccolo-bass-and-drums duo playing heavy, improvisational blues rock on this planet, at least for now. There's no way all this would have happened for me without the loving support from my mom, my sister, Paula, and my dad. That support, coupled with a reliance on a higher power, whom I choose to call God, has given me a life beyond my wildest dreams. For this I am so truly blessed and forever thankful."

Leslie Ann Jones

skysound.com/bio/lajones.html

Leslie Ann Jones is a multiple Grammy Award–winning recording engineer. She works as director of music recording and scoring at Skywalker Sound, a Lucasfilm Ltd. company. Leslie is a past chair of the National Academy of Recording Arts and Sciences board of trustees, the organization that awards Grammys.

Jones's extensive credits include numerous works for PBS, HBO, and CBS, including *Soldiers of Conscience* (PBS), *If These Walls Could Talk* (HBO), and the Grammy Awards (CBS). She has received Grammy Awards for her work, including Eliesha Nelson and John McLaughlin Williams—*Quincy Porter: Complete Viola Works* and the Kronos Quartet—*Berg: Lyric Suite* (Nonesuch). Jones has worked with, among others, Bobby McFerrin, Herbie Hancock, Jane Fonda, Miles Davis, Quincy Jones, Boz Skaggs, Kim Carnes, B. B. King, and Dee Dee Bridgewater. A sampling of her video game scores includes those for Star Wars: The Old Republic, Socom 4, Pirates of the Caribbean—Armada of the Damned, Star Wars: The Force Unleashed II, Dead Space 2, and God of War 3.

Raphella Lima

Raphaella Lima is music supervisor at Electronic Arts Guild, where she oversees the selection of licensed music and the creation of custom songs for several EA franchises, including FIFA, NBA, Fight Night, NHL, Rugby, FIFA World Cup, Tennis, NFL Tour, Def Jam, Active, and Cricket. Lima is also involved in the music for franchises such as Madden, The Sims, and FIFA Street.

Lima also heads the production of EA Recordings, a division responsible for digital releases of all EA-owned music assets, having released over a hundred score soundtracks that include blockbuster franchises like Medal of Honor, The Sims, Mass Effect, and Need for Speed.

Lima's knowledge of emerging artists and upcoming musical trends, particularly within the international and urban arenas, has helped to globalize the music featured across EA games.

Howard Massey

whenim64.com

Howard Massey is a music journalist, musician, and recording engineer/producer. He was formerly an editor at *Musician* and *Performing Songwriter* magazines.

Massey is the author of fifteen books, including two collections of interviews, entitled *Behind the Glass* and *Behind the Glass, Vol. II* (Backbeat Books). In 2006, he co-authored the critically acclaimed memoir of legendary Beatles engineer Geoff Emerick, entitled *Here, There, and Everywhere* (Gotham Books). Massey's latest book, co-authored with baby boomer expert Marvin Tolkin, is called *When I'm 64* and focuses on retirement planning.

Ted Masur

scoredesign.com

Masur is a classically trained composer and conductor who has composed music for numerous television shows, feature films, short films, documentaries, and commercials. He has been a contributing composer for the Diamond E Music Library since 2010, where he is the primary provider of underscore for *Entertainment Tonight, The Insider, Dr. Phil, Rachael Ray,* and *The Doctors.* Masur's television credits include music for *One Life to Live* and *Cold Case.* His feature film credits include *The Best and the Brightest* (2010) and *Cop Dog* (2008).

Masur was the recipient of the inaugural Steve Kaplan Award at the ASCAP Film Scoring Workshop, an Aspen Music Festival film scoring fellow, first runner-up for a BMI Pete Carpenter fellowship, a finalist for the TCM Young Film Composer Competition. Masur earned an MM at Indiana University, Bloomington, in composition and conducting, and a BA from Yale University in American studies.

Scott Mathews

scottmathews.com

Scott Mathews is a music producer, composer, song doctor, multi-instrumentalist, and entrepreneur. He has produced music for many clients, including A&M, BMG, Capitol, Epic, EMI, EMusic, Geffen, Imago, Island, Liberty, MCA, Polydor, RCA, Reprise, Sire, Sony,

Universal, Virgin, and Warner Bros. Mathews's work in movies ranges from the multiple Oscar-winning *One Flew Over the Cuckoo's Nest* to the Oscar-nominated *Wag the Dog.* His songs have sold millions for recording artists in all fields, from Barbra Streisand to Robert Cray. Mathews has had several Top 10 records in pop, alternative rock, R & B, country, and Americana, and has participated in Grammy and Oscar Award–winning projects.

Mathews's resume is too large to post in this book, but a partial list includes: the Beach Boys, the Blind Boys of Alabama, David Bowie, Zac Brown, Jimmy Buffett, Eric Clapton, Elvis Costello, Ry Cooder, Robert Cray, Sammy Hagar, Herbie Hancock, John Hiatt, John Lee Hooker, Etta James, Mick Jagger, Booker T. Jones, Patti LaBelle, Huey Lewis, Nick Lowe, Taj Mahal, the Mamas and the Papas, Steve Miller, Eddie Money, Van Morrison, Aaron Neville, Roy Orbison, Van Dyke Parks, Steve Perry, the Pointer Sisters, Bonnie Raitt, Joey Ramone, Keith Richards, Todd Rundgren, Carlos Santana, Joe Satriani, and Neil Young.

Mathews owns and operates Tiki Town Studios, and Hang On to Your Publishing, a music publishing company with more than 3 million units in combined sales. He is spearheading a new large-scale program for the United States Library of Congress in the Performing Arts Department.

Arnold McCuller

arnoldmcculler.com

Arnold McCuller is a longtime featured vocalist who has worked with top recording artists such as Phil Collins and James Taylor. He is also one of the music industry's most popular session singers, who is credited on hundreds of recordings, including those of Aretha Franklin, Diana Ross, Luther Vandross, Bonnie Raitt, Linda Ronstadt, Bette Midler, Brenda Russell, Lionel Ritchie, Dave Koz, Billy Idol, Lyle Lovett, and Beck.

An appearance on *Saturday Night Live* led to a phone call from singer-songwriter James Taylor, and they have continued to perform and record together for thirty years. In between world tours, McCuller has appeared in the films *Beaches, Without You I'm Nothing, Crossroads, Hollywood Knights, American Hot Wax,* and *What's Love Got to Do With It;* he sang the national anthem in *The Sum of All Fears.*

Randy Mease

thatsoundssweet.com

Randy Mease has worked as an audio engineer in the Central Florida area since 1998. He studied at Full Sail, and has worked with engineers, producers, musicians, and voice talent throughout the country. Mease works primarily with advertising agencies to record and mix various marketing materials utilizing the Pro Tools platform. He specializes in music/voice editing and sound design.

David Newman

davidnewmancomposer.com

David Newman has scored for over one hundred films, ranging from *War of the Roses, Matilda, Bowfinger,* and *Heathers* to *The Spirit, Serenity,* and *Alvin and the Chipmunks: The Squeakquel.* Newman's music has enhanced the critically acclaimed dramas *Brokedown Palace* and *Hoffa;* top-grossing comedies *Norbit, Scooby-Doo, Galaxy Quest, The Nutty Professor, The Flintstones,* and *Throw Mama from the Train;* and the award-winning animated films *Ice Age, The Brave Little Toaster,* and *Anastasia.* Newman has received top honors from the music and motion picture industries, including an Academy Award nomination for his score for the animated feature *Anastasia.* He was the first composer to have his piece, *1,001 Nights,* performed in the Los Angeles Philharmonic's Filmharmonic series, conducted by Esa-Pekka Salonen.

Newman headed the Sundance Institute's music preservation program and during his tenure wrote an original score and conducted the Utah Symphony for the classic silent-motion picture *Sunrise,* which opened the Sundance Film Festival in 1989. In 2007, he was elected president of the Film Music Society, a nonprofit formed by entertainment industry professionals to preserve and restore motion picture and television music.

Newman is the son of nine-time Oscar-winning composer Alfred Newman. He was born in Los Angeles and trained in violin and piano from an early age. He has worked extensively in the motion picture and television industry as a violinist, playing on such films as *E.T., Twilight Zone—the Movie,* and the original *Star Trek* film.

Adam Parness

thebordercops.com

Adam Parness is the senior director of music licensing at Rhapsody International Inc., where he oversees the company's music publishing operations. Since joining Rhapsody in 2006, Parness has negotiated and managed the company's relationships with thousands of music publishers, licensing agencies, and record labels for the award-winning Rhapsody music subscription service. He has managed dozens of high-profile Rhapsody television campaigns. Parness is responsible for a broad range of Rhapsody's business matters, including database technology and development, strategic partnerships and audits.

Parness received a bachelor of music degree from New York University and is an accomplished musician both onstage with the Border Cops and in the recording studio.

Harold Payne

haroldpaynemusic.com

Harold Payne is a multi-platinum and Posi Award–winning songwriter, who has written songs for artists, including Rod Stewart, Peter, Paul & Mary, Patti Labelle, the Temptations, Snoop Dogg, and Bobby Womack. Recently, Kelly Rowland of Destiny's Child recorded a version of the Payne/Womack song "Daylight" that climbed high on the UK / BBC singles chart and the *Billboard* dance charts.

Over several decades, Payne has maintained a schedule averaging over 200 performances per year, at just about every imaginable venue. He has opened for, among others, Van Morrison, Kenny Loggins, and Hawaiian legend Iz (Israel Kamakawiwo'ole). In 2001, he launched the Power of Positive Music series, which led him to regular performances at New Thought churches and with various motivational speakers like Mark Victor Hansen and Robert G. Allen. Payne has performed in India, Japan, Russia, Hawaii, Cuba, Ireland, Bali, and Bora Bora, developing his own style of audience interaction, including song improvisations. He plays both solo and with the group Gravity 180.

Conrad Pope

conradpopemusic.com

Conrad Pope is one of the most in-demand scoring professionals. He is supervising orchestrator and co-producer for the scores to *Harry Potter and the Deathly Hallows* parts I and II. He has worked as an arranger, orchestrator, and conductor for John Williams, Alexandre Desplat, James Newton Howard, Jerry Goldsmith, James Horner, Alan Silvestri, Danny Elfman, John Powell, Hans Zimmer, and Mark Isham.

Pope was classically trained at some of the world's finest music conservatories, and arrived in Hollywood with the ability to re-create numerous styles of music. This led to arranging source music for diverse films, guiding him, ultimately, to the orchestrating and ghost writing of many major motion pictures. A sampling of the films to which Pope has contributed includes the most recent installments of the *Star Wars* films (*The Phantom Menace, The Attack of the Clones,* and *The Revenge of the Sith*), the Harry Potter series, *Indiana Jones and the Kingdom of the Crystal Skull, Pirates of the Caribbean, The Matrix* films, *Memoirs of a Geisha, Julie and Julia, The Curious Case of Benjamin Button, A Christmas Carol* and *The Adventures of Tintin: The Secret of the Unicorn.*

Pope has received, among other awards, a Leonard Bernstein fellowship and a Fulbright fellowship. Pope was also awarded first prize in the Pacific Composers Forum Composition Competition.

Steve Porcaro

Steve Porcaro, a songwriter/keyboardist, was a founding member of the Grammy-winning, platinum-selling rock band Toto. Toto's first album, *Toto* (1977) went platinum; in 1982, *Toto IV* swept the Grammys, winning Album of the Year, Record of the Year ("Rosanna"), and Producer of the Year. Porcaro's credits include the pop hits "Hold the Line," "Rosanna," and "Make Believe." He also co-wrote "Human Nature" on Michael Jackson's 30 million-selling *Thriller* album. In addition to work with Toto and Michael Jackson, Porcaro also topped the charts with Don Henley, Elton John, Boz Scaggs, and Barbra Streisand.

After Toto disbanded in 1988, Porcaro launched a film-scoring career. He studied composition with Allyn Ferguson and has collaborated with James Newton Howard. Porcaro contributed to movies, such as *Metro* starring Eddie Murphy and *Hope* with Christine Lahti. He also scored the UPN-TV series *The Sentinel* and ABC's *Gideon's Crossing*. While Porcaro is still called regularly for pop studio and stage projects, Steve's passion and primary focus is music for film. His most recent projects were the NBC series *Raines* and the Touchstone pilot *Football Wives*.

Porcaro started piano lessons at age four, and played in various bands with his brothers, drummer Jeff Porcaro and bassist Mike Porcaro; the three went on to play together in Toto.

Kevin Quinn

Emmy-nominated songwriter/producer Kevin Quinn has composed hundreds of songs for television, records, and motion pictures. Credits include the theme song for the popular sitcom *Sister, Sister,* featured songs in Disney's *High School Musical,* and a string of national commercials for Target stores. The eclectic list of artists who have recorded his work includes Vince Gill, Robin Williams, Betty White, Zac Efron, and Kermit the Frog. Quinn is currently the lead singer/songwriter for the indie-folk band Boho Chapeau.

Quinn's credits include the following for Disney: *High School Musical* trilogy, *Brandy and Mr. Whiskers,; Teacher's Pet, 101 Dalmatians, Goof Troop, Bonkers, Hercules* (over fifty featured songs for the ABC series), *Recess* (theme song), *The Little Mermaid* (ABC series), *Jungle Cubs* (ABC series), *Kim Possible* (ABC series), *Lion King II; Aladdin and the King of Thieves, The Return of Jafar, The Hunchback of Notre Dame II, House of Mouse, Pepper Ann, Here's to You Mickey Mouse, Sing Me a Story, Disney Afternoon,* and *A Goofy Movie.*

His credits at Paramount include *Sister, Sister; Fired Up;* and *Carol & Marilyn: Real Friends.* At Hanna-Barbera, they include *Bill and Ted's Excellent Adventure, Gravedale High,* and *Two Stupid Dogs.* At Lorimar, *Nearly Departed;* at MGM, *All Dogs Go to Heaven;* at NBC, *California Dreams.* He has also written for a number of direct-to-video movies, including *Timmy the Tooth.*

Bjorn Roche

bjornroche.com

Bjorn Roche is an independent software developer, who has provided services to the music and pro audio industries. He has worked for Z-Systems Engineering, a maker of high-end pro-audio hardware Sterling Sound, a major mastering studio, and Indaba Media, a social networking site for musicians. He has also contributed to the open-source project called PortAudio, which allows audio software to function on multiple platforms without having to be rewritten. He specializes in DSP, internet-related music software, and desktop pro-audio software. He wrote one of the first, and still most powerful, audio editors that runs entirely in a web browser. Recently he has been working hard on his own project, called Xonami, which is both a desktop audio editor and a service that will allow musicians to collaborate in real time from anywhere around the globe.

Forest Rodgers

Forest Rodgers is a self-employed musician who plays guitar, banjo, Dobro (round-neck), and mandolin. He is a member of ASCAP. From 1984 to 1998, Rodgers led and played in the Cheyenne Stampede at the Cheyenne Saloon and Opera House in Orlando. The band was featured on TNN and the *Citrus Bowl Half Time Show* on CBS, and won the True Value/GMC Truck *Country Showdown* in 1991.

Rodgers is a Taylor Award winner, and won honorable mention in *Guitar Player* magazine's Fourth Annual Sound Page Competition (1991). He was featured in the book *Working Musicians* by Deems (Harper Entertainment, 2002). Rodgers is the author of *Pedal Steel Licks for Guitar,* an instructional DVD/Book (Centerstream/Hal Leonard).

Todd Rundgren

Todd Rundgren is a songwriter, video pioneer, producer, recording artist, computer software developer, conceptualist, and, most recently, an interactive artist (re-designated TR-i) who has made a lasting impact on both the form and content of popular music. Rundgren's production credits include albums by Patti Smith, Cheap Trick, Psychedelic Furs, Meatloaf, XTC, Grand Funk Railroad, and Hall & Oates. Rundgren composed the music and lyrics for Joe Papp's 1989 Off-Broadway production of Joe Orton's *Up Against It*, the screenplay commissioned by the Beatles for what was intended to be their third movie. He also has composed for a number of TV series, including *Pee Wee's Playhouse* and *Crime Story*.

Rundgren began playing guitar as a teenager in Philadelphia, going on to found and front the Nazz, the '60s cult group. In 1969, he left the band to pursue a solo career, recording his debut album, *Runt*. On 1972's *Something/Anything?* he played all the instruments, sang all the vocal parts, and was his own producer. This was followed by the LPs *The Hermit of Mink Hollow*, *A Wizard*, and *A True Star*, and the hit singles "I Saw the Light," "Hello It's Me," "Can We Still Be Friends," and "Bang the Drum."

In 1998, Rundgren introduced PatroNet technology, which for the first time allowed fans of a musical artist to subscribe directly to the artist's musical output via the Internet. Rundgren is responsible for many multimedia innovations, including the first interactive television concert in 1978; the first live nationally broadcast stereo radio concert in 1978; the opening of Utopia video studio in 1979; the creation of the first color graphics tablet, licensed to Apple in 1980; the production of "Time Heals," the second video to be played on MTV; the first live national cablecast of a rock concert in 1982; the release of the world's first interactive record album on CD-I; and the world's first interactive concert tour in 1995.

Michael Semanick

redmachinemm.com/msemanick

Michael Semanick is a two-time Academy Award winner and has been nominated six other times for Achievement in Sound Mixing. Semanick was nominated for all three Lord of the Rings films and won for *Return of the King*. He received his second Oscar for Peter Jackson's *King Kong*. Semanick was also nominated for his work with Pixar on *Ratatouille* and *Wall-E*, for his efforts on *The Curious Case of Benjamin Button*, and for *The Social Network*.

Semanick received a scholarship to attend the Berklee College of Music. Upon graduation with a BA in music production and engineering, Semanick returned to the Bay Area to work in the music recording industry, first at Hyde Street Studios in San Francisco, then at Berkeley's Fantasy Studios. Semanick worked with Ronnie Montrose, Joe Satriani, Starship, Todd Rundgren, En Vogue, Greg Kihn, Tesla, Y&T, and Grammy winner MC Hammer.

Semanick began working in movies in the early 1990s and has built an extensive collection of credits. In addition to the Lord of the Rings trilogy, Semanick has worked on *Stars Wars Episode II: Attack of the Clones* with director George Lucas, *Mystic River* and *Space Cowboys* with

Clint Eastwood, *Signs* and *Unbreakable* with M. Night Shyamalan, *Magnolia* and *Punch Drunk Love* with Paul Thomas Anderson, *Romeo + Juliet* with Baz Luhrmann, *Fight Club*, *The Game*, and *Se7en* with David Fincher, and many more films. Semanick credits his high school drama instructor for giving him the inspiration and motivation to pursue his interests.

Andrew Sherman

gimmebutter.com

Andrew Sherman is a creative director/composer at Butter. He has scored thousands of commercials, for which he has won Clios, AICPs, LIAAs, Lions, and Pencils. His compositions have been recorded on the Virgin/EMI/EastWest/Shanacie labels and include songs for the Latin Grammy–winning "This Side of Paradise" by Nestor Torres.

Sherman attended the Berklee College of Music and the BMI Musical Theatre Workshop. His career writing for theater began in 1998 at Moonwork in New York, where he composed the scores for Shakespeare's *What You Will* and *A Midsummer Night's Dream*, and Edgar Lee Masters's *Spoon River Anthology*. Off-Broadway, he composed the score for *Debbie Does Dallas*. Sherman has also toured as a sideman with Patti Austin, Walter Beasley, Jonathan Butler, Mariah Carey, George Duke, Julia Darling, Dizzy Gillespie, Lalah Hathaway, Brian McKnight, Redtime, and the Brooklyn Boogaloo Blowout, among others. In his spare time, Andrew composes for the 52nd Street Project, a nonprofit children's after-school program in New York City's Hell's Kitchen, and continues to perform with his band, the Brooklyn Boogaloo Blowout.

Gregory Sill

Sill earned a BA in sociology with a minor in music from Humboldt State University, California, in 1976. From then through the 1990s, Sill held the following posts in succession: music coordinator at Columbia Pictures Television and Films, director of music at American International Pictures, director of film and television music at CBS Songs, senior director for film and television music at Warner/Chappell Music Inc., and vice president for music at Warner Bros. Television.

Sill's credits as a music supervisor are extensive. They include *Justified* (SONY), *Prince of Motor City* (Touchstone), *Canterbury's Law* (SONY), *Cane* (CBS Paramount), *Football Wives* (Touchstone), *Life* (NBC Universal), *Burn Notice* (pilot) (FOX), *To Love and Die in LA* (NBC/Broadway), *Raines* (NBC), *In Plain Sight* (NBC), *Heist* (NBC), *Conviction* (NBC), *Beauty and the Geek* (WB), *The Jenna Elfman Show* (Touchstone), *Black Donnelly's*, *Killer Instincts*, *The Cell*, *Elvis*, *Hawaii*, *American Family* (PBS), *American Dreams* (NBC), *Boomtown* (NBC), *That's Life* (NBC), *ER* (NBC), *Friends* (NBC),

Sisters (NBC), *The Drew Carey Show* (ABC), *Reefer Madness* (Showtime), *Faith of My Fathers* (Sony), *Campus Bookies* (TNT), *Monday Night Mayhem* (TNT), ~~*Creature Features* (HBO)~~, ~~*Door to Door* (TNT)~~, ~~*Boss of Bosses* (TNT)~~, *Passing Glory* (TNT), *Pirates of Silicon Valley* (TNT); *Freedom Song* (TNT), *Running Mates* (TNT), and *Strange Frequencies* (VH1).

David Simoné

primarywavemusic.com

David Simoné is a partner at Primary Wave Music Publishing. He was formerly president of Arista, Mercury, and MCA Records in the UK before moving to the US, where he was the president of UNI Records, president of PolyGram Music Publishing, and EVP of Geffen Records. Simoné has worked with numerous artists and songwriters, including Elton John, Jon Bon Jovi, Desmond Child, and Bono.

Simoné and his partner, Winston Simone, formed Deston Songs, an independent publishing company.

Lee Sklar

Lee Sklar, a Hollywood session bassist since the 1970s, has recorded more than 2,000 albums. His credits include work with Linda Ronstadt, James Taylor, Hall & Oates, Jackson Browne, Phil Collins, Clint Black, Reba McEntire, George Strait, Willie Nelson, Steven Curtis Chapman, Nils Lofgren, and Lisa Loeb. Sklar has also played for television, including the shows *Hill Street Blues*, *Knight Rider*, and *Simon and Simon*, as well as for movies, including *Forrest Gump*, *Ghost*, *Kindergarten Cop*, and *My Best Friend's Wedding*.

Sklar started playing piano at age four, and began string bass in junior high school.

After he graduated from California State University—Northridge with a degree in music/art, Sklar began to play with James Taylor; when Taylor's "Fire and Rain" became a hit, Sklar's career was launched.

Adam Taylor

apmmusic.com

Adam Taylor is president of Associated Production Music (APM), where he reinforces the company's standing as one of the largest and most diverse collections of original production music available anywhere in the world. For over two decades, Taylor has helped companies, organizations, and individuals manage and extract value from their intellectual property in the form of copyrights, trademarks, and patents.

Prior to taking the helm at APM, he was the founding partner of Goldman/Taylor Entertainment, where he developed numerous properties, including the television series *Confessions of Crime* for Lifetime Network, and the PBS series *Joseph Campbell—Mythos,* hosted by Academy Award winner Susan Sarandon in partnership with the Joseph Campbell Foundation.

Damon Tedesco

scoringmixer.com

Damon Tedesco is an independent music-scoring mixer for film and television. He's worked for Warner Bros., scoring as a union stage manager, and 20th Century Fox as a scoring stage assistant, before building a 5.1 mix studio at his home and launching his career as an independent scoring mixer.

Tedesco earned his BA in communication arts at Loyola Marymount University. During college, he worked at Evergreen recording studio, which specialized in recording live music for films and TV; he started full-time after graduation, and his experience and connections at Evergreen led to many opportunities. Tedesco assisted on sessions and watched composers such as Michael Kamen, John Williams, Elmer Bernstein, and Jerry Goldsmith craft a score with live orchestras. He learned from scoring mixers such as Armin Steiner, Dan Wallin, Bobby Fernandez, Al Schmitt, Dennis Sands, and Shawn Murphy.

Russ Titelman

Russ Titelman is an independent record producer and songwriter who has won three Grammy Awards. He earned his first producing assignment on the Steve Winwood song "Higher Love," and his second and third for Eric Clapton's *Journeyman* and *Unplugged* albums. Titelman also produced Clapton's *24 Nights* live album of 1990 and the all-blues album *From the Cradle*, released in 1994.

Since the 1960s, Titelman has worked with musicians such as the Monkees, Dion Dimucci, George Harrison, Bee Gees, Little Feat, Christine McVie, Meat Loaf, Paul Simon, Brian Wilson, the Allman Brothers Band, James Taylor, Rickie Lee Jones, Chaka Khan, Ry Cooder, Randy Newman, Gordon Lightfoot, Eric Clapton, and Gerry Goffin. Titelman worked for Warner Bros. Records for twenty years.

Titelman has an independent music label, Walking Liberty Records, in New York. One of his first productions for the label was the debut album by the Oklahoma-based singer-songwriter

Jared Tyler. Released in 2005, *Blue Alleluia* included guest appearances from Emmylou Harris, Mac McAnally, and Mary Kay Place.

John Vester

johnvester.com

John Vester is a singer-songwriter. He grew up in Cincinnati, Ohio, where he started playing guitar in bands at age sixteen. Vester relocated to California in 1978, where he attended the Grove School of Music, played in bands, and began to write his own material. Vester delivered his first album, *My Heart Is in Your Hands* in 1998, followed by *Half a World Away* (2002), *Things I Wish I Would Have Said* (2004), and *All the Way Out West* (2007), the latter three albums co-produced with Michael Lennon. John has also written and co-written a number of songs on the last seven albums by the band Venice, including *2 Meter Sessies*, which earned a gold record in Holland in 2003. Together with Mark Lennon, Vester released *2 Voices, 1 Guitar, a* tour promo CD, in 2005, and the John Vester/Mark Lennon Holland live tour concert DVD/CD in 2006.

Steven Winogradsky

winogradskysobel.com

With over thirty years experience as an attorney in the music industry, Steven Winogradsky is a partner in Winogradsky/Sobel in Studio City, California, providing global media and music business affairs and legal support for composers, songwriters, music publishers, recording artists, and television, film, video, and multi-media producers.

Prior to being in solo practice with the Winogradsky Company, Mr. Winogradsky had served as director of music business affairs for Hanna-Barbera Productions, Inc.; managing director of music, legal, and business affairs for MCA Home Entertainment; director of music licensing and administration for Universal Pictures and Universal Television; and vice president of business affairs for the Clearing House, Ltd.

Daniel Zaccagnino

indabamusic.com

Daniel Zaccagnino is co-founder of Indaba Music, and part of its senior management team. Zaccagnino is a member of the Recording Academy. He has spoken at the SXSW music conference, the User-Generated Content Expo (UGCX), New York University, Duke

University, the International Association of Jazz Education Conference (IAJE), and numerous other industry conferences.

Zaccagnino graduated from Harvard University, where he co-founded the student-run record label Veritas Records. Throughout college he also worked for Blue Note Records and Virgin Records. Zaccagnino is a musician, songwriter, and instrument collector. He serves as chair of the Steering Committee for Education Through Music, a nonprofit.

about the author

MICHAEL REDMAN is a musician, composer, and serial entrepreneur, who has started over ten companies, including the Hard Rock Academy, RedHouse, AdJacket, MyMusicSource, Powerhouse Music, Reeltracs, and others. His passion is, and has always been, music and technology.

He is currently an author, a technology consultant, runs a music company with a primary focus on music content and licensing, and still finds a little time to write and record the music he loves. In his career, he has held many of the jobs listed in this book, including recording engineer, producer, live sound mixer, session musician, studio owner, among others. Michael lives in Santa Fe, New Mexico, and Cleveland, Ohio.

musicPRO guides

Quality Instruction, Professional Results

978-1-4584-1657-5	A Cappella Arranging	$29.99
978-1-4768-1701-9	The Best Jobs in the Music Industry. . . .	$24.99
978-1-4234-9279-5	The Complete Pro Tools Shortcuts, second editon	$29.99
978-1-4234-9671-7	The Complete Pro Tools Shortcuts, second editon – Spanish edition	$29.99
978-1-4234-6339-9	The Craft of Christian Songwriting	$24.99
978-1-4584-0374-2	Desktop Mastering.	$29.99
978-1-4234-6331-3	The Desktop Studio	$27.99
978-1-4234-4343-8	The Drum Recording Handbook	$29.99
978-1-4234-9969-5	The Future of the Music Business, third edition.	$29.99
978-1-4234-4190-8	How to Make Your Band Sound Great . .	$29.99
978-1-61774-227-9	Making Your Mark in Music: Stage Performance Secrets.	$29.99
978-1-4234-3850-2	Mixing the Hits of Country	$59.99
978-1-4234-9944-2	Modern Guitar Rigs	$24.99
978-1-4234-8445-5	Moses Avalon's 100 Answers to 50 Questions on the Music Business . . .	$19.99
978-1-4584-0289-9	Music 3.0.	$24.99
978-1-4234-5458-8	The Music Business Contract Library. . .	$24.99

978-1-4234-7400-5	The Music Producer's Handbook	$34.99
978-1-4234-3874-8	The Musician's Guide to Brides	$24.99
978-1-4234-8444-8	The Musician's Video Handbook	$34.99
978-1-4234-5440-3	1000 Songwriting Ideas	$19.99
978-1-4584-0039-0	Pro Tools Surround Sound Mixing, second edition	$39.99
978-1-4234-8896-5	The Recording Guitarist.	$24.99
978-1-4234-3483-2	The Reel World, second edition.	$27.99
978-1-4234-9278-8	Rockin' Your Stage Sound	$24.99
978-1-4234-8448-6	Secrets of Negotiating a Record Contract.	$19.99
978-1-4234-8847-7	Sibelius	$29.99
978-1-4234-6341-2	The Studio Musician's Handbook	$34.99
978-1-4234-5699-5	Succeeding in Music, second edition. . .	$24.95
978-1-4234-9236-8	The Touring Musician's Handbook	$34.99
978-1-61780-557-8	The Ultimate Church Sound Operator's Handbook, second edition . .	$39.99
978-1-61780-559-2	The Ultimate Live Sound Operator's Handbook, second edition . .	$39.99
978-1-4584-7449-0	Welcome to the Jungle.	$24.99

Prices, contents, and availability subject to change without notice.

Hal Leonard Books
An Imprint of Hal Leonard Corporation
www.musicproguides.com